Informal Finance in China

Informal Finance in China: American and Chinese Perspectives

Edited by
Jianjun Li and Sara Hsu

OXFORD
UNIVERSITY PRESS

2009

OXFORD
UNIVERSITY PRESS

Oxford University Press, Inc., publishes works that further
Oxford University's objective of excellence
in research, scholarship, and education.

Oxford   New York
Auckland   Cape Town   Dar es Salaam   Hong Kong   Karachi
Kuala Lumpur   Madrid   Melbourne   Mexico City   Nairobi
New Delhi   Shanghai   Taipei   Toronto

With offices in
Argentina   Austria   Brazil   Chile   Czech Republic   France   Greece
Guatemala   Hungary   Italy   Japan   Poland   Portugal   Singapore
South Korea   Switzerland   Thailand   Turkey   Ukraine   Vietnam

Published by Oxford University Press, Inc.
198 Madison Avenue, New York, New York 10016

www.oup.com

Oxford is a registered trademark of Oxford University Press

Library of Congress Cataloging-in-Publication Data

Informal finance in China : American and Chinese perspectives / edited by Jianjun Li and Sara Hsu.
    p. cm.
Includes bibliographical references and index.
ISBN 978-0-19-538064-4
1. Finance–China.   2. Financial institutions–China.   3. Informal sector (Economics)–China.   I. Li, Jianjun.
II. Hsu, Sara.
HG187.C6154   2009
332—dc22   2009000252

9 8 7 6 5 4 3 2 1
Printed in the United States of America
on acid-free paper

Preface

In December 2005, Dong Tao, the chief Asia economist of Credit Suisse First Boston, called me to let me know that an American scholar named Sara Hsu would come to Beijing to talk to me about informal finance. At the time, many foreign writers and scholars would come to my school to discuss Chinese informal finance and to interview me as I had just completed a research project on the scale and impact of underground finance in China and had published some papers on this topic. I agreed to meet Sara Hsu on December 29, 2005.

That morning, Sara came to my office and asked me several questions about my research and told me that she was doing her PhD dissertation on Chinese Small and Medium Enterprise (SME) financing. She wanted to do a survey and fieldwork in Nanjing and Shanghai. I was to perform the second national survey on informal finance from January through March 2006, so we exchanged questionnaires. Her survey questionnaire left a deep impression on me and finally, we decided to do a joint investigation.

Since then, we began to collaborate, and Sara introduced me to Professor Kellee Tsai, who is an American pioneer and a scholar in informal finance. I wanted to study abroad in order to learn international academic methodology. From September 2006 to September 2007, I did research on informal finance as a visiting scholar at Johns Hopkins University under Professor Tsai's supervision. Shortly after I arrived in the United States, Sara earned her PhD and came up with the idea of publishing a book of essays about informal finance in China, since she had contacted several Chinese and American scholars in this field as she worked on her dissertation. She suggested that we invite Xuzhao Jiang, Shuxia Jiang, Kellee Tsai, and Jianwen Liao to write chapters based on their prior studies. I thought this was a very good idea, because more and more people, including foreign scholars, government officials, foreign bankers, and graduate students want to know about Chinese informal finance, but only a few books are available on this topic.

Since 1996, several Chinese and American scholars have performed research on Chinese informal finance from different perspectives. The scholars use different methods to research the same topic, so their research cores and contents are different. Professor Xuzhao Jiang studied the types of informal finance from a historical and regional perspective. Professor Shuxia Jiang did his research from a historical and cultural perspective. My research focuses on the scale and impact of informal finance from a macroeconomic perspective. Professor Kellee Tsai looked at informal finance from a local perspective, presenting a political explanation for the private economic sector and enterprise informal financing. Professor Jianwen Liao studied the enterprise venture financing in China from a capital management perspective. Professor Sara Hsu looked at SME financing structure and efficiency based on her survey in Nanjing and Shanghai. I felt that if we put these scholars' research works together in one book, we could present a clear picture of informal finance in China. This book is written by these scholars based on their prior studies and hence has some new views, presenting the history and status of informal finance in China; the deciding factors of development and rules of evaluation; the causes, costs, and profit of enterprise informal financing; the scale and impact of informal finance; Chinese government policy on informal finance changes in the past; and possible policy choices for the future.

I want to thank all the authors of this book for their spirit of cooperation and for having finished their work on time: Kellee Tsai, Jianwen Liao, Sara Hsu, Xuzhao Jiang, Shuxia Jiang, Qiang Fu, and Guangning Tian. Thanks are also due to Joyce Keller, Yejing Huang, Dong Tao, and Stephen Reynolds, who helped us finish this book. And finally, I express my heartfelt thanks to the president of Central University, Professor Guangqian Wang; my dean, Professor Liqing Zhang; and my research advisor, Professor Jian Li; who gave me much encouragement and support in my research.

Jianjun Li
August 18, 2008

Contents

List of Figures

List of Tables

List of Abbreviations

AID	Agency for International Development
ANOVA	Analysis of Variance
CMA	Capital mutual assistance associations
CUFE	Central University of Finance and Economics
CBRC	China Banking Regulatory Commission
EMAI	Economic Movement Alert Index
EPQ	Entrepreneurial Profile Questionnaire
ICMB	Industrial and Commercial Management Bureau
IFCI	Informal Financial Conditions Index
IFCBCF	Informal Cross-Border Net Financial Investment
IFL	Informal Loan Indicator
IFNFI	Informal Net Financial Investment
MLE	Medium and Large Enterprise
MOA	Ministry of Agriculture
MCI	Monetary Conditions Index
NFI	Net Financial Investment
NGO	Non-Governmental Organization
OFE	Other Factor Effects
PBC	People's Bank of China
RIFE	Real Informal Economic Factor
RMB	Renminbi
ROSCA	Rotating Credit and Savings Association
RCF	Rural Cooperative Fund

RCC	Rural Credit Cooperative
RFS	Rural Financial Services
RMAA	Rural Mutual Aid Associations
SME	Small and Medium Enterprise
SETC	State Economic and Trade Commission
SOBK	State Owned Bank
SOE	State Owned Enterprise
SNA	System of National Accounts
UCB	Urban Cooperative Bank
UCC	Urban Credit Cooperative
VC	Venture Capital
WTO	World Trade Organization

List of Contributors

American Authors

Sara Hsu (Editor)
Visiting Assistant Professor
Trinity University
Department of Economics
sara_hsu@yahoo.com
801-755-0725

Jianwen Liao (Contributing Author)
Associate Professor
Illinois Institute of Technology
Stuart School of Business
liao@iit.edu
312-567-3895

David Pistrui (Contributing Author)
Associate Professor
Illinois Institute of Technology
Stuart School of Business
pistrui@iit.edu
312-567-3948

Kellee S. Tsai (Contributing
  Author)
Professor
Johns Hopkins University
Department of Political Science
ktsai@jhu.edu.
410-516-7972

Harold Welsch (Contributing
  Author)
Professor
DePaul University
Department of Management
hwelsch@depaul.edu
312-362-8471

Qian Ye (Contributing Author)
PhD Candidate
University of Louisville
College of Business
Department of Management
qian.ye@louisville.edu

Chinese Authors

Qiang Fu (Contributing Author)
Director and Associate Professor
Social Simulation Lab
Central University of Finance and
    Economics
Department of Financial Engineering

Shuxia Jiang (Contributing Author)
President
Xiamen Chamber of Commerce
Professor
Xiamen University
Department of Finance
shuxia.jiang@xiamen.edu

Xuzhao Jiang (Contributing
    Author)
Dean and Professor

China Ocean University
School of Economics
Shandong University
jxz2000@beelink.com
 + 86 531- 88361686

Jianjun Li (Editor)
Assistant Dean and Professor
Central University of Finance and
    Economics
School of Finance
ljjlsh@gmail.com

Guangning Tian (Contributing
    Author)
Assistant Professor
North China Electric Power
    University
School of Business

Informal Finance in China

Chapter 1

Introduction

Sara Hsu

Informal finance consists of nonbank financing activities, whether conducted through family and friends, local money houses, or other types of financial associations. Informal finance has provided much-needed financing to small and medium enterprises (SMEs) in particular, in the face of a tightly constrained, overburdened formal banking system. Unable to obtain a bank loan, firms have relied upon individuals and informal organizations outside of the banking system to obtain financing for their ventures. Informal finance has played an important role in China's economic boom in the last 30 years.

This book describes the evolution, characteristics, and variation of informal finance in China from an American and Chinese perspective. Literature by Jiang Shuxia, Jiang Xuzhao, and Li Jianjun has heretofore been available only in Chinese, while work by Kellee Tsai, Jianwen Liao, Harold Welsch, David Pistrui, and Sara Hsu has been available only in English. For the first time, we come together to discuss informal financing and its many aspects.

Much of the work stems from detailed surveys conducted locally as this type of data is not normally collected by the government. Informal finance is a local and personal activity, but it also affects the macroeconomy—particularly in China, where it is pervasive.

In this chapter, we first discuss existing literature on informal finance and then discuss the details in the following chapters.

Informal Finance in the Literature

The study of informal finance in developing countries began in the late 1960s and early 1970s, with the study of nonbank financial institutions in countries such as India, Bolivia, Indonesia, Somalia, Niger, and Papua New Guinea. This work stemmed from studies performed by the Agency for International Development (AID) on small farmer credit programs, and from the recognition, by Gunnar Myrdal (1956) and other economists, that the development of savings institutions was critical to the growth process. Yet it was also recognized that developing countries often required an intermediate step between no credit and savings institutions, and formal credit and savings institutions (Geertz 1962).

The middle ground consisted frequently of Rotating Credit and Savings Associations (ROSCAs), found in different variations across regions of the world, and drawing upon traditional practices and relationships in order to pool and provide capital. In the ROSCA, a fund is rotated among contributing individuals at different points in time. ROSCAs have long been in existence in African, Asian, and Latin American countries. They have become an institution in some parts of China, and remain so even today.

The economist Dale Adams has been a leader in the study of ROSCAs and other informal financing practices. Dale Adams and Delbert Fitchett come to several conclusions regarding informal finance across the globe (1992, 3):

1. Informal finance pervades developing countries, particularly urban areas.
2. Informal finance is inclusive of both poor and rich individuals in these countries.
3. Informal financing methods are flexible and easily adapted to changing circumstances.
4. Informal financing provides individuals with opportunities to save where other institutions may not.
5. Informal finance is not normally exploitative.
6. Informal finance improves the efficiency of resource allocation.
7. There are links between informal and formal finance that are often unexpected.

These are interesting observations as they are based on research conducted across continents, and since many are contrary to the image that is usually associated with informal finance. Adams and Fitchett's work concludes that informal finance is quite beneficial to individuals in developing nations. Wherever there is a lack of formal financial channels, these extremely flexible and relatively efficient institutions have emerged.

There is a wide variety of informal financing methods. The existence of these institutions has served to fill a specific need and/or complement the socioeconomic culture in which economic transactions take place. These other types of informal finance include lines of credit with supply chain networks, pawnshops, sharecropping, land pawning, and borrowing between friends and family. Lines of credit with supply chain networks allow suppliers and purchasers to conduct business on a continuous basis, without interruption due to cash-flow issues. Pawnshops allow individuals with little access to formal financing to obtain loans by pawning an item as collateral (before the loan is due) or payment (at the time the loan is due). Sharecropping contracts specify that the tenant shall pay the landlord in kind. Land pawning is a practice found in countries such as the Philippines, Bangladesh, and India, and involves the temporary transfer of land or cultivation rights to the lender during the course of a loan, and a permanent transfer of land or cultivation rights if the borrower cannot pay back the loan (Nagarajan, David, and Meyer 1992). Borrowing from friends and family may or may not include interest, by demand or favor. It is the most common means of financing for many businessmen, and is usually the best resource (ceteris paribus), after own savings, for private financing.

Although there is little advanced theoretical literature on informal finance outside of risk modeling, perhaps because some economists consider informal finance to be outside of the market arena (Besley 1995), or at least outside of the *formal* market arena in which data is regularly recorded, academics do give informal financial institutions an important place within the context of financial development as a whole. Bala Shanmugam (1991) discusses the importance of the ROSCA as a means of savings, as well as a means of directing funds toward more profitable areas. ROSCAs and other informal financial institutions are seen as a progression toward capital institutions, as well as social organizations. Informal financial institutions often provide poorly established or non-asset holding individuals with a means of making large purchases for investment or consumption. They are viewed as being quite different from formal savings and credit institutions because they often occur between interest groups or neighbors, and because they often have a social purpose beyond funding. Social interchange and business networking occur in many instances.

Informal financing methods have also been judged as important means of reducing financial risk to the individual. The practice of sharecropping reduces risk both to landlord and tenant by cushioning the impact of negative shocks. Social networks among informal financial institutions that extend beyond the loan also lessen the existence of asymmetric information and bring down enforcement costs as lenders are more likely to know the borrower. Inductive analyses of risk in informal financing practices with particular characteristics have been made by Christopher Udry (1994) in his work on informal credit and risk sharing in Nigeria. Deductive analyses of risk with regard to informal financing practices have been carried out by Monsoora Rashid and Robert Townsend (1992) with regard to India and Thailand, respectively.

Informal financial institutions may arise anew or continue to exist alongside formal financial institutions. There are differing theories on why this may be the case. One theory states that government ceilings on interest rates prevent capital from being efficiently allocated. Another theory states that high costs of contract enforcement in formal financing edge out the poorer individuals through collateral or income requirements. In both these cases, an informal financial sector arises to cater to the underserved portion of the population (Mohieldin and Wright 2000). These theories attempt to explain the continuing existence of informal financing areas like rural China, as well as the new formation of informal financing institutions among minority groups in the United States. The reasons for the existence of informal finance may be diverse and may vary for every region. This makes policy implications more difficult to assess.

Finally, a related area of study and practice has been on microcredit institutions in developing countries. Such institutions are largely nonprofit and directed toward the very poor. The purpose of informal finance and microcredit institutions is often similar—both types of institutions may reduce financial risk to individuals and may provide persons who do not own collateral with a means of obtaining financing. In addition, the structure of lending within microcredit institutions may mirror that of informal financing institutions. In some cases, as Jonathan Morduch (1999) notes, the microcredit institution was established based on local informal financing practices. The practice of group borrowing, with joint liability, in particular, is a practice that has been implemented in microcredit organizations based on local traditions. The study of microcredit institutions, with regard to efficiency and risk, is amassing a great amount of literature, and in some ways is related to the field of informal finance.[1]

Chinese Informal Finance

Informal finance has played an increasing role in China's transition from a planned economy to a market economy. Informal finance was reborn during the reform and opening-up period, and has since been a major factor in China's economic success in the last 30 years.

There have been only a handful of major studies on informal finance in China: Jianjun Li's two research projects (2005, 2006) and publications on informal financing throughout China; Kellee Tsai's research project (2002) in Fujian Province, the city of Wenzhou, and Henan Province; Shuxia Jiang's research project (2000) in the cities of Fuzhou, Xiamen, Beijing, and Shanghai; and Xuzhao Jiang's research projects (1996, Jiang and Ding 2004), which covered the cities of Jinan, Qingdao, and Weifang. There is also at least one smaller study at the individual city level, including a review of informal financing in the city of Wuhan by Jianwen Liao, Harold Welsh, and David Pistrui (2003).

Li (2006) describes in detail the relationship between informal finance and business by using narratives about individuals in different regions of China. The individuals include moneylenders, ROSCA participants, criminals, and entrepreneurs and come from all regions, but they all have in common the fact that they are trying to improve their situation in life and cannot do so through the formal banking system. Li surveys 1150 SMEs and individuals engaged in commerce. The results reveal that most businesses in these regions view informal financing as having a good deal of influence on their businesses.

Li (2005) analyzes in detail the macroeconomic effects of informal finance on China's economy, using data on China's M_2, GDP, provincial data on the use of informal finance, and fixed asset investment, among other variables. The goal of this research project was to assess the impact of informal finance on bank deposits, currency, capital, and GDP. Informal finance takes on various roles in the economy, and is a source of savings and investment as well as a base for income generation. This book arrives at the result that the informal sector amounted to a nonnegligible portion of GDP in 2003—at 7.6%–8.6% of GDP and 3.6%–4% of M_2. Informal financing, then, is a major factor for consideration in monetary policy.

Tsai's book (2002), *Back-Alley Banking*, is based on surveys conducted in 1996 and 1997, and on research that extended over a period of several years. Tsai administered 374 surveys in Henan Province, Fujian Province, and the city of Wenzhou. From his work, it can be concluded that there is no single method of informal finance in China. Informal finance may take on diverse forms and varies from region to region.

Shuxia Jiang (2000, 2003) conducted research on Chinese informal finance, supported by the National Natural Science Foundation of China and the Ministry of Education from 1998 through 2003. She and her research team did a national survey of underground finance in different areas of China and compared Chinese informal financial types, evolution, and functions with those in other countries or regions in East Asia. In 2000, she published the book, *China's Underground Finance*. Then she turned her attention to the social and cultural background of informal finance in China and did another in-depth study. Jiang published the results in her second book, *China Informal Credit-Analysis of the Social and Cultural Background* (2003).

Xuzhao Jiang was the first Chinese scholar to study informal finance in China from a historical point of view. He did a survey on the types, characteristics, determining factors, and effects of informal finance in different areas of China in 1994–1995 and published the book, *The Research of Informal Finance in China* (1996). He later led a research team in another survey on informal finance in Shandong, Jiangsu, and Henan Provinces and published a paper about the evolution of informal financial organizations and their functions in local economic development (2004).

Liao, Welsh, and Pistrui (2003) focus specifically on entrepreneurial financing, with 222 surveys being performed in Wuhan, China using the

Entrepreneurial Profile Questionnaire (EPQ). The researchers found that most venture financing was obtained from personal savings and financial support of family and friends, followed by the mortgage of one's own assets. Entrepreneurs' demographics with regard to financing methods, such as age, gender, years of education, and working experience vary. The results are interesting as they provide insight into the borrowing patterns of entrepreneurs as a whole, and also in terms of social groups.

Why has there been so little written about informal finance? There is a copious amount of literature on formal financial institutions and reforms needed in that area, but little on informal finance. This is in large part due to the fact that there is little original, detailed data available. Studies on informal financing, at this time, must survey businesspeople, which requires more funding and time. With the exception of the literature above, original research on informal finance in China has been limited to date.

Informal finance in China has largely arisen due to lending constraints in the formal banking sector. Banking reforms, to date, have not been sufficient to allow formal institutions to supply funds to all enterprises. We next briefly discuss the major banking reforms and why they are found lacking.

Banking Reforms in the Formal Financial Sector

The pattern of reform in China is to experiment with a reform before expanding its scope. Reform was carried out in three major stages: from December 1978 to September 1984, from October 1984 to December 1991, and from January 1992 until the present (Gao 1999).

The first and second stages of reform saw the establishment of a two-tier banking system consisting of a central bank and four specialized banks owned by the state. The People's Bank of China became the Central Bank. Direct grants to enterprises were replaced by interest-bearing loans.

The banking structure in the third stage of reform, which ushered in the establishment of a socialist market economy, was further separated into a three-tier system consisting of four specialized banks, three policy lending banks, more than 100 commercial banks, 42,000 rural credit cooperatives, 3000 urban credit cooperatives, and 190 foreign bank branches (Shirai 2002). Reforms in 1995, among other measures, abolished loan quotas, created asset management companies to deal with nonperforming loans, and introduced a gradual tightening of accounting regulations.

In December 2003, post-creation of asset management companies, $22.5 billion was pumped into China Construction Bank and Bank of China to boost the viability of these banks (Herrero, Gavila, and Santabarbara 2005). This was done to write off existing nonperforming loans, so that capitalization did not improve substantially, although asset quality indeed did. In June 2004, $15.6 billion and $18.1 billion in nonperforming loans were auctioned off from the same two banks. In 2005, $15 billion was pumped into the Industrial and Commercial Banks. These funds, used to improve asset quality, originated from China's official international reserves through the transfer of U.S. government bonds.

Foreign banks were allowed to compete in the Chinese banking sector and also to purchase ownership shares in major Chinese banks as of 2006.

Banking reforms, although extensive, have not culminated in the desired result. Banks still remain largely controlled by the state, and the treatment of nonperforming loans has been rather superficial. The very existence of non-performing or poorly performing loans to State Owned Enterprises (SOEs) may create an incentive for banks to continue a relationship with SOEs in the hope that the finances will be repaid (Gorton and Winton 1998). This makes the process of making banks profitable much more difficult, as credit to private enterprises continues to be restricted, and as bad loans to SOEs continue to be granted.

Because banks still struggle with nonperforming loans and lack a profit-oriented mentality, SMEs have been unable to obtain sufficient funding for growth. Sustained economic growth in this area has largely been funded by informal finance. In this book, we describe and discuss informal finance and its role in China's economy.

Overview of Chapters

This book is organized in the following manner. Chapter 2, by Shuxia Jiang, details the evolution of Chinese informal finance, describing the different types of informal finance that have eased constraints posed by the formal financial sector. Chapter 3, by Jianjun Li, looks at characteristics of informal finance across China based on a national survey of firms and banks. Chapter 4, by Xuzhao Jiang, discusses various forms of informal finance that have arisen in the north and in the south of China, and compares the different forms this has taken in the two regions. Chapter 5, by Kellee Tsai, examines the main types of informal finance in terms of legality and local variation, and finds that the more institutionalized forms of informal finance depend on political bargains struck between financial entrepreneurs and regulators at the local level, and are, to some degree, path-dependent in their evolution. Chapter 6, by Jianwen Liao, Qian Ye, David Pistrui, and Harold P. Welsch, looks at venture financing among entrepreneurs in Wuhan, and finds that informal finance comprises a large part of start-up capital. Chapter 7, by Sara Hsu, compares informal and formal finance in terms of costliness of obtaining and keeping loans, and finds that formal finance should be preferred by firms that are better credit risks. Chapter 8, by Jianjun Li, concludes with the rules of informal finance and policy recommendations.

Appendix A, by Qiang Fu and Jianjun Li, takes on a macroeconomic perspective to analyze the impact of informal finance on monetary and economic movements. The authors compile informal financial indexes and build economic models that show the effect of informal finance on monetary and economic movements. Appendix B, by Guangning Tian, presents a typical story of an entrepreneur's financing dilemma in Shanxi, and his experience with informal finance.

There are three main themes in this book. The first is that informal financial development, including its organizational structure and regional character, varies widely to fit local needs. Informal finance reflects the local culture in different areas of China. The second is that informal finance both affects and is affected by macroeconomic policy. Policymakers must take into account the existence of nonbank financing before implementing new monetary policy. The third theme is that enterprise informal financing has specific benefits and costs, depending on the financial and social situations of both the borrower and the lender. It is critical to understand the benefits and costs of informal finance in order to properly regulate this important sector.

China seems to be deepening its financial reform to assist the legalization process for informal financial institutions, forming a multi-institutional financial system. More information about specific types and effects of informal financial institutions can only assist this process.

Note

1. Microcredit cannot be seen as an alternative to informal financing for two reasons. First, microcredit institutions are seldom financially viable and rely on the contributions of nongovernmental organizations. Second, the size of the loans granted by microcredit institutions is often too small to finance small businesses in rapidly growing countries like China. It is an interesting consideration in terms of institutional structure but it is not a solution to China's financial issues.

References

Adams, Dale W. and Delbert A. Fitchett, eds. 1992. *Informal Finance in Low-Income Countries*. San Francisco: Westview Press.

Besley, Thomas. 1995. Nonmarket institutions for credit and risk-sharing in low-income countries. *Journal of Economic Perspectives* 9(3): 115–27.

Gao, Shangquan. 1999. *Two Decades of Reform in China*. London: World Scientific.

Geertz, Clifford. 1962. The Rotating Credit Association: a 'middle rung' in development. *Economic Development and Cultural Change* 10(3): 241–63.

Gorton, Gary and Andrew Winton. 1998. Banking in transition economies: does efficiency require instability? *Journal of Money, Credit and Banking* 30(3(2)): 621–50.

Herrero, Alicia Garcia, Sergio Gavila, and Daniel Santabarbara. 2005. China's banking reform: an assessment of its evolution and possible impact. *Bank of Spain Occasional Papers #502*.

Jiang, Xuzhao. 1996. *The Research of Informal Finance in China.* Shandong: Shandong People's Publishing House Press.

———— and Changfeng Ding. 2004. Theoretical analysis of informal finance: conception, comparison and institutional change. *Journal of Financial Research* 8: 100–11.

Jiang, Shuxia. 2000. *China Underground Finance.* Fuzhou: Fujian People's Press.

————. 2003. *China Informal Credit-Analysis of Social and Cultural Background.* Beijing: China Press of Finance and Economics.

Li, Jianjun. 2005. *Research on the Volume of Underground Financing and Its Economic Effects.* Shanghai: China Financial Publishing House.

————. 2006. *The Survey of Underground Financing in China.* Shanghai: Shanghai Renmin Press.

Liao, Jianwen, Harold Welsch, and David Pistrui. 2003. Patterns of venturing financing: the case of Chinese entrepreneurs. *The Journal of Entrepreneurial Finance and Business Ventures,* 8(2): 55–69.

Mohieldin, Mahmoud S. and Peter W. Wright. 2000. Formal and informal credit markets in Egypt. *Economic Development and Cultural Change* 48(3): 657–70.

Morduch, Jonathan. 1999. The microfinance promise. *Journal of Economic Literature* 37: 1569–614.

Myrdal, Gunnar. 1956. *An International Economy: Problems and Prospects.* New York: Harper.

Nagarajan, Geetha, Cristina C. David, and Richard L. Meyer. 1992. Informal finance through land pawning contracts: evidence from the Philippines. *Journal of Development Studies* 29(1): 93–107.

Rashid, Monsoora and Robert Townsend. 1992. Targeting credit and insurance: efficiency, mechanism design, and program evaluation. Washington DC: World Bank.

Shanmugam, Bala. 1991. Socio-economic development through the informal credit market. *Modern Asian Studies* 25(2): 209–25.

Shirai, Sayuri. 2002. Banks' lending behavior and firms' corporate financing pattern in the People's Republic of China. ADB Institute Research Paper 43.

Tsai, Kellee S. 2002. *Back-Alley Banking: Private Entrepreneurs in China.* Ithaca, NY: Cornell University Press.

Udry, Christopher. 1994. Risk and insurance in a rural credit market: an empirical investigation in northern Nigeria. *Review of Economic Studies* 61(3): 495–526.

Chapter 2

The Evolution of Informal Finance in China and Its Prospects

Shuxia Jiang

In this chapter, we discuss the following: why informal finance is important, how it has evolved, and what can be further done to improve informal finance.

Chinese informal finance is a wonderful phenomenon. Informal finance refers to a kind of direct private credit relation that takes the form of a loan in currency or goods, but credit provided by banks is excluded from this arena (Da Huang 1990; Zhao 1999). Informal finance is referred to as unofficial credit, and it includes informal loans, commercial credit, and *hehui* (rotating savings and credit associations) (Zeng and Wang 1993). From the Xi-Zhou Dynasty in 1046 BC until the establishment of New China in 1949, informal finance has never ceased to evolve. Informal finance has been rejuvenated since the reform and opening-up policy in the 1980s, as China has experienced the transition from a planned economy to a market economy as well as from single-ownership to multi-ownership, and seen a rapid boom of the private economy.

The Economic Influence of Informal Finance in China

The Impact of Informal Finance on Supporting the Private Economy in China

Essentially, informal finance is the product of a special "war" between old forms of institutional arrangements and the newly born market economy. Since the reform and opening-up of China, private enterprises have been playing a rather important role in promoting the development of the market economy.

Although the direct measurement of the scale of informal finance is not feasible, through investigation, the sum of informal finance can be roughly estimated. In 2004, through an investigation by a research team at the Central University of Finance and Economics (CUFE),[1] the scale of informal finance in 2003 was estimated to be between 740.5 and 816.4 billion yuan (Li 2006). According to official records, the scale of informal finance was around 950 billion yuan, accounting for 6.96% of GDP and 5.92% of total loans.[2] These two estimates roughly match.

Small- and medium-sized enterprises (SMEs) have relied on informal finance to fund their businesses, in part or in whole. SMEs have been playing a rather important role in China. However, since they are not transparent enough and are short of assets that can be used as collateral, they often encounter difficulties in obtaining formal finance. Therefore, various informal financial sources, such as rotating savings and credit associations, informal moneylenders, loan brokers, informal credit unions, and pawnbrokers, play a critical role in assisting SMEs to start up and to take advantage of business opportunities. As for the SMEs in Taiwan, which have been the mainstay of the Taiwanese economy, informal finance has been an indispensable source for SMEs to finance their operations. According to some scholars' research, more than 35% of the SMEs' domestic debt comes from informal financial sources (Weiying Zhang 1994; Xin Wang 1996; Zhou and Lin 1999). And in Zhejiang province, China, informal finance has existed extensively since the reform that began in the 1980s. For example, in Wenzhou, Zhejiang Province, as Tsai (2001) and Shi and Ye (2001) noted, it is not only start-up businesses that depend mainly upon internal funds and informal finance but also those with substantial size and market power, where informal finance is still an important source of external funds (Lin and Sun 2003).

The Impact of Informal Finance on Reducing Rural Poverty in China

During the last 20 years, historical progress has been made in easing poverty in China; however, to reach its goal of constructing an affluent society, it still has a long way to go. Going by the international poverty standard of $1.00 per day (in 1985 purchasing power parity dollars), the poverty line in China should be 924 yuan per year, and there are 7.58 million rural residents living below that line. Going by the poverty standard of the World Bank, there are 300 million rural residents still living in poverty. Therefore, reducing poverty in China is quite a challenge.

Many believe that a major solution to the poverty problem is the supply of capital. Currently, "governments' public investment is an important resource for supporting the growth of the rural economy and reducing poverty and regional inequality" (Boqiang Lin 2005). However, depending entirely on fiscal support to solve the poverty problem in China is a bad idea. In particular, the lag of reform in the rural financial system causes serious problems to rural financial institutions in performing financing functions; capital resources are flowing out of, rather than into, rural areas. The outflow of capital reaches on average 70–80 billion yuan every year. Due to the absence of formal financial institutions, informal finance, with its advantages of reducing transactions costs, uncertainty, and risk, is one of the important sources of capital flowing into rural areas.

Informal finance plays a particularly large role in rural areas. According to an investigation by Guangwen He (1999), more than 75% of the debt of rural households comes from informal financial sources. The IFAD (2002)[3] report also points out that the number of informal loans taken by rural households is four times greater than that of formal loans. Informal finance is thus irreplaceable when it comes to reducing rural poverty. Without informal finance, businesses cannot function, since informal finance often provides off-farm or farm-based businesses with directly needed working capital. Households can neither afford to purchase higher priced items such as bicycles or TV sets nor pay education fees for their kids on their own. With the help of informal credit, businesses and households in poor areas can raise their living standards above the poverty level with less difficulty.

Although informal financing methods in rural areas are quite varied, these methods have significant features in common. The first two features are convenience and flexibility: rural informal finance is based on regional, occupational, and familial relationships, which rules out asymmetric information. Because of these personal relationships, it is easy for lenders to collect information about borrowers and make a proper decision in time, without spending much effort on credit investigation when the loan request is made. In addition, the sum, term, and even interest rate of credit loans can be flexibly negotiated without necessarily knowing how the loan will be used. The other two features include low information and supervision costs: rural financing is small-scale and frequent, with imperfectly documented information, and few assets that can be used as collateral. For formal institutions, it is quite expensive to carry out these types of financial transactions. The entire transaction fee may be consumed before, during, and after the deal, costing the formal institution more than the profit it can obtain through the deal. By contrast, informal financial transactions generally take place among agents who are very familiar with each other, so personal information of debtors can be acquired by the lender at little cost, before the loan takes place, and the fee for contract implementation and supervision is also normally low. The final feature includes strong moral constraints. Although it lacks legal protection and formal regulations, with moral constraints, the informal financial system is still effective in recovering loans. All of these features make informal finance the most important external source of funds for rural areas.

The Historical Evolution of Informal Finance in China

The Primary Development of Informal Finance

Informal finance dates as far back as the Xi-Zhou Dynasty, with the emergence of the private lending contract.

Private Lending

Private lending consists of direct loans from family or friends without intermediaries involved. It is one of the most ancient informal financial activities and has not been interrupted since the day it appeared, even under the traditional planned economic system. After the reform and opening-up of China, more and more people became involved in private lending, especially in rural areas. According to an inference from a typical survey of the Research Center for the Rural Economy (Cao 2001), the total sum of private lending among farmers in 2000 did not exceed RMB 140 billion, accounting for 68.8% of the total sum of loans; moreover, about 47.7% of private lending was in the form of interest-bearing loans.

Categorized in terms of debit and credit conventions, private lending can be divided into four types: borrowing money and paying back money; borrowing money and paying back goods; borrowing goods and paying back money, and borrowing goods and paying back goods. The first type is the most common one. Categorized in terms of interest that is repaid, informal finance can be classified in terms of no interest loans, low interest loans, and high interest loans. These are therefore defined as "white," "gray," and "black" finance, respectively (Xuzhao Jiang 1996).

Pawnbrokers

Pawnbrokers, loan organizations that require collateral, date back to the Nan Qi stages in the South and North Dynasty, during which, after the war years, in order to ease fiscal pressure, as well as to bring people out of their misery, the government authorized temples to run pawnshops, which became the prototype for pawnbroking. From then on, pawnbroking prevailed, and turned out to be one of the most important types of informal finance in China.

Hehui

The *hehui* (also known as the ROSCA) is a fund based on regional and familial relationships, dating back a long time ago. It can be found all over the world, whether in underdeveloped or developed countries. It goes by different names in different regions and countries; however, it is now mostly known as Rotating Savings and Credit Associations (ROSCAs). ROSCAs consist of a group of individuals who come together and make regular cyclical contributions to a common fund, which is then given as a lump sum to one member in each cycle. The member who receives the lump sum amount this way from the group pays back the amount by way of regular further monthly contributions. Depending on the cycle in which a member receives his or her lump sum, members alternate between being lenders and borrowers. That is, there is a mutual give-and-take involved in ROSCAs.

Money Houses (*Qian zhuang*)

Historically, there were many types of money houses, and the simplest type was called *yinbei*, or loan broker. A loan broker is an intermediary between lenders and borrowers. Loan brokers do not lend their own funds but bridge the gap between lenders and borrowers, using their advantages in information and credit. Brokers receive a commission as their reward.

Rural Credit Cooperatives (RCCs)

Created during the agrarian reform campaigns right after Liberation, rural credit cooperatives (RCCs) in China are a special financial institution with the specific target of developing a truly local cooperative system which enables peasants to avoid high-interest money lenders and to develop their own capital resources to meet their production and personal needs. Through the mandatory implementation of the government, with the effort of national banks, by 1957 the RCCs had evolved into a large national system of local cooperatives lending in 88,368 associations. A total of 98.45 million peasant households, accounting for 81.2% of rural households, were members of this system, either as actual shareholders or as depositors. The total funds raised by this system reached 310.18 million yuan by 1957. By then, the cooperative movement of rural credit was basically realized.

The RCCs, from their inception, were products of a political movement rather than a spontaneous product of economic and social development. Although, to some extent, RCCs satisfied the financing demand of farmers at the beginning, fundamentally speaking, they did not really belong to an informal financial organization for the following reasons: (a) from the perspective of ownership, most members were forced to join the RCCs instead of voluntarily doing so and did not really possess the rights which a real owner should have; (b) from the perspective of credit, a farmer who deposited his money into RCCs was actually placing confidence in the government, for he considered RCCs to be state-owned financial organizations; and (c) from the perspective of management, nonprofit oriented RCCs had a strong political complexion. All the characteristics of RCCs mentioned above foreshadowed their mutation.

The Decline of Informal Finance after the Foundation of the People's Republic of China in 1949

After the foundation of the People's Republic of China, all types of traditional informal finance nearly disappeared during the process of abolishment initiated by the government. Meanwhile, a new type of informal finance, the rural credit cooperative association, grew rapidly through the promotion of the government. However, due to changes in the political and economic system, informal finance languished after only a short period of development. Although it did not vanish completely under the planned economy, it went underground and its scale dramatically dwindled.

The Ban of Pawnbroking

Before the War of Resistance against Japan, there were many pawnshops in China. There were 114 pawnbrokers and 455 pledge houses in Shanghai.[4] During the war, the pawnbroking business was demolished by the Japanese. In rural areas, the pawnbroking business hardly existed; however, in some cities, the pawnbroking business had never stopped running until the Liberation. The reason that pawnbroking survived for such a long period is due to the financial gap between unsatisfied capital demands for daily expenditures and low incomes. The gap never closed, therefore pawnbroking continued to be valued.

After the Liberation, unaware of the necessity of pawnbroking in the financial market, along with the influence of extreme ideology and improper propaganda, pawnbroking was banned.

The Reform of Money Houses

In early 1949, there were over 1032 money houses around China, mainly operating in Shanghai, Tianjin, and Hankou. Later, the central government stepped into the development of money houses and initiated reform of the money houses. The government built state and private joint venture banks and cooperative financial institutions and let most private houses continue to do business. After reform, all private money houses finished rebuilding under a socialist frame. This process included four stages.

In the first stage, in order to guide idle money to serve the economy through money houses, as well as maintain room for the development of money houses, the Money Houses and Trusts Joint Lending Office of Shanghai was established by the government on September 24, 1949. Later, on December 14, 1949, the Public–Private Financial Industry's Joint Lending Office of Shanghai was founded. Because of their successful performance, the idea of Joint Lending was then promoted nationwide by the government in no time.

In the second stage, Joint Lending developed into Joint Operation. After February 1950, the breakdown of industrial production in Shanghai made money houses suffer greatly, and some small ones went into bankruptcy as a result. Thus, on July 1, 1950, the first and the second money houses' joint operations were established, and right after that the third and fourth joint operations were established. The number of money houses involved in this reform accounted for 69.2% of the total number of money houses (Jianhui Huang 1994).

In the third stage, Joint Operation evolved into Joint Management. Although most of the money houses joined the Joint Operation, the joint funds provided by money houses only accounted for 10% of their total deposits, and blind competition among them still existed. In order to solve this problem, in August 1950, the People's Bank of China decided to merge the Joint Operations. A year later, in July 1951, the first and the second joint operations in Shanghai merged and were called the No.1 Office of Joint Management. Later that year, in November, the third and the fourth joint operations merged into the No.2 Office of Joint Management.

In the final stage, the Public–Private Joint Management was formed. The Public–Private Joint Management is the highest form of state capitalism. After the reform and opening-up, four banks, Xinhua, Shiye, Shangtong, and Siming, were grouped into the Joint Office and became the first Public–Private Joint Banks.

During the Three Antis and Five Antis movements, speculation and illegal conduct of money houses, such as illegal arbitrage of exchange, tax evasion, stealing state economic information, and blind expansion of credit, were exposed. Therefore, their credit as well as their business lapsed. In May 1952, the People's Bank of China decided to "completely reform the joint banks, as well as abolish the money houses." In December 1952, the Office of Public–Private Joint Management was founded, and the financial industry of Shanghai accomplished public–private joint management for the first time. A year later, the national public–private joint bank was merged and the joint office was moved from Shanghai to Beijing. From then on, money houses did not exist any more and the public–private joint bank, as a private business arm of the People's Bank of China, gradually evolved into an irreplaceable part of the national banking system.

The Mutation of Rural Credit Cooperatives

The features of Rural Credit Cooperatives (RCCs) have always been controversial. Usually, RCCs are thought of as cooperative financial organizations that are democratic and flexible, aimed at serving *sannong* (three areas): *nongcun* (rural areas), *nongye* (agriculture) and *nonghu* (rural households). If RCCs can be perceived of as historically first performing their function of solving the financial problems of farmers and supporting agriculture, with reform these institutions evolved on their own, changing their features over time. After 1958, RCCs became semi-state-owned financial organizations, whose ownership and risk all belonged to the central government rather than to an informal financial organization.

Since their establishment in 1950, RCCs have developed greatly. By the end of April 2001, there were over 158 trillion deposits and over 105 trillion loans owned by RCCs, accounting for 12% of total deposits and 10% of the total owned by all kinds of financial agencies, respectively. RCCs had become irreplaceable in the financial system of China (Sheng, Ying, and Huang 2001).

A Rough Analysis of the Decline of Informal Finance

At the end of the socialization, especially after the Great Leap Forward in 1958, state ownership was dominant. The private economy was nearly cleared up, leaving the household as the only unit of the private economy, which owned little household property. Hence, the ownership foundation of informal finance hardly existed, for informal finance is based on private ownership to some extent.

Everyone was grouped into various kinds of publicly owned organizations, and one's identity as a social being was greatly enhanced through all kinds of group activities; however, one's identity as an individual was at the same time greatly undermined as the consequence of the decline in economic activities. Hence, the societal foundation of informal finance hardly existed, for informal finance is based on the financial interactions between individuals.

Most of the national income flowed into the exchequer of the central government as construction investment, while only a small percentage was paid as daily expenditures to individuals who worked in community or state-owned companies. Because individuals or households did not engage in production, they only consumed daily necessities. Even if they wanted to consume more, taking into consideration the supply shortage and limited repayment ability, there would not be a strong motivation to lend money to individuals. Only a few private loans among relatives or neighborhoods occurred sporadically.

Ideologically, informal finance was regarded as heresy in an environment of state ownership. Correspondingly, a monopolistic financial system comprised only of the People's Bank of China was established. Informal finance was intensively fought against and nearly disappeared.

The Course of the Rejuvenation of Informal Finance

Since the reform and opening-up policy in the 1980s, China has experienced a transition from a planned economy to a market economy. With the development of the market economy, the private economy has boomed rapidly. Further growth of the private economy posed financing needs which could not be fulfilled by the undeveloped formal financial system. Meanwhile, with the growth of the economy, national income and therefore potential capital supplies of informal finance have largely increased. Under these circumstances, modern informal finance has gradually developed.

At the beginning of the reform and opening-up, informal finance stayed underground, and its scale and influence were limited. From the 1980s to the 1990s, because of the limitation of government administration, informal finance had developed rapidly. The traditional forms of informal finance, such as private lending, money houses, *hehui*, and pawnbroking, came alive again. At the same time, informal collecting, cooperative funds and private equity funds were created one after another.

From then on, as the reform and opening-up process deepened, the government turned a blind eye to informal finance, so its scale grew day by day, especially in those regions with a developed private economy. In the twenty-first century, however, informal finance still remains largely underground.

Because the development of informal finance was beyond the expectations of the government and challenged the monopoly position of state-owned financial institutions, informal finance has to continue to stay underground and has never been recognized by authorities, which also puts it outside of formal financial supervision. Without supervision, the operation of informal finance is hard to trace in time, which renders a huge difficulty in its regulation and management, as well as increases social costs, especially when damage is done.

There are many forms of informal finance in China, including not only the traditional forms, such as financing through private banks and pawnshops, but also innovative forms, like financial services in rural areas, rural cooperative foundations, rural mutual funds, and so on. Among those various forms of informal finance, some, such as informal loans, are sporadic and lack particular organizational structures, while some are organized and roughly shaped, such as private banks and rural cooperative foundations. From the simple to complex and from the low levels to high levels, informal finance has gradually evolved (Xiaoyi Wang 1999).

During the economic transition period, due to the fierce confrontation between the planned economy and the market economy, a wide range of "underground" finance arose in the financial arena. The discrimination of types of informal finance is crucial. Categorized by its economic foundation, informal finance can be divided into two types: "gray finance" and "black finance." "Gray finance" has not been recognized by authority, but its existence satisfies the institutional demand and accelerates the progress of the economy. Moreover, after proper regulation and guidance, it can become a component of formal institutions; on the contrary, the purpose of "black finance" is to serve illegal behaviors or even crimes, which would endanger the harmony and stability of society, and should therefore be banned. Simply labeling informal finance as "illegal" is inappropriate. Only after careful discrimination, can an effective reform be carried through and proper guidance be administered to informal finance. Then the benefits of informal finance can be felt and disadvantages can be overcome (Shuxia Jiang 2001).

Private Lending

Whether in developed or in underdeveloped regions, it is easy to find the influence of private lending. In the developed regions it is mainly used in the areas of production, while in the underdeveloped regions it is mainly used for special living expenditure.

Pawnbrokers

Although it had been gone for nearly 40 years, the first post-reform pawn-shop, the Chengdu Huamao Pawnshop, was revived in Chengdu in January 1988. After that, more and more pawnshops came forth around China. Pawnbroking as a type of informal finance is now widespread.

In the early stages of the development of pawnbroking, a few problems arose. First of all, limitations of the financing term led to a high percentage of bad debts. Secondly, the loan interest rates of pawnbroking, ranging from 28% to 72%, were much higher than those of banks. Last but not least, the pawn-broking market was quite uncontrolled. In order to put things straight, the People's Bank of China (PBC) promulgated the Notice on Strengthening the Control of Pawnbroking in 1993, and later the Provisional Regulations of the People's Republic of China on the Control of Pawnbroking in April 1996. In 2000, the Industry and Commerce Bureau took charge of pawnbroking. And currently, pawnbroking is the only informal institution operating publicly.

Hehui

After the reform and opening-up in China, *hehui* first appeared on the Southeast Coast, where the commodity economy was relatively developed, particularly in Zhejiang, Fujian, Guangzhou and Sichuan Provinces. However, *hehui* in these areas transformed, for the worse, into pyramid-like structures, called *taihui*, in which loan sources for old members are funded by the growth in the number of new members.

In order to keep this kind of association running, two conditions need to be fulfilled: the growth of new members must continue and the credit of existing members must remain strong. The failure of one condition could lead to the immediate collapse of this pyramid-like scheme. There is a paradox in this kind of association: the association cannot be formed without an attractive interest rate and it is impossible to keep the number of new members constantly growing. Once the number of new members decreases, the fund will collapse because of a resource shortage; if the holder of the association promises an attractive interest rate, he will face the problem of not being able to afford the interest by investing in normal ventures with the collected funds. The interest can only be paid by new fund member contri-butions that turn it into a mathematical game doomed to collapse. This has often caused social problems, such as divorce, suicide, and murder. Therefore, it is important to keep *hehui* under control.

Money Houses

As the reform and opening-up of China's economy progresses, the regions with active commodity economies strongly demand a convenient and efficient financial market. Corresponding to this request, in the 1980s, many money houses emerged in Zhejiang, Fujian, and Guangdong Province, where the private economy was developing rapidly. Having prevailed for hundreds of years as important financial organizations in those regions, money houses were once again resurrected and accepted immediately by local people.

The Old Lady Bank in Wenzhou is the typical representation of a *yinbei*. This spreads across several villages of Wenzhou, where loan brokers are located. These individuals hold information on capital resources, voluntarily informed by the people who have idle funds. Businessmen who are short on money will get in touch with these loan brokers. After a risk evaluation, the brokers may decide to extend loans, and they will collect all the idle funds they can obtain and collect a brokerage commission as a reward. Millions of idle funds can be collected in no time; however, the brokers in charge of this process are middle aged women up to 60 years of age, who have little education. According to a statistics report from the Central Bank, by the end of 2007, there were more than RMB 10,000 billion of idle funds in the informal financial market. In Zhejiang Province, for example, the scale of idle funds was as much as RMB 8300 billion. Idle funds are collected underground and can be attracted to new ventures by the prospect of a little profit.

The most common type of money house is an institutional or semi-institutional private intermediary organization. The operators of money houses use their own money as security for low interest loans, and then, according to the risk and the time range they face, lend it at different high interest rates.

Some money houses are running under the name of associations or funds, such as the Old Men's Association, the Informal Mutual Aid Association, and so on. At first, these operated as cooperative associations, only collecting funds from their members and disbursing funds to those who needed it. As time passed, they became profit-oriented money houses, which also absorbed funds from non-members.

With a few exceptions, most of the money houses were unpublicized and unauthorized; however, because of some extreme bias held by state-owned local financial organizations, those publicized and authorized money houses were banned by the government on May 1986. From then on, all money houses were unpublicized.

Informal Money Collection

After the reform and opening-up, private enterprises emerged and thrived. However, most of the banks were owned by the state and therefore provided limited financial support to the development of private enterprises. As a result, informal money collection was innovated as a new channel to finance the development of private enterprises. Informal money collection is a type of financial activity in which the money borrower collects money directly from financial markets by all means possible. For the money borrower, money collection is a crucial way to solve financial problems; for the money lender, money collection is an innovative way to invest. During the 1980s, money collection prevailed, creating informal stock and bond markets. It also brought about the idea of partnerships and shareholding companies.

Right at the beginning of the reform process, there were different types of money collection. Categorized in terms of validity, money collection can be divided into three types: that which is authorized by the PBC, that which is authorized by the local government, and that which is non-authorized. Money collection can also be categorized by the interest rate into the following types: no interest collection, low interest collection, and high interest collection. Thirdly, it can be categorized by ownership type as enterprise ownership, local government ownership, and state ownership. Lastly, it can also be sorted into a profit-oriented type and a nonprofit-oriented type.

Obviously, money collection of local-government owned and state-owned types actually does not belong to the category of informal finance. Only non-state-owned enterprise money collection counts. Informal money collection plays a supplementary role in social economic development. Its contribution to the prosperity of non-state-owned enterprises and to the exploration of shareholding companies is incomparable.

Initially, most of the informal money collection is performed upon the request of the producer. However, in order to collect sufficient money, the money collector usually promises a high interest rate, which increases the risk of default. Once the investment has produced a lower than expected return, or has even failed, due to lack of social norms and legal regulation, on the one hand, the debtor cannot deliver his promise or even "escape from debt;" on the other hand, the lender cannot find a way to pursue his rights. Credit losses from informal money collection can be found everywhere, in which the default of a single debtor has limited influence. Some collections are merely shell games—by creating a shell company in the name of real estate investment or something similar, with a high promised interest rate, the criminals successfully persuade people to "invest." Using mathematical tricks, that is, paying high interest to a small group of people by borrowing from a larger group of people, the reputation of the shell company keeps growing, as does its scale. With more and more people involved in this game, some who learn the truth may even became the accomplices in order to "earn" their money back.

However, this unsustainable structure cannot continue. Once it collapses, many people will suffer from it, depending on its scale. Furthermore, as a financial crime, without proper supervision and a powerful legal system, it will spread rapidly, jeopardizing the order of financial markets, and threatening the security and stability of the entire society. Moreover, 80% of the collected money is drawn from banks, which leads to shortages in the credit resources of bank, therefore challenging the financial status of formal finance, especially during periods of monetary tightening. Eventually, this phenomenon of "capital circulating outside the formal system" was regulated and restricted in the early 1990s.

Private Equity Funds

Private Equity Fund is a special term created in the late 1990s in China, referring to a type of unauthorized collective investment that is not publicly advertised and is recruited from particular investors. There are basically two types of such funds: one is the contract-based collective investment fund formed through investment trust contracts, and the other is the company-based collective investment fund formed through establishment of a joint stock company.

With the development of a stock market and a futures market, more and more agencies engage in the private equity business; as a result, private equity funds have experienced a stage of expansion. According to a survey performed by Xia Bin in 2001, of all the companies with the highest possibility of operating private equity businesses in Beijing, including investment management companies, investment consulting companies, financial management companies, and financial consulting companies, 52% admitted that they were doing "financial planning" for their clients—running a private equity business in fact. Calculated based on the number of clients and the money involved in each deal, the funds recruited per company average around 1.5 billion yuan, which means the total sum of Beijing, Shanghai and Shenzhen could reach 544.35 billion yuan. According to an investigation performed by the China Securities Regulatory Commission, one financial planning subsidiary that belonged to a Nanjing securities company recruited investment funds of more than 10 billion yuan and there were many securities companies running businesses of similar types, which means the total sum is more than 200 billion yuan. If the funds that trust companies collected are taken into consideration, it would be more than 700 billion yuan (Xia Bin 2001). And according to the China Private Equity Report issued by Zero2IPO Group, in the first quarter of 2008, more than $19.99 billion was recruited by 16 Private Equity Funds in China. When compared with the recruited funds in the first quarter of 2007, it has increased by 163.3%.

Rural Financial Organizations

Rural financial organizations refer to those financial organizations that existed from the mid-1980s to the mid-1990s, including Rural Cooperative

Funds (RCFs), Rural Mutual Aid Associations (RMAA) and Rural Financial Services (RFS), among which RCFs were the most popular organization.

RCFs first showed up as the innovational form of security organization in Jiangxi Province in December 1982, and used the RMAA as their prototype. The RMAA's innovational form of security organization was recognized and further promoted by the Ministry of Civil Affairs. During this stage, these organizations gradually developed into RCFs.

RCFs appeared as a consequence of the particular historical background of the rural economic institutional reform and the rural economic development at that time: on one hand, as the rural credit cooperative association gradually dissimilated, farmers lost their credit source for agricultural production, and in order to meet the needs of the rural economy, they struggled to find a new financial channel to get out of this predicament; on the other hand, the agricultural household responsibility system became nationwide, while the traditional people's commune (PC) system was finally broken. Along with the sudden demise of the PC, the original and newly accumulated rural collective funds were vastly eroded because the original collective management system and methods did not continue to work well and meanwhile, a new management system had not yet been established. In 1984, after liquidation of the original collective assets, the local governments of Jiangsu and Hubei Provinces began to explore new measures to manage collective assets. During that time, RCFs were brought to the attention of the Agricultural Monitoring Station as well as of the local government and therefore became nationally promoted. By the end of 1996, according to official statistics, 21,000 townships and 25,000 villages, accounting for 47.6% of all townships and 3.4% of all villages, respectively, had established RCFs while the funds raised totaled 108.28 billion yuan. Cumulative fund lending totaled 152.73 billion yuan. The RFS was actually an "advanced" form of RCFs, providing financial services to nonagricultural departments.

Without a proper monitoring system and strong regulations, and with poor management, RCFs suffered payment crises from time to time. For the sake of the stability of the financial system, the central government promulgated several documents to strengthen the management of RCFs. In 1996, the State Council promulgated the Decision on the Reform of the Rural Financial System, in which a thorough cleanup of RCFs was announced, and actions were taken thereafter.

The Fundamental Defects of Informal Financial Institutions in China

According to the theory of institutional demand, the creation and evolution of informal finance follow a logical formula, from the perspective of both the imperfect formal financial institution and the informal financial institution.

According to the theory of institutional supply, informal finance is actually a spontaneous innovation aiming at overcoming the defects of the formal financial arena as well as a method of adjusting the financing system to benefit the development of private enterprises. However, with the deepening reform in the market economy, informal finance is suffering a great concussion. Unable to resist economic temptation, individuals commit immoral deeds, violating the interests of others. This is fundamentally due to defects in informal financial institutions, which are based on the traditional credit culture that cannot sustain the expansion of financing scale only by its moral constraints.

For financial activities, there are three kinds of constraints that ensure the proper rights of lender and restrict the behavior of borrower: firstly, legal constraints are imposed when a legally binding contract is signed; secondly, economic constraints implement the use of collateral to ensure the proper rights of the lender; finally, moral constraints impose mental pressure and social pressure on the debtor to restrict his behavior.

Most informal financing activities are based only on an oral agreement and lack collateral, while even those having a written contract are weakly protected by the legal system since informal finance is still an underground activity. Therefore, one often finds that moral constraints are the only type of constraints that prevails. If the moral constraint imposed is powerful, risks associated with informal financing will be reduced and efficiency will be enhanced; otherwise, chaos in the informal financing market will set in and the stability of society will be undermined. Different from formal credit, informal finance takes place without any detailed investigation and is only based upon personal relationships. As the financing scale grows and the number of members increases, personal relationships fundamental to informal finance break down and the problem of asymmetric information between lender and borrower emerges. The effective and safe recovery of loans becomes quite difficult. Meanwhile, some illegal activities, such as high-interest lending, or even financial crimes have greatly affected the moral foundation of informal finance and could lead to the invalidation of the informal financial system. Bilk, payment crisis of money houses, and the collapse of some *hehui* all correspond to moral loss.

Taihui, a transformation of *hehui*, is an informal financial activity in the southern region of Zhejiang Province. In 1986, the national economy was booming, but formal finance could not meet the demand of expanding economic activities. As a result, some resorted to borrowing or lending high-interest loans. Because of attractive returns, the scale of high-interest loans sharply increased and turned into the form known as *taihui*. Nearly 80% of the holders of *taihui* were illiterate countrywomen, whose advantages were their local connections and their shrewd minds. Without moral constraints, tempted by enormous pecuniary, *taihui* developed into a pyramid-like structure, where loan sources for old members were funded by the growth in the number of new members. From 1985 to the spring of 1987, in 9 counties of Wenzhou City, 300,000 people were involved in this money collecting game and the money involved reached as much as RMB 1.2 billion. In the spring of 1986, when the *taihui* started to collapse, the panic spread like the plague from town to town. After the collapse of the *taihui*, nearly 80,000 farm households lost every penny in their pockets and were mired in deep debt.

As can be seen from the analysis above, the moral constraints of informal finance are only appropriate for small-scale financing between individuals who know each other well and have high moral standards. However, with the development of the economy, the scale of financing has enlarged. The traditional moral constraints cannot hold up the entire informal financial system.

In addition, the institution of informal finance has been innovated through repeated negotiations among market participants rather than through imposed reformation. Informal finance and its institutional risks are not often recognized by the government.

The Features of Societal Transition in Informal Finance in China

Informal finance is the product of the mutual interaction between demand and supply of money, and was reborn during the special transition period when China switched from a planned economy to a market economy. As a social phenomenon, informal finance is a result of cultural inheritance and social transition, based on low-level informal loan relations.

There are several features of societal transition in informal finance:

Firstly, informal finance is the product of the interaction between overall changes and local changes. Things are evolving with time, and so is informal finance. However, the process of evolution for informal finance has been a long journey that could not be achieved in a short time. And only with the local changes of structure, ideology and operation, could the organization of informal finance evolve.

Secondly, informal finance may bring a benefit or a danger to society. The breakup of the direct connection between the borrower and the lender, the establishment of the benefit-oriented core values and the appearance of intermediaries favor the development of the individual, the organization, and the society. However, because of the private nature of its ownership, informal finance has never been recognized by authority and can only be operated underground. Without appropriate supervision and guidance, it may turn into "black finance" and therefore bring instability or even danger to the development of individuals, organizations, and society.

Finally, informal finance is a combination of a spontaneous change and a planned change. The spontaneous change mostly happens in the second phase of transition, while the planned change mostly happens in the first phase. Following the first phase of transition, a relatively stable organization of informal finance is established. Now, it is at the crossroads of further development: one pathway entails operating under formal regulations and making a greater contribution to the development of the market economy; the other pathway leads to "black finance" and ends in the collapse of the whole system, as well as in social unrest. Only with planned guidance and reform can informal finance be coaxed into sustainable and sound development.

Taking a panoramic view of the development of the societal transition of informal finance, it can be clearly seen that informal finance is an institutional arrangement spontaneously induced by the potential for economic gain. As a consequence of the induced institutional change, informal finance is more sensitive to market signals than formal institutions. Moreover, although there is a lack of formal regulations, informal finance can allocate capital resources efficiently, because through its allocation, the positions of the capital demander and the capital supplier are improved. Informal finance fills the gap between the capital supply provided by formal institutions and the capital demand of the market.

Cause of the Distortion of Informal Finance in China—Culture Lag

In the past 1000 years, diverse forms of credit culture have emerged and evolved in China. The Analects of Confucius written 2400 years ago states that "without trust, the people cannot establish their stance," which means, if the people lose their faith in government, then the government loses its foundation of existence. There are still many statements about credit such as "I do not know how a man without truthfulness is to get on," "they are determined to be sincere in what they say, and to carry out what they do," and so on.

Though it has a 1000 years of history, why has informal finance become such a big issue now? The reason is because the "culture lag," which was generated during the social transition period, has jeopardized the personal religion which was the foundation of the credit culture. The traditional credit culture mentioned above is more related to the personal religion, or more specifically personal moral objectives rather than to norms of social behavior. Without its religious foundation, the traditional credit culture can easily break up under economic temptation. A "lag" is thus generated between distorted traditional cultural characteristics and modern economic life. This is what we call "culture lag."

The Causes of Culture Lag

During the economic transition period, the traditional culture concept was under great attack. The traditional credit culture, of which Chinese people used to be proud, has now become subordinate to the market economy. The causes of this change can be analyzed with both objective and subjective factors.

Objectively speaking, under the planned economy, as a result of regulated planning, the rules of contract and credit relationships are distorted; therefore, the lag between traditional credit culture and modern contract culture is generated. At the beginning of the development of the market economy in China, the effect of this lag was not apparent, for the primary aim of the central government was the growth of economy rather than the establishment of market rules. With the development of the market economy and the extension of the merchandise exchange area, the effect of culture lag is exposed. The lack of market rules becomes the bottleneck of the modernization process.

Subjectively speaking, the frequent political movements, especially the "cultural revolution," have dramatically jeopardized the inheritance of traditional culture and the continuance of ideology and have generated the lag between ideological change and institutional change of the economy.

The above two factors have caused the fade-out of the traditional credit system, which is based on traditional moral culture.

The Lack of the Construction of the Modern Contract Credit System during the Transition Period

On the one hand, the underdeveloped market economy could not sustain the modern contract credit system. After the reform and opening-up, although economic development has achieved remarkable success, the domestic market has not been entirely established and regional development is diverse. Therefore, a functional platform of the modern contract credit system could not be implemented.

On the other hand, the legal system in China has had its own inevitable disadvantages since the old times. Famous for its concept of "rule by law," the Legalist School still had some shortcomings. It exaggerated the effect of law and underestimated the influence of "rite." And some of its extreme thoughts affected the formation of objective and scientific attitude of "rule by law." At present, during the process of modernization, the shortcomings of the legal system are manifested mainly in its incapability of satisfying personal rationality as well as providing proper incentives. The evolution of traditional credit culture lags behind the development of modern economic life, while the imperfect legal system cannot perform its function of instruction and regulation. Therefore, the phenomenon of credit loss is an institutional problem as well as a cultural problem.

The traditional credit culture has become subordinate to modern culture, but the modern contract credit system is yet to be established. Under these circumstances, credit loss emerges as a result of the culture lag.

To Meet the Demands of the Credit Culture, New Types of Informal Finance Were Generated

As the culture lag became a phenomenon ubiquitous throughout society and the new foundation of the modern market economy, which is based on the law of value although large-scale market exchange has not been established, people became alert to lending activities. Meanwhile, facing institutional constraints, some individuals and SMEs could not obtain finance through formal financial institutions. In order to catch up with the wheels of economic change, some started to resort to new types of informal finance, which evolved from the traditional credit culture, that is, small-scale credit financing based on regional, occupational, and familial relationships, which help in supervising the loan process and therefore can reduce the risk of adverse selection and moral hazard.

While discussing the merits of traditional credit culture, we should point out that there are some great weaknesses. Traditional credit culture simply relies on small-scale personal relationships, which could easily break up as its scale is enlarged. A credit system in the modern sense has yet to be established and its primary target is to teach social members what to pursue and what not to pursue, as well as which behavior will be rewarded and which behavior will be punished. Meanwhile, the legal system has to be improved. This is not only necessary for moral reasons, but also for the development of the market economy.

The Potential of Informal Finance as a Financial Industry in China

After the reform and the opening-up, with the deepening reform of the market economy, some traditional forms of informal finance have been brought back to the financial market. At the same time, new forms have been created. At the beginning, because it was unrecognized by authority and due to the payment crises of some money houses and *hehui*, informal finance was mostly regarded as an underground organization that needed to be banned. With the boom of the private economy in recent years, people have started to see the great contribution made by informal finance. Meanwhile, in order to effectively reduce poverty in China, particularly in rural areas, informal finance is a useful tool to employ. Moreover, if informal finance can be legalized, and then further properly regulated and guided by the government, its potential as a financial industry will be exploited.

Recently, private firms are still suffering serious financing issues: first of all, they have very little access to bank credit. Most private enterprises are in their nascent stages. Their scale of business, operations, and potential risk control do not match the standards requested by commercial banks. Meanwhile, there are too many state-owned enterprises competing for the capital resources from state-owned banks. Secondly, private enterprises still find it is very difficult to obtain funding from venture capital. The Chinese venture capital industry, although begun in the mid-1980s, is still in the start-up phase after years of sluggish development, and its scale of investment remains small. In addition, venture capital currently never lacks new ventures. Most private enterprises cannot obtain start-up venture capital. Thirdly, private firms have difficulty in financing through the stock market. The fundamental purpose of the establishment of the stock market is to optimize the allocation of capital resources. However, the initial motives of the establishment of the stock market in China were to serve the development of state-owned enterprises. This one-way political relationship deeply impacts most private entrepreneurs who dream of financing through stock market. Finally, private firms' attempt to get fiscal support is in vain. Capital is a scare resource which is impossible to obtain simply by earning the sympathy of the government. At the same time, with the growth of the economy, there are many more "idle funds" accumulated by common citizens, who would rather invest than save in a bank. With the strong demand and expectations, informal finance encounters innovation, providing capital to private enterprises, while creating investment channels for "idle funds." The optimal allocation of capital resource is thus realized with the help of informal finance. Meanwhile, the regulation environment has been better improved. From the holding of an Annual China International Private Equity Forum to the promulgation of the Proposals on adjusting and relaxing the market-entry policies for the banking institutions in rural areas so as to support the construction of the new socialist countryside by the China Banking Regulatory Commission (CBRC), the government has made efforts to create a sound environment for the healthy development of informal finance. Thus, informal finance with a modern meaning was generated after the reform and thrives on the development of private enterprises.

The Scale of Informal Finance—Local Investigations

The underground nature of informal finance leads to statistical trouble in estimating the scale of informal finance, which is off the record. We know that the scale and influence of informal finance was much greater in the southeastern coastal areas where the commodity economy was relatively developed; thus, a local investigation of these areas reflected the scale of informal finance around China.

Take Wenzhou, for example. From the beginning of reform until the 1990s, the scale of informal finance largely increased and the forms also diversified. By the end of August, 1992, 40% of the capital resources of private enterprises came from informal finance, which was twice as much as the formal credit supplied by banks and trust associations. According to the report of the Wenzhou Branch of the People's Bank of China, by the end of 2001, there was 17 billion yuan of external financing coming from informal finance, accounting for 42.5% of the total sum (Yunfan Wang 2002). The sample survey of 66 rural households in Wenzhou showed that 83.3% of them were involved at some point in informal financing activities. And in

2002, the percentage of informal finance out of the overall financial market in Wenzhou was around 33%. In some rural areas, where the financial market was less developed, this figure was as high as 66%. In Fujian Province, 240 billion yuan was involved in informal finance in 2001 (Cui, Li, Wu 2002). According to the research of the Hangzhou Branch of the People's Bank of China, during the Tenth Five-year Plan Period, 830 billion yuan was involved in the operation of informal finance (Deng 2002). According to a routine investigation by the Guangzhou Branch of the People's Bank of China, the capital resources of informal finance accounted for 5% of deposits in formal financial institutions and 7% of the operating capital. At one time, 30% of rural households and 56% of self-employed households were involved in private lending (Jianjun Zhang 2002).

Reforming the Formal and Informal Financial Systems

Matching Up the Defects of Formal Financial Institutions and Promoting the Development of Rural Financial Markets

After the WTO accession, the four major state-owned banks have gradually drawn away from the rural financial market and have served only as deposit collectors in those areas. In addition, rural credit cooperatives do not devote to serving the *sannong* (three areas). Because most of the agricultural production activities are small-scale and low-profit businesses with high risk, once the government loosens its control on RCCs, their business scope will expand to the nonagricultural fields to maximize their profit. Farmers cannot obtain necessary credit funds from the formal financial market.

According to statistic reports by financial institutions, there are few formal credit funds in rural areas and most of them cannot reach SMEs, not to mention rural households. According to an estimate by the Banking Regulatory Commission, in 2000, bank credit only accounted for 7% of agricultural loans, much lower than the percentage of bank credit used for industrial and commercial industries. Millions of funds that come from rural areas are now being used in other industries rather than in agriculture, so the capital demand of farming is not met and the poverty problem cannot be solved.

Informal finance can not only satisfy the capital demand of farms, but it can also stimulate RCCs to improve their management, and can optimize the capital resources in rural areas through fair competition with RCCs. The reform of RCCs is the most important part of the reform of the rural financial system, but it is not the only part. Only by recognizing the legal status of informal finance and granting it the opportunity to fairly compete, can a healthy rural financial system with fair competition and multiple participants be established.

Informal finance should cooperate with local rural credit cooperatives. Through cooperation, its system can be standardized, its operation and management can be rationalized and legalized and its historical defects can be overcome. On the other hand, RCCs can learn from informal finance with respect to risk management, operation insurance, information exchange, and cost reduction, which can help RCCs realize sustainable development in rural areas.

Because of the advantage in obtaining rural capital resource information, informal finance could also be used to build up a credit evaluation and guarantee system in rural areas. For instance, an informal financial organization or an individual who meets certain conditions can take a lead in founding a credit guarantee association, while some specific policies can be made to attract informal financial organizations or individuals to provide paid services about credit guarantees.

Developing a Multilevel Financial Market, Promoting the Upgrade in the Structure of the Financial Industry, and Optimizing the Ecological Environment of Finance

Various economic components outside institutions developed and a fair competition environment for all kinds of production industries formed before the full reform of the formal institutional economy. The financial industry, however, is still under monopolistic control by state-owned banks, which ignores the existence of the informal finance and lacks a mechanism for competition. Currently, with regard to financial markets, 70% of all financial resources are under the control of state-owned banks, whose branches have spread all over China. Although permitted to enter the financial market to some extent, private banks are still at a disadvantage. Without a well-established market entrance mechanism, competitors cannot be pulled into the market. Therefore, the scale of the financial market will not expand and the development of financial markets will be lagging. The construction of a multilevel financial market requires the contribution of private banks. The reform of the marketization process and the development of market competition are greatly dependent on the development of competition in the private economy. The competition of private banks can impose huge pressure on the inefficient state-owned financial institutions. And by example, private banks can promote the further commercialization of state-owned financial institutions. Moreover, through the exchange among multi-party ownership, capital resource allocations can be optimized and the structure of the financial industry upgraded.

In 2006, China agreed to allow foreign financial institutions to enter China's financial market. This is also a great opportunity for informal finance to develop, because there is no reason to keep China's financial market closed to national informal capital. Without historical burdens, informal financial institutions can easily learn from foreign financial institutions, which have advanced management skills and business practices. And after years of practicing, they will be able to compete with foreign financial institutions in the financial market. Furthermore, financial innovation advocated by international financial institutions will bring large benefits in terms of reducing risk and uncertainty to society. Large commercial banks in China are actively exploring this area, but as they are larger, more deeply embedded institutions, a slight mistake in operation may lead to a disaster. Informal financial institutions, comparatively small and independent, can be the experimental units of financial innovation. If they are successful, the development of financial innovation will be promoted; if they fail, the damage will be minimal. Therefore, informal financial institutions can play a significant role in optimizing the ecological environment of finance.

In late 2006, the China Banking Regulatory Commission (CBRC) promulgated the Proposals on adjusting and relaxing the market-entry policies for the banking institutions in rural areas so as to support the construction of the new socialist countryside (hereinafter referred to as the Proposals). Later, Sichuan, Qinghai, Gansu, Neimenggu, Jilin, and Hubei Provinces were taken as experimental units, where entry threshold was lower. According to the Proposals, a village or township bank shall meet the following requirements for establishment: (a) The controlling shareholder or sole shareholder of a village or township bank must be a domestic banking institution. The controlling shareholder who is a banking financial institution shall hold at least 20% of the bank's total equity. (b) The individual natural persons or the independent legal entities shall hold no more than 10% of the bank's total equity and the individual nonbank financial institutions or non-financial enterprises shall hold no more than 10% of the bank's total equity. (c) The registered capital of a county based village or township bank shall be no less than RMB 3 million and that of a township based village or township bank shall be no less than RMB 1 million. (d) Village or township banks shall not grant loans to individuals or entities other than local borrowers, while a lending company with no less than RMB 500,000 registered capital can only be set up by a domestic banking institution.

It is an important reform in China's rural financial institutional arrangement and has positive implications for the increase of peasant income, the development of agriculture, and the development of the rural market. The establishment of village or township banks better supports the *sannong* by solving the problems of low coverage of banking outlets, inadequate variety and supply of financial products and services, and insufficient competition.

The Development Opportunities and the Future of Informal Finance in China

Informal finance can be divided into two types: "gray finance" and "black finance." "Gray finance" should be permitted, promoted and standardized, for its existence has made outstanding contributions to the private economy. "black finance" should be banned, for its existence highly increases the level of financial crimes such as financial swindle, the evasion of foreign exchange control, the practice of money laundering, and so on (Shuxia Jiang 2001).

If the development of informal finance is suppressed by the government, informal financial institutions will easily move underground. The existence of intensive underground activities results in the circulation of a great deal of currency outside the formal financial system, increasing pressure through currency withdrawal and making macroeconomic control by the central bank more difficult. If "gray finance" can be recognized by the authorities, and then regulated, supervised, guided, and protected, its positive influence can be improved, that is, it can make use of idle money and support the development of SMEs. Furthermore, with the development of informal finance, "black finance," which as an illegal financial activity endangers the stability of the financial system and society as a whole, will be constrained to some extent; at the same time, macroeconomic control can be better achieved.

Brought about by the demands of the market economy, informal finance is developing in a distorted manner under government suppression. This makes it different not only from traditional informal finance, but also from informal finance in western countries. Currently, all kinds of informal finance, except pawnbroking, are operating underground and out of the scope of supervision. Nonetheless, all the troubles in the informal financial arena are caused by the formal institutional arrangement. As was laid out in Article 28 of the Provisional Regulations of the People's Republic of China on the Control of Banks and promulgated by the State Council (1986): "the individual is not allowed to establish banks or other financial institutions, nor to operate financial businesses." Finance has since been closed to individuals and private organizations. Therefore, although created in response to great demand, private financial organizations can only operate and develop by eluding supervision.

In addition, informal finance has had a lot of difficulties because of inconsistent governmental policies. Although, since the reform and opening-up, government has been suppressing the development of informal finance, its attitude toward informal finance has been changing all the time. When informal finance is considered to favor the development of the economy, the government will turn a blind eye; when informal finance is considered a threat to the monopolistic position of state-owned financial institutions, or a source of disorder in financial markets or a disturbance to monetary policy, it will be resisted or banned.

Different local governments, even different departments of local governments, have different attitudes toward informal finance. Taking the local economy into consideration, the local government tends to protect and encourage the development of informal finance. However, as a financial administrator, the central bank tends to suppress the development of informal finance. Overall, the development of informal finance is the equilibrium result of a multi-agent game, which involves informal financial suppliers, informal financial demanders, state-owned financial institutions, the central government, local governments, and different departments of local governments, where the determining force is the central government.

Authority must realize that informal finance is an institutional innovation, initiated by grassroots activities, serving grassroots populations, and having economic and social foundations. Although informal finance has been cleared up and banned several times, it still exists and keeps developing. Evidence shows that pure suppression can only lead to unattainable supervision, underground operation, or even illegal operation rather than the full eradication of informal finance. Meanwhile, it should also be noted that the current types of informal finance are ancient and inferior informal institutional arrangements with insurmountable endogenous defects, and are therefore transitional, since they cannot meet the demand of the further development of the market economy and should be replaced by formal institutional arrangements.

In summary, the government must discard outdated thoughts that government-owned institutions are the only valid type of financial institutions and pay careful attention to secondary institutional arrangements induced by the market. The government should regard informal finance as a "weather-vane," which can "forecast" the credit demand of the financial market; an innovation, which can optimize the allocation of institutional resources; and an induced institutional arrangement, which can fix the problems brought about by state-oriented financing institutional change. Only after adjusting credit policy and improving financial regulation, as well as legalizing, standardizing, and guiding informal finance, can the government truly contribute to the development of the market economy and a harmonious society.

Generally speaking, there are two strategies for standardizing and guiding informal finance. One is by gradually absorbing the capital in informal financial markets into the formal financial market, and thus realizing a diversification of ownership of formal institutions. Meanwhile, through accelerating the management structural reform in formal financial institutions and expanding the business scope of formal financial institutions, the demand that informal financing faces can be met. For example, in rural areas, as the dominant formal financial institution, RCCs need to be coordinated with the local industrial development plans and patterns, and the scale of small and short-term loans needs to be increased and made to serve the rural households. In urban areas, banks need to change their thoughts about ownership, reform the management structure, reduce the cost of small loans, and satisfy financing demands by SMEs and other private enterprises. Through these interactions, the incorporation of informal finance and formal finance can be accomplished. The negative "black finance" activities should be fought against, even as the positive informal financial activities are brought into the formal financial system and given appropriate supervision.

The role government shall play in the process of establishing a stable, unbiased foundation for informal finance is critical. With an appropriate policy, through recognizing, legalizing, and guiding informal capital into the financial industry, informal finance, as well as finance as a whole, will have a bright future.

Notes

1. CUFE surveyed more than 90 SMEs as well as more than 1100 individual industrial and commercial households in 82 cities and 200 villages of 20 provinces.

2. Note: quoted from the speech of Xiao-ling Wu at "China's Macroeconomic Tends and Industry Development Summit Forum," http://business.sohu.com/20050723/n240186724.shtml.

3. Fund for Agricultural Development, *Rural Poverty Report*—2002.

4. Note: quoted from "Pawnbrokers in Shanghai," *Journal of Society*, 1(12), Dec.1929.

References

Cao, Liqun. 2001. A study of the subject behavior in current financial market in rural areas. *Financial Forum* 5, pp. 6–11.

Cui, Lijin, Jiang Li, and Liang Wu. 2002. The underground financial market in Zhejiang, Fujiang and Guangzhou Provinces. *International Financial News*, January 18, p. 4.

Deng, Yuwen. 2002. What is standing in the way of the development of private banks? *China Economic Times*, September 25.

He, Guangwen. 1999. A perspective of rural residents' credit activity: financial restraint and financial deepening in rural areas. *China Rural Economy* 10, pp. 42–48.

Huang, Da, ed. 1990. *The Encyclopedia of Finance in China*. Beijing: Economy and Management Publishing House Press.

Huang, Jianhui. 1994. *Banking History in China*. Shanxi: Shanxi Economy Publishing House Press.

Jiang, Shuxia. 2001. *Informal Finance in China*. Fujian: Fujian People's Publishing House Press.

Jiang, Xuzhao. 1996. *The Research of Informal Finance in China*. Shandong: Shandong People's Publishing House Press.

Li, Jianjun. 2006. *The Investigation of China's Informal Finance*. Shanghai: Shanghai People's Publishing House Press.

Lin, Boqiang. 2005. Government expenditure and poverty reduction in China. *Economic Research Journal* 1, pp. 27–37.

Lin, Justin Yifu and Xifang Sun. 2003. Information, informal finance, and SME financing. China Centre for Economic Research in Peking University Working Paper (September), No. C2003025, pp. 2–34.

Sheng, Songcheng, Borong Ying, and Xiang Huang. 2001. Retrospect and prospect of China's rural credit cooperatives. *Journal of Financial Research* 5, pp. 42–49.

Shi, Jinchuan and Min Ye. 2001. Financial arrangements in the environment with institutional distortion: Wenzhou case. *Economic Theory Business Management* 1, pp. 63–68.

Tsai, Kellee. 2001. Beyond banks: The local logic of informal finance and private sector development in China. Presented at the Conference on Financial Sector Reform in China, www.ksg.harvard.edu/cbg/Conferences/financial_sector/BeyondBanks.pdf.

Wang, Xiaoyi. 1999. The investigation of rural informal finance during the industrialization. *China Rural Survey* 1, pp. 5–7.

Wang, Xin. 1996. What can Mainland learn from the experience of SME financing in Taiwan? *Comparative Economic and Social Systems* 5, pp. 36–42.

Wang, Yunfan. 2002. Where did 160 billion informal capital in Wenzhou go? *21st Century Business Herald*, June 10.

Xia, Bin. 2001. A report on the private funds in China. *Journal of Financial Research* 8, pp. 18–31.

Zeng, Kanglin and Changgeng Wang. 1993. *On Credit.* Beijing: China Financial Publishing House Press.

Zhang, Weiying. 1994. Capital structure of SMEs and financial system in Taiwan. In *Taiwan Economy and the Economic Reform in Mainland China*, ed. Yi Gang and Xu Xiaonian. Chapter 7, Beijing: Chinese Economy Publishing House Press.

Zhang, Jianjun. 2002. On the inter-personal credit and private-governed financing. *Journal of Financial Research* 10, pp. 101–9.

Zhao, Rulin, ed. 1999. *Dictionary of Market Economics.* Beijing: Economy and Science Publishing House Press.

Zhou, Tiancheng and Zhicheng Lin. 1999. *The Development Mechanism of SMEs in Taiwan.* Lianjing: Lianjing Publishing House Press.

Chapter 3

Informal Finance, Underground Finance,

Illegal Finance, and Economic Movement:

A National Analysis

Jianjun Li

During the new turn of macroeconomic regulation and control that started in 2003, the Chinese economy, under a process of deregulation, witnessed the appearance of different economic phenomena. Price levels rose, despite monetary policy, which was implemented to push them down. Repeated government efforts were unable to curb the increase in investment and consumption prices. These issues urged scholars to review the wisdom of the past, in order to influence the economy with theoretical innovations. This research involving a nationwide investigation was launched on such a basis from a different point of view that was not previously examined. This is from the perspective of informal finance, underground finance, and illegal finance, which provide foundational references for structural and economic influence in terms of macroeconomic regulation and control, as well as economic decision-making. These three types of unobserved finance prevented monetary policy from working effectively during these years of heightened economic growth.

The beginning of this study started nearly 3 years ago, in September 2003, even as deregulation began, but the effects of the initial studies were certainly not obvious since tight monetary policy was implemented. The People's Bank of China (PBC) improved the deposit reserve rate several times and increased the basic interest rates to control formal commercial banks' credit expanse, but most enterprises still could be financed by other types of finance, which are not observed by the financial authority. Unobserved finance was supporting fixed asset investment growth at a high speed to some extent. Price levels and the economic rate of growth have not diminished, and strong economic growth continues. The reasons for these are worth consideration.

―――――

Background

We will first review the regulative policy measures and their effects, describing a series of macroeconomic controls that did not have their expected impacts. In the fourth quarter of 2003, the price level in China increased, in conjunction with economic growth, particularly in the areas of financial investment services, production of electrolytic aluminum, and production of cement. In order to prevent the economy from over-heating, the currency was stabilized. On September 21, 2003, the bank reserve ratio was increased from 6% to 7%, in order to ensure the stability of banks. This, in turn, suppressed fixed asset investment and dampened excessive growth, weakening the pressure for prices to continue to rise. But rather than falling, as would be expected, price levels continued to rise, and after 6 months, namely in the first quarter of 2004, investment and consumption prices rose together, as the price level rose by 2.8%. Interest rates also rose. In response, the PBC decided to adopt interest rate regulation, which was implemented for short-term loans from March 25, 2004. Adjustment within finance raised the interest rate again to 0.63 of a percentage point, simultaneously surrendering to the state the rediscounting interest rate of 0.27 of a percentage point. In April 2004, prices continued to rise by 0.5%, which surpassed the bank demand deposit interest rate. Therefore, the PBC announced increase in the reserve fund rate once more, starting on April 25, 2004. On this date, the bank reserve rate grew from 0.5% to 7.5%.

As informal finance went into an active period, much money went out of the banking system because the deposit interest rates on the curb market were higher than formal bank's rates and private enterprises therefore received more informal financial support. Beginning in May 2004, the public anticipated that the central bank would increase interest rates, but the PBC did not do that immediately and took a careful attitude. In October 29, 2004, when the anticipation of raising interest became weak, the PBC announced interest rate increase, such that the 1 year time deposit interest rate was increased by 0.27%. Except for the legal reserve requirement policy and the interest rate policy, the PBC also contracted the money supply by issuing central bank notes since 2004. But as a result of the exchange rate mechanism system, outside the universally anticipated renminbi (RMB) exchange rate revaluation, foreign funds flew into China and the official foreign exchange reserves grew rapidly and caused a larger release of basic money into circulation.

Under the pressure of rapid money supply increase, the PBC continued to issue notes and use open market operations to call back currency from circulation. In the same year on July 21, the PBC, authorized by the State Council, reformed the RMB exchange rate, announcing the implementation of changes in the exchange rate system to a new mechanism which is based on market supply and demand, with reference to a basket of currencies in a managed floating exchange rate system, revaluing the RMB 2.1% to the US dollar. The RMB exchange revaluation could affect the domestic Chinese economy; although it cannot be called monetary policy per se, it is in fact advantageous to the suppression of an overheated economy, controlling continued price rises.

Since the beginning of 2006, the economic growth rate has been even quicker, despite efforts to dampen the overheated economy. In the first half of the year, GDP growth achieved 10.9%, and the consumer price index (CPI) rose by 1.5% on trend. On July 5, 2006, the PBC announced increase in the deposit reserve ratio of 0.5%. On July 21, the PBC again conducted reserve adjustment policy, and the legal bank reserve ratio was increased by 0.5% once again since August 15, 2006, achieving a ratio of 8.5%. And at the same time, the central bank notes were issued quickly and hugely. It was anticipated that the central bank would increase the interest rate again and on August 19, the PBC increased the basic rate by 0.27%.

Chinese economic growth has been based largely on fixed asset investment. This type of growth requires the support of the monetary supply. The question that remains, then, is when the PBC installs a tightening policy, which would raise the cost of investing, why does investment still continue to grow quickly, particularly in the energy and real estate industries? We found that informal finance, underground finance, and illegal financial activity have been weakening macroeconomic regulation and controlling its effects.

Because informal finance is in demand outside the mainstream money market, the interest rate is higher than the regular bank deposit interest rate (PBC 2005). The private economy is supported by unobserved finance, and to a certain degree unobserved finance has counterbalanced monetary policy effects. Money circulates between individuals and businesses, to a large extent without interacting with the banking sector. Therefore, the government has limited control over monetary effects (Li 2005).

Definition, Types, and Cases of Unobserved Finance

We next discuss what exactly unobserved finance is and some real examples of this nonbank financing method. Unobserved finance is a financial activity that is accounted for with difficulty under the system of national accounts and the financial statistics system, including informal finance, underground finance, and illegal finance. Below, we illustrate cases that were looked at during our surveys in 2004 and 2006, which illustrate these three types of unobserved finance.

Until now, the phrase 'unobserved finance' has not been used widely. The phrase 'unobserved economy' appeared not long ago and was used by an official for the first time in 2001, when it was published in official files made by OECD in order to guide different countries in the SNA system (OECD/ IMF/ILO/CIS 2002). After that, the United Nations also used this phase in its published books (United Nations Economic Commission for Europe 2003). The unobserved economy includes the informal economy, underground economy, hidden and shadow economy, and illegal economy, which have generally been discussed in the informal finance literature. These words or phrases used by different people have held different meanings, making it hard to compare the research conclusions arrived at by different authors. The same issue exists in the area of financial research—informal finance, underground finance, and illegal finance overlap. Therefore, it is necessary to define and distinguish these phrases.

There are different versions of the definition of informal finance. Xuzhao Jiang, a Chinese scholar, wrote that it should be defined from the ownership perspective, such that all non-state or nonpublic financing activities and financial organs belong to informal finance (Xuzhao Jiang 1996). He revised the definition of informal finance later and stated that informal finance should be judged by the rule of corporate law; the financial institutions that did not register in the State Ministry of Industry and Commerce belong to informal finance (Jiang and Ding 2004). Foreign scholars define that informal finance is also based on the standard of financial supervision and management, where all financial activities outside the scope of official supervision belong to informal finance (Isaksson 2002). Informal financing practices range from casual interpersonal borrowing and trade credit among wholesalers and retailers to more institutionalized mechanisms such as rotating credit associations, grassroots credit cooperatives, and even full-service yet unsanctioned private banks (Tsai 2002).

Chinese scholars cited the World Bank's definition and decided that those lenders (pawnshops, businessmen) that supply money to the noncorporate sector (farmers, individual entrepreneurs, retailers, etc.) should be referred to as participating in informal finance; institutional informal financial types circulate money outside the banking system, conduct economic transactions with cash, raise funds at a high interest rate, and transfer money from banks to private financial institutions (Lu 1995, 1997). Informal finance escapes official supervision and management, and avoids taxation and financial statistics (Cai 1996). Informal finance is on the opposite side of formal finance, including all financial activities outside the official financial supervision and management system (Zuo 2001). It is a civil financial sector spontaneously formed outside the official financial system and formal banking organization (Jun Zhang 2002). Informal finance is one part of that financial system, which is not accepted by legal and financial rules and exists outside of the formal financial system, and it includes underground finance (Ning Zhang 2002, 2003). From the above definitions of informal finance, we can see that it has not truly been distinguished from underground finance and illegal finance.

The phrase "underground finance" appeared in China in the 1990s, and most scholars since assumed that underground finance holds the same meaning as informal finance. The first Chinese scholar in the underground finance research field, Shuxia Jiang, stated that underground finance is part of finance and has general financial characteristics; it is formed in a special economic environment and is based on some form of credit (Shuxia Jiang 2001). So it is critical to define the 'underground' in the phrase "underground finance."

Underground finance is unprotected by law. It has five characteristics related to being outside the legal system: it is outside official supervision; it is not included in official statistical statements; it is illegal; those involved in it do not pay taxes; and it is hidden (Shuxia Jiang 2001). Underground finance can be divided into "gray finance" and "black finance." The former is beneficial to economic development and could be replaced with formal finance, while the latter is illegal finance, which is not suited to economic demand and is forbidden by law (Zhu and Hu 1997). Underground finance is illegal financial activity forbidden by official financial supervision and mainly exists at the border areas between towns and rural developing areas to assist the rural economy (Zhu 2003). From the above perspectives, underground finance has been defined mainly based on its sometimes illegal nature, although underground finance includes "gray finance."

In past research, illegal finance was included in underground finance, in which the narrow concept of underground finance equaled illegal finance. We assume here that illegal finance is financial activity forbidden by law, including criminal acts in formal financial institutions (Xia and Liu 2001). Underground finance, then, is not the same as illegal finance.

Informal finance, as we define it, refers to financial activity or financial organizations that society spontaneously produces, like borrowing between personal acquaintances, borrowing between enterprises, creation of cooperative fund organizations, and creation of mutual economic assistance organizations. It has financial institutions similar to banks, credit associations, negotiable securities organizations, insurance organizations, and so on. Informal finance does not have legal rules written about it and frequently finds cutting edge solutions, supporting private sector development.

Case 1: Informal Finance, Chuai–Shuitou Anti-Poverty Financing Association in Linxiang, Shanxi Province

Chuai–Shuitou is the seat of town government located in Lin Xian, Shanxi Province. More than 1800 inhabitants live there. Most inhabitants are poor since the natural environment is not good for agricultural production, which depends on the weather, especially rain. In 2003, there was a drought, and the crops were nearly totally destroyed. So finding antipoverty solutions became a large mandate for the local government. Chuai–Shuitou Anti-Poverty Financing Association was formed on September 15, 2001. The main investors came from big cities, while others were local rich householders. As of March 31, 2004, the total number of investors was 83. The funds balance reached RMB 291,462 from RMB 13,000 sponsored by the founder, Mr. Yushi Mao.

The financing association was an informal social financial organization. The association issued microloans to peasants in poor areas for health care, children's education, and agricultural production. The financing association was welcomed by farmers in this area.

It was financed by two kinds of funds, one being an antipoverty fund and the other being an interest-payment fund. The former operated without interest to the sponsors, and the latter was used by the association for at least 1 year, after which time the investors were paid 6% interest per year, including a 20% income tax on the profit. The antipoverty fund could not be withdrawn, but the interest-payment fund could be withdrawn if the investors gave notice to the foundation at least half a year in advance. If the income from the interest-payment fund was less than the interest that should be paid to investors, the difference in volume would be paid from the antipoverty fund. The Foundation issued two kinds of loans: interest-bearing loans and interest-free loans. Interest-free loans were used for medical treatment and school study, while interest-bearing loans were used for agricultural production. The loan periods included a 3-month period, a 6-month period, and a 1 year period. The interest rate was higher than the rural credit society's rate but was lower than the usury rate. Before March 31, 2004, the foundation issued 402 loans and the total loan amount reached RMB 568,700, including 42 loans with RMB 40,900 for medical treatment; 38 loans for school study with RMB 43,200; 315 loans for production with RMB 478,200; and another 7 loans with RMB 6400. The foundation made interest income of RMB 26,867 and expenditures of RMB 23,567. Many poor inhabitants benefited from the foundation.

Case 2: Informal Finance, Bidding Association in Fu-an, Fujian Province

The bidding association is one of the oldest types of mutual financing organizations in Zhejiang and Fujian. In fact, the bidding association provides loans based on the common savings of members to other members in turn. The loan interest rate is determined by members' bidding, with the member offering the highest rate getting the loan. The bidding association follows rules, and one person as the "head" organizes meetings for a certain purpose (such as medical treatment, a marriage, or a funeral) to collect money, and the first period's funds go to the head. Members may get money in the next periods by bidding. The meeting usually is held every month or every quarter according to the number and agreement of members. In every periodic meeting, all members contribute or save the same balance of money and one member gets the total money. In the next meeting, the members who received money in past meetings would pay one member principal and interest. When every member is refunded, the bidding association ends; it is not a permanent organization. The head of the bidding association is in charge of collecting members' money, as well as of accounting, recovering, and bidding. If one of the members does not pay the principal and interest, the head is responsibile for compensation. As a compensation for risk, the head does not pay the interest for his or her loan obtained at the first meeting.

On May 16, 2004, a bidding association head named Zhu Li went to the local Public Security Bureau to give himself up for organizing a bidding association that went bankrupt for nonrefundable money. Li did this in order to avoid being harmed by the association's members. From the primary investigation, Li's association financed about RMB 90 million from more than 1800 members. The effects of the association's bankruptcy spread quickly, and consequently most of the bidding associations in Fu-an went bankrupt. The total amount of funds of those bankrupt bidding associations was more than RMB 1 billion and about 80% of families in the city were involved in this financial disaster. The local population was 160,000 and local government income was just RMB 230 million in 2003. In this bidding association case, every resident in the city lost on average more than RMB 6000. A financial calamity caused by bidding association bankruptcies swept over the little city of Fu-an.. This case is a typical example of informal finance and the rotating credit association.

Underground finance is a financial concept. Underground financial activity and illegal organizations include unlicensed institutions like secret credit organizations. These types of organizations, like illegal money shops and usury, have market demand, but the law forbids this kind of financing.

Case 3: Underground Finance, Private Money House in Nanyang, Henan Province

Jingui Chao was the agent of the supply and marketing cooperative in Liang Erzhai Chun, Rengu Town, Tangying County, Nanyang City, Henan Province. In 1998, the central government allowed the Shopping Society to issue shares to all supply and marketing cooperative members, but in some places, there were cases in which the supply and marketing cooperative agents damaged the members' benefits by operating in illegal ways, and the government consequently forbade the policy. After that, Jingui Chao continued to absorb the public deposits in other ways and the supply and marketing cooperative turned into a private money house, which provided loan and deposit services. Jingui Chao made profits by mobilizing deposits and then paying interest several times above the official rate set by the PBC. The certificates of deposit that Chao gave depositors were just self-made two-sheet notes with the tax seal of the Liang Erzhai Shopping Society Branch.

By 2004, the total volume of funds absorbed by Jingui Chao reached RMB 770,000. The depositors came from 180 families in Liang Erzhai and its neighboring villages. Among these deposits, the largest deposit was RMB 170,000, while the largest loan was RMB 180,000. Out of the whole depository of RMB 770,000, over RMB 400,000 could not be refunded for bad loans. Because Jingui Chao destroyed some certificates before the case was disclosed, the local government met with big problems in dealing with refund affairs, and public benefits were damaged to some extent.

Illegal finance refers to enterprises without financial service permits that may be corrupt, engaging in financial crime or financial fraud. This can include the transfer of public deposits to illegal funds, in the gathering of deposits without authorization. These funds can take the form of outstanding shares, bonds, trust plans, certificates of deposit, and more. Another illegal practice is when bank staff members or administrative personnel divert customer funds, make illegal loans, or swindle bank credit. This kind of finance is sometimes observable, even if there is no obvious difference between the actual loan and the loan on the bank's books, if the transaction process is misrepresented.

Case 4: Illegal Finance, Wanxiang Company in Shengyang, Liaoning Province

Beginning in March 2002, Wanxiang Biological Planting Company signed trust contracts with investors for planting mushrooms (*Lingzhi*). The contract items showed that all investors only paid RMB 25 per month to the company as a planting fee. After 10 months, the company would refund the money to investors through bank transfers and investors could gain 35% interest in the next 4 months. Under the high profit trepanation (planting in shallow holes), many people signed contracts with Wanxiang Company and in a few days, there were about 200 people waiting in line at the company door to sign contracts. On December 12, 2003, Wanxiang Company transferred some money into partial investors' accounts, but investors received nothing from Wanxiang from the next day. In the 2 years between the company's founding and its closing, more than 10,000 investors in Shengyang and other regions of Liaoning Province were cheated out of their money. The financing volume of Shengyang Wanxiang was RMB 900 million. On December 12, 2003, the Shengyang Public Security Bureau froze Wanxiang Company's bank accounts. Through October 2004, refunds amounted to less than half of the illegal financing number.

The cases above articulate the subtle differences between informal, illegal, and underground financing. Informal finance is mutual cooperative financial organizations, which is moved by individuals in rotating associations or foundations, and not illegal. Underground finance includes belowground financial activity and organizations that lack a legal form, some of which are entirely forbidden by law. Illegal finance is also forbidden by law, but the institution has a legal form and engages in financial business outside of its permitted scope. We now go on to analyze the size of these nonbank financing methods.

National Survey on Unobserved Finance

In order to keep abreast of Chinese unobserved finance, in terms of its influence on economic movement, the Central University of Finance and Economics formed a research group that carried out a 3-month investigation, engaging in field work in 2006 in 27 national provinces, an investigation similar to that which was carried out at the beginning of 2004 (Li 2006), which was used as a basis of comparison. The most recent investigation was much larger, and the number of provinces studied was increased from 22 to 27. The number of surveys administered also rose from 7300 to 20,800, with 4705 private enterprises as survey respondents up from 1789 in 2004.

The survey personnel made field visits in order to administer the questionnaire survey, asking questions from the form in order to obtain the first materials. The investigation was carried out in 27 provinces, including the autonomous regions and the municipalities. The areas under investigation included five levels of administrative areas with a minimum sample size in each in order to guarantee coverage. The provinces under review were as follows: in the eastern area 10 provinces were looked at, including Liaoning, Hebei, Beijing, Tianjin, Shandong, Jiangsu, Zhejiang, Fujian, Guangdong, and Hainan; in the middle area there were 8, including Heilongjiang, Jilin, Shanxi, Henan, Anhui, Hubei, Hunan, and Jiangxi; and in the western area there were 9, including Inner Mongolia, Shaanxi, Sichuan, Yunnan, Guangxi, Ningxia, Gansu, Tsinghai, and Xinjiang.

This investigation provided 30,000 surveys, with 28,664 completed surveys and 20,896 effectively asked surveys, bringing the ratio of qualified surveys to 72.9%. The city and countryside surveys consisted of 7420 surveys, or 35.5% of the total; the enterprise surveys consisted of 4705, or 22.5% of the total; the financial institution surveys consisted of 4857, or 23.2% of the total; and the government department surveys consisted of 3914, or 18.7% of the total.

The investigation samples were chosen according to location coverage rules. We chose at least five districts in equidistant distribution in every province, autonomous region, and municipality, chose at least five counties or cities also in equidistant distribution in every district, and chose at least 10 villages or communities in the same way in every county and city. In every county and city, we randomly chose 200 inhabitants, 20 enterprises, 20 financial institutions, and 10 kinds of government department to complete the questionnaires. We also performed fieldwork on informal financial associations, illegal financing cases, and private moneylenders.

The Scale of Nonbank Financing in China

We estimated the size of informal finance, underground finance, and illegal finance from three angles: first, from the dependency of enterprises on nonbank financing, in which the target is to obtain financing on a scale similar to that obtainable from banks; second, from the government estimates of hidden financial activity; and third, from inhabitant participation in informal finance and underground finance from both a deposit and a loan perspective. These comprise nonbank financing to varying degrees.

Enterprise Nonbank Financing

During the enterprise financing investigation, we established two types of topics to determine the enterprise's extent of dependency on nonbank financing, in terms of where the financing is obtained and to what degree that financing is used.

First we looked at enterprise borrowing from informal channels and its extent in relation to bank lending. We investigated enterprises through survey feedback. After finding our sample population, we then calculated the value of different sector borrowing according to our sample population, and finally we added together the products, finding the average proportion of nonbank financing.

The investigation results showed that in eastern China's 10 provinces, enterprise nonbank financing accounts for 42.41% of all financing; in middle China's eight provinces the enterprise mean value is 41.39%; in western China's nine provinces the enterprise mean value is 38.31%; and overall in the 27 national provinces, the mean value is 40.7%. In other words, viewed from the national average level, enterprises obtain approximately 28.9% (40.7% over 140.7%) of financing from nonbank channels.

In another related topic of investigation, we looked at the level of dependency on different financing methods. In the formal lending channels, commercial credit societies, including regular banks, publicly raise funds in the form of outstanding shares and bonds. The nonbank financing method includes borrowing from personal networks and gathering capital internally (for example, obtaining regular financing through commercial bribes). We investigated inter-enterprise lending, commercial credit, and society funds, finding that the level of dependency was 22.3%, 19.5%, 15.1%, respectively. Usury and internal funding amounted to 13.4% and 17.3% of borrowing. If other financing methods are considered, 27 national provinces have enterprises that achieve a

42.4% level of dependency on informal financing. Eastern China's enterprises have a dependency level of 39.9%; middle China's enterprises are at 45.3%; and western China's enterprises are at 44.2%.

Second, we looked at estimates from financial institutions and governmental departments about the scale of unobserved financing. Stemming from industry competition, financial institutions have a direct understanding of informal financing, underground financing, and illegal financing, in terms of government finance, taxation and statistics, industry and commerce, and judicial and public security organs. It is possible to directly or indirectly observe financial activity through these three types of institutions. Therefore, by looking at financial institutions and the government's inquiries, we established the scale of deposit loans which informal finance, underground finance, and illegal finance are believed to occupy in the formal financial system. Though approximate, the numbers are close to the level of nonbank financing.

Financial Institutions' Estimates

The subjects of this investigation mainly included the PBC, commercial banks, policy banks, credit associations, negotiable securities organizations, trust investment companies, insurance organizations, and financial supervising and managing branches. The investigation question was, according to your experience, what is the proportion of all loan business occupied by informal finance, underground finance, and illegal financial activity (please choose the numeral which corresponds to 1–10—with 10 being the highest proportion)? The summation of the scales in all local groups gives us an idea of how extensive nonbank financing is in terms of deposits occupied in banks. The results showed that informal finance, underground finance, and illegal finance occupy a proportion of bank deposits on a national scale (27 provinces) of 32.34%. In eastern China's 10 provinces this occupied 33.95%; in middle China's eight provinces this occupied 30.43%; and in western China's nine provinces this occupied 32.24%. Comparing various provinces, Yunnan and Fujian's proportions were highest, achieving 37.7% and 37.4%, respectively, while those in Shanxi and Hainan were lowest amounting to 25.1% and 25.6%, respectively.

Government Department's Estimates

Compared with financial organization estimates, there is not much difference in the government department's estimation of nonbank financing. Governmental projections stated that the national mean value was 33.12%. Mean value of eastern China's 10 provinces was 32.9%; mean value of middle China's eight provinces was 33.6%; and mean value of western China's nine was 32.9%.

There were two estimates of bank deposits for nonbank financing that had differences of only a few percentage points. In the eastern area the difference between our investigation estimate and the government estimate was 1.05%; in the middle area it was 3.66%; and in the western area it was 0.66%. It can be said that in the eastern and western areas the estimates are consistent, while in the middle area the difference is bigger.

What, then, is the actual number for the middle area? Looking from the enterprise investigation results that enterprise nonbank financing occupies a proportion of 42.7% to the regular financing scale, we see that it is higher than the western area mean value and lower than the 45.3% level of dependency in the eastern part. From this perspective of analysis, the government department's estimate approaches the actual statistic. This is because the government department surveyors are based in the statistical department and in the judicial and public security institutions, as well as in business management and finance and taxation, and they directly or indirectly have contact with unobserved finance, so that their estimate is somewhat more objective.

The result of these two investigations is that we are able to obtain estimates of the scale of local informal finance, underground finance, and illegal finance in various provinces. The results showed that in eastern China's 10 provinces the mean value was 33.43%; in middle China's eight provinces the mean value was 32.02%; in western China's nine provinces the mean value was 32.57%, and in the national 27 provinces the mean value was 32.73%. It can be said that informal finance, underground finance, and illegal finance provide banks with a loan business scale of about one-third.

The Ratio of Inhabitant Participation in Nonbank Financial Activity

The proportion of local inhabitant participation in nonbank financing was then investigated. In our survey, we asked the following question: does your business use an organization outside the formal financial system to deposit or borrow funds (such as an enterprise, personal foundation, personal money house, underground bank, etc.)? It was found that the national average ratio of inhabitant participation in nonbank financial activity was 16.1% in terms of deposits, and 12.5% in terms of loans. Inhabitants in eastern China's 10 provinces participate in nonbank financial deposits at a rate of 15.48%, loans at a rate of 9.41%; in middle China's eight provinces the number for deposits is 16.31%, for loans 14.38%; and in western China's nine provinces the number for deposits is 16.6%, for loans 14.33%. In the eastern area of Fujian, the middle area of Henan and the western area of Tsinghai, inhabitant participation in informal and underground finance is quite high, but in Liaoning, Hainan and Jilin, inhabitant participation in informal and underground finance is quite low. In the majority of provinces, however, inhabitant participation in deposits is higher than participation in loans (according to funds). In this sense, nonbank and bank financing are the same. Inhabitant banking provides funds to other branches of the economy, often channeling money from the banks to be used in the nonbank finance sector.

The Structure of Unobserved Finance

The investigation assessed the proportion of financing that is occupied by informal finance, underground finance, and illegal finance. The results showed that, within the national 27 provinces, the mean values of each category respectively are 34.3%, 32.4% and 33.3%, respectively.

This part of the investigation included inhabitants in the city and countryside; privately operated, collective, state-owned, joint stock system enterprises; financial institutions, including banks; and government department including industry and commerce ministries, public finance and taxation bureaus, state statistics bureau branches, procuratorates, courts, and public security organs. These institutions and individuals are directly or indirectly involved in informal finance, underground finance, and illegal finance. Basic questions and additional questions were asked in degrees to comprise an index. Afterward, partial proportions were calculated by using this index. Table 3.1 contains the results.

Compared with figures for informal finance in the eastern area, estimated by the local government department, the results of our investigation are lower, with the government estimates being at 38.4% for inhabitant informal finance use, while the enterprise and the financial institution estimates are completely consistent. The four kinds of investigation on informal finance in the middle area were basically consistent, and the confidence level is highest for this area. There was a very low difference between our investigation results and government estimates for the western area. In terms of informal finance in the eastern area, the eastern area government's view is obviously lower than that of the other three kinds of investigations, at 30.7%, but estimates for the inhabitants, enterprises, and financial organs are above 33%. Tacit governmental approval of informal finance is quite high, as was explained by the local eastern area government. Mechanisms and policies are quite flexible in the middle and western areas as well. Four investigations (households, enterprises, financial institutions, and governmental departments) in the middle and western areas showed that there was not a large difference in findings. In terms of illegal financial activity, three of the four investigations were in agreement.

From three different local investigations in which a credibility analysis was undertaken, it was found that the standard error of data in the middle areas was smallest in terms of informal finance, underground finance, and illegal finance. For the western area, the standard error was also quite small and results were basically consistent. There were differences in the eastern area in terms of informal finance, mostly because in each place the development of informal finance is quite varied, more developed in provinces like Zhejiang and Fujian, but less developed in provinces like Liaoning and Hebei, while informal finance in Beijing is not very large-scale.

In 27 national provinces, across all four investigations on informal finance, underground finance, and illegal finance, the standard error is

Table 3.1
Estimation of China's Unobserved Finance Structure

Informal Finance	Households	Enterprises	Financial Institutions	Governmental Department	Average
Eastern China's 10 provinces	33.6%	33.8%	34.1%	38.4%	35.0%
Middle China's 8 provinces	33.3%	33.5%	34.0%	34.0%	33.7%
Western China's 9 provinces	34.3%	34.9%	34.1%	33.3%	34.2%
National 27 provinces	33.7%	34.1%	34.1%	35.2%	34.3%

Underground Finance	Households	Enterprises	Financial Institutions	Governmental Department	Average
Eastern China's 10 provinces	33.0%	33.2%	33.2%	30.7%	32.5%
Middle China's 8 provinces	32.1%	31.5%	32.5%	31.6%	31.9%
Western China's 9 provinces	32.8%	31.9%	33.4%	33.0%	32.8%
National 27 provinces	32.6%	32.2%	33.0%	31.8%	32.4%

Illegal Finance	Households	Enterprises	Financial Institutions	Governmental Department	Average
Eastern China's 10 provinces	33.4%	33.0%	32.7%	30.9%	32.5%
Middle China's 8 provinces	34.6%	35.0%	33.5%	34.4%	34.4%
Western China's 9 provinces	33.0%	33.2%	32.5%	33.7%	33.1%
National 27 provinces	33.7%	33.7%	32.9%	33.0%	33.3%

consistently between 0.005–0.006, and the informal finance proportion is slightly higher than the illegal finance and underground finance proportions.

China's Informal Finance Interest Rate Level

One of the main objectives of this investigation was to review the impact of unobserved finance upon the interest rate. For inhabitants, enterprises, and financial institutions, we compared different values from the sector product to the sum of its components, in order to find what was missing so that we could obtain some local average interest rate levels. Afterward, two types of investigations were carried out to confirm this local interest rate level.

The results showed that the mean interest rate level of informal finance, underground finance, and illegal finance interest rate was 16.4% overall, while the eastern areas' mean level was 15.6%, the middle areas' mean value was 16.7%, and the western areas' mean value was 17%. The lowest level for inhabitants was 15.6%, while the enterprise level was highest at 16.93%, and the government department's level comes at 16.6%. Inhabitants' estimated interest rate level was lower than the level which the government and the enterprise estimated, because underground finance mainly absorbs deposits from inhabitants. In general, the deposit interest rate is lower than the loan rate not only in the formal financial institutions but also in the informal financial institutions. But the interest rate level estimated by enterprises was highest, since enterprises find it difficult to obtain loans from public banks and must pay a higher cost to obtain loans from the informal financial market. The government department interest rate levels were somewhere in the middle. As for the provinces, Jiangxi Province's overall interest rate was highest, at 22.48%, while Hainan Province's was lowest at 12.3%.

Case 5: The Informal Interest Rate and Formal Financing Cost in Zhejiang

Next, we discuss if the interest rates in informal finance and formal finance reach similar levels. Here is a case to illustrate that they do. The Zhejiang Land Development Company uses a financial manager who has good relations with a local bank manager, who was once a bank staff member. The bank agreed to provide loans of RMB 30 million, with deposit mortgage as collateral. In addition, the manager obtained the loan qualifications from one company in Hong Kong of a RMB 30 million deposit, and after that, the company in Hong Kong moved the deposit out of this bank. The real estate company's interest rate was a monthly interest rate of 1.2%, giving to the bank a monthly loan interest rate of 0.55%, with a surplus of 0.65% given to the manager as a consultation service fee. Finally this transaction reached an agreement. Based on this transaction, the bank loan annual interest rate was 6.6%, but the enterprise's final loan cost was 14.4%, including attorney fees, the insurance premium, and so on, so that the loan cost actually approached 15%. By comparison, the informal lending rate in Zhejiang Province estimated by enterprises, inhabitants, and financial organs was 19.4%, 16.3%, and 18.9%, respectively; the mean value was 18.21%. This is a typical example that shows that there is, then, not a big difference in interest rates between the informal lending sector and the formal lending sector.

Analysis of Unobserved Financial Funds Industrial Inflow Patterns

Next we will discuss which industries informal funds flow to and what influence this has on the movement of the national economy.

Industrial Inflow Patterns of Unobserved Financial Funds in Different Areas

In the investigation process, we inquired about unobserved finance, asking questions separately for the enterprise, the government department, the financial institution, and the city and countryside inhabitants. For these questions, we used 5 as a cardinal number, in order to index the flow of these funds, with 5 being 100% nonbank financing and 0 being 0% nonbank financing. This index reflects informal finance, underground finance, and illegal finance in the agriculture, mining, manufacturing, architecture, business and dining service, and real estate industries, as well as in the education, science and technology, culture, health, and nonprofit industries.

The results showed that, if 5 expresses a 100% flow to some industry, then flows to the real estate industry measure 2.56 (51%), while in eastern China's 10 provinces the real estate indexes are highest, in middle China's eight provinces the indexes are next highest, in western China's nine provinces the indexes are lower than the middle area. The real estate industry overall has been doing well, with housing prices increasing. The restaurant industry index is also quite high, with a national average index of 2.6 (52%), while the middle area index is slightly higher than that of the west. There are many inflows from the informal financial sector into the restaurant industry, for in this profession capital faces a quick turnover and requires timely funding. (Obtaining loans from banks may take a long time, at least 1 month, and on average 3 months.) Therefore, borrowing demand has been quite exuberant in recent years, particularly in the informal financial sector. The architecture industry index is ranked third in the nation at 2.39 (48%), with the same levels in the middle areas and western areas and a higher level in the eastern areas. Agriculture is particularly big in terms of informal finance in Heilongjiang, Jilin, and Henan. The index for the mining industry is slightly lower than in agriculture, at 2.24 (45%) in the western area, which is higher than the middle areas, as well as the eastern areas, in which the index is lowest, since coal and petroleum are mainly distributed in the middle and western provinces. This year, the provinces of Shanxi, Inner Mongolia, and Jilin increased their wealth in coal and oil mining, attracting many informal funds, and officials have even invested in coal stock as one of the key industries in 2005 and 2006. The manufacturing industry informal finance index has come to occupy sixth, with few differences among eastern and western China. The lowest index for informal financing was found among the education, science and technology, culture, health, and nonprofit organizations, since this domain is not yet completely open to the informal capital hence depending heavily on government investment. In recent years, the privately operated capital has been used to purchase businesses like hospitals and movie theaters.

To some degree, unobserved finance patterns can be used to show short-term speculation. Speculation funds in high-return industries such real estate, natural resource mining, and so on are financed by unobserved finance in some extent.

Industrial Inflow Patterns of Unobserved Financial Funds Estimated by Other Credible Sources

From the estimates of other credible sources, the real estate industry had some of the highest levels of nonbank funding inflows, in which the index was 2.79 (56%), and the estimates of inhabitants and government interviewees were nearly the same. Enterprise interviewees thought that the architecture, manufacturing, mining, and agriculture industries were more attractive to informal funds. Because enterprises directly or indirectly invest in these industrial areas, this estimate is more believable. In recent years, the central bank controls commercial banks' lending size by using tightening policy tools such as the reserve rate and interest rate, so that most private enterprises turn to informal institutions for borrowing money, which they get to know well. Government estimates of informal finance are lower than those of the other three investigations for two reasons: one is that the government is unable to gather full information particularly on informal finance, underground finance, and illegal finance, since these dodge government supervision and management. The other is the government department underestimates the degree of informal financing in order to maintain social stability. Financial institutions and inhabitants' estimates were quite consistent, because these two kinds of investigations were able to detect indirect participation or had grasped some information related to informal, underground, or illegal finance. In brief, the different investigations had certain limitations, but in terms of estimating the scale of these types of finance in various industries, all investigations were consistent.

Regardless of the estimates of different types of interviewees, informal finance, underground finance, and illegal finance have some general characteristics of industrial inflow patterns. The real estate industry is the most attractive industry to informal funds; next is the business and restaurant industry, which has a short investment cycle; third is the mining industry. Agriculture has always been very active in nonbank finance, since formal finance has been scarcer in the countryside. Unobserved finance is growing in the fuel industry as well. Unobserved finance in the western area is on quite a large scale, although local financial resources are scarce and therefore nonbank interest rates are quite high. This can be shown in the prominence of Qinghai, Yunnan, and Sichuan in interest rate ranking across the nation.

Conclusions and Implications

Chinese Informal Finance, Underground Finance, and Illegal Finance Have a Certain Scale

The short-term nature of informal finance, underground finance, and illegal finance means that the scale of unobserved finance is currently not entirely adequate but is appropriate for current capacity. The current capacity is the volume at a certain time. The scale of unobserved finance occupies the formal loan scale of 32.7%, according to the 99.7% probability interval computation.[1]

In the first quarter of 2006, compared with 2005, the deposit and loan balance in the formal financial sector increased. Net deposits added up to RMB 4.798 trillion (not including government deposits), while net loans added up to RMB 2.093 trillion. Informal financial deposits are estimated to be between RMB 1.556 trillion and RMB 2.955 trillion, with a median estimate of RMB 2.255 trillion. Estimates for the informal financial sector loans are between RMB 472.6 billion and RMB 897.7 billion, with a median value of RMB 685.2 billion.

Informal finance, underground finance, and the illegal finance are equally divided in terms of deposit and loan amounts. Again using a 99.7% probability interval computation, in informal finance, the sale of deposits is estimated between RMB 618 billion and RMB 929.2 billion, with a median value of RMB 773.6 billion, while the loans are estimated between RMB 187.7 billion and RMB 282.3 billion, with a median value of RMB 235 billion. In underground finance, deposits are estimated between RMB 588.7 billion and RMB 872.8 billion, with a median value of RMB 730.8 billion, while the loan scale is between RMB 178.8 billion and RMB 265.2 billion with a median value of RMB 222 billion. In illegal finance, deposits are estimated between RMB 593.1 billion and RMB 902.2 billion, with a median value of RMB 747.7 billion, and the loan scale is estimated between RMB 180.2 billion and RMB 276.1 billion, with a median value of RMB 228.2 billion (see Table 3.2).

Table 3.2
The Scale of Informal Finance, Underground Finance, and Illegal Finance in 2005

Financing Category	Scale Range	Deposit Range and Mean (in billions of RMB)	Loan Range and Mean (in billions of RMB)
Informal finance	27.4%–41.2%	618–929.2, 773.6	187.7–282.3, 235
Underground finance	26.1%–38.7%	588.7–872.8, 730.8	178.8–265.2, 222
Illegal finance	26.3%–40.3%	593.1–902.2, 747.7	180.2–276.1, 228.2
Unobserved finance	22.6%–42.9%	1555.7–2955.1, 2255.4	472.6–897.7, 685.2

Note: Calculated on the survey result and China Financial Yearbook's data issued by PBC (2006).

Negative Effects of Unobserved Finance

Without a doubt, in the past 3 years, the rapid development of the Chinese real estate industry and real estate price increases have become a topic of social discussion in many social circles. Property developers use many kinds of channels to obtain funds, since real estate prices have been much higher than the cost of development, allowing developers to obtain a high level of profit. Some national departments responsible for regulating real estate prices tightened the money market by levying real estate taxes, including a business transaction tax and an income tax, but real estate prices still rapidly rose. Because of this, unobserved finance continues to supply enough funds to the real estate sector.

In the energy mining sector, informal finance is abundant, and so are profits, which attract not only the common people but also civil servants to invest in stocks for small coal mines and oil fields. Because the prices of energy and raw materials, including coal, petroleum, and non-ferrous metal have been rising, the mining industry has witnessed a rapid and dramatic rise in profits, resulting in many nouveau riche. These newly rich individuals, who acquired capital in a mere 2 to 3 years, increase their wealth yet again by investing in other sectors, like real estate.

In the agricultural industry, unobserved finance makes up for a lack of financing and has played a positive role in the development of agriculture. But agriculture is a national industry, with a low investment repayment rate in small-scale production, and higher investment income is difficult to obtain. When a bumper crop is produced, farm prices cannot rise, but agricultural production prices are continuously rising. For example, in 2006 the Shanxi Yuncheng watermelon wholesale price was 7 ¢ per 500 gram, whereas usually the price is 20–40 ¢ per 500 grams, so that farmers must withstand huge funding pressure. In the harvest season of 2005, fishermen in Guangdong Zhongshan faced stocks of dying fish due to a nearby factory dumping pollutants. Some fisherman borrowed more than RMB 100,000 from the informal sector (through usury) for fish raising, while also losing funds as a safeguard and verging on bankruptcy. Obviously, the high interest rates faced by farmers in informal finance, underground finance, and illegal finance are disadvantageous to the sustainable development of the agricultural economy.

Unobserved Finance's Effects on Macroeconomic Regulation and Control Policy

From the analysis of interest rates in unobserved finance, the average level is above 16%. But the interest rate in the formal financial sector is at about 5%. The central bank interest rate is based on its future policy, and it can either increase financial institutions' legal bank deposit reserve ratio or adopt regulative measures. The effects of these results are hard to measure in the short term. Compared with profits in the investment industry, interest rates in the unobserved finance sector are not high. Unobserved finance fills a void in financing left over from the formal financial sector, in order to satisfy enterprises' demand for financing, but in the process this has an effect upon macroeconomic regulation and control.

Therefore, the government must pay attention to the influence of unobserved finance in the macroeconomic regulation and control process, in which funds from the formal sector can promptly flow to the unobserved sector. The scale and the structure of the unobserved sector must be constantly assessed, with the knowledge that regulations imposed on the formal financial institutions can affect transaction behavior in the informal sector. A standing monitoring mechanism must be implemented, in order to find out the effects of the informal sector upon policies. This is an essential subject to regularly investigate and study.

Note

1. Average value $U \pm 3$ sigma standard difference, according to the results, we calculated the standard difference $\sigma = 3.4\%$.

References

Cai, Tiejun. 1996. On informal finance in the transition economies. *Guizhou Institute of Finance and Economics Journal* 3: 8–14.

Isaksson, Anders. 2002. The Importance of Informal Finance in Kenyan Manufacturing. United Nations Industrial Development Organization (UNIDO) Working Paper 5.

Jiang, Shuxia. 2001. *China's Underground Finance*. Fujian: Fujian People's Press.

Jiang, Xuzhao. 1996. *Research on China's Informal Finance*. Jinan: Shandong Peoples Press.

———— and Changfeng Ding. 2004. Theoretical Analysis of Informal Finance: Conception, Comparison and Institutional Change. *Journal of Financial Research* 8: 100–111.

Li, Jianjun. 2005. *Research on the Volume of Underground Financing and its Economic Effects.* Beijing: China Financial Publishing House.

————. 2006. *A Survey of Underground Financing in China.* Shanghai: Shanghai People's Press.

Lu, Xianxiang. 1995. China's Financial Control and Informal Finance. *Zhongnan University of Economics Journal* 1: 59–62.

————. 1997. China's Institutional Informal Finance. *Finance and Trade Economics* 5: 31–34.

OECD/IMF/ILO/CIS STAT. 2002. *Measuring the Unobserved Economy: A Handbook.* Paris: OECD.

Tsai, Kellee S. 2002. *Back-Alley Banking: Private Entrepreneurs in China.* Ithaca, NY: Cornell University Press.

United Nations Economic Commission for Europe. 2003. *Unobserved Economy in National Accounts: Survey of National Practices.* Geneva: United Nations.

Xia, Bin and Wenlin Liu. 2001. *Illegal Financial Business Cases.* Beijing: China Finance Press.

Zhang, Jun. 2002. Financial Diversification and Economic Growth. *Shanghai Finance* 5: 4–6.

Zhang, Ning. 2002. Study of Informal Finance. *Modern Finance* 11: 34–38.

————. 2003. China's Informal Financial Situation and the Main Perspectives Correction. *Management World* 3: 53–60.

Zhu, Delin and Haiou Hu. 1997. *China's Black and Grey Finance: Market Situation and Rational Thinking.* Lixin: Lixin Accounting Publishing House.

Zhu, Ze. 2003. *China's Underground Finance Development and Control Measures.* South Rural 5: 12–14.

Zuo, Baiyun. 2001. Study of Informal Financial Issues. *Financial Theory and Practice* 5: 21–22.

Chapter 4

A Comparative Analysis of Regional Informal Financial Organizations in China

Xuzhao Jiang

This chapter focuses on the comparison of informal finance in northern and southern China by discussing the status of China's informal finance and the reasons for its inception and development.

Informal finance includes various types of nonformal financial institutions, which cannot be observed by the governmental sector. This chapter points out that there are many differences in phases of economic development, credit systems, cultural characteristics, historical backgrounds, business cultures, and topographies across regions. Therefore, demand and supply must embody various characteristics that have given rise to different kinds of informal finance in north and south China.

As a whole, in southern China, especially in southeast China, the volume of informal finance is bigger and the categories are more numerous than in other areas. The main reason for this is that due to the better developed private economy, the economy in southern China is better developed. We find that the better developed the private economy is, the greater the demand for informal finance and the greater the supply of private capital, and therefore the more numerous the categories of informal finance will be.

The specific type of informal finance reflects the different characteristics in northern and southern China. In northern China, the main types of informal finance are private loans and enterprise funds. Rotating savings and credit associations (ROSCAs), illegal private banks, and private investment groups dominate southern China. Enterprise lending, pawnbrokers, private note issuance, and privately raised funds can be found in both southern and northern China, but the volume of these funds are greater in the southern areas. Further elaboration of informal financing types and reasons for their evolution and development are laid out in this chapter.

Informal finance presents different characteristics in northern China and southern China because there are many differences between the two regions in terms of the credit system, historical background, business culture, social characteristics, geography, enterprise organization, and government power.

The Main Types of Informal Financial Organizations in Northern China

Private lending and enterprise fundraising are the main types of informal finance in northern China.

Private lending is the unorganized lending and borrowing among individuals. The lender and borrower perform financial transactions directly or through the help of a broker (*qian zhong* or *yinbei*). It is direct financing, and the lowest level of informal finance. Private lending is very important in northern China where the private economy and the credit system are underdeveloped, and most people do not dare to venture. As a result, the volume of the supply of this kind of informal finance is not large and a perfect credit system cannot be created, since this would require frequent financing. So in northern China, people inclined to the lowest level of informal finance in which the credit system is very simple.

According to the interest rate level, private lending can be divided into the following categories: friendship lending, gray lending (middle-level interest rate lending) and black lending (high interest rate lending and borrowing) or usury. Friendship lending is small-volume lending and borrowing among relatives, friends and neighbors. This kind of informal finance is mainly used for living and consumption, and the interest rate is very low or almost zero. Friendship lending exists all over the country, but is more prevalent in areas of low income levels. Interest rates in gray lending are between those of friendship lending and high interest rate lending and are often higher than the bank's interest rate. This kind of informal finance provides money for production or production circulation. Therefore, it often exists in areas where the private economy and individual economy are developed to some extent. High interest rate lending exists not only in private lending but also in other kinds of informal finance, which we shall discuss in the following sections.

A Legend of "Zero Bad Loans" in 12 Years of Lending

In a village named Shenwucun in Jinan, Shandong Province, an old man named Yuncheng Li has a record of extending "zero bad loans" in 12 years of lending.[1]

Yuncheng Li's lending is important to rural enterprises. As he said, "my capital is not much, the scale is not large. My lending does not compete with formal finance and also cannot be included in formal finance but can complement formal finance to some extent. Although it does not complement bank loans much, it is important to the enterprises."

Li believes that "the warrantor is more important than the borrower. As long as the warrantor has the ability to repay, even if the borrower flees or goes into bankruptcy, there will be no loss for the lender." Only after the three parties, the borrower, the lender (Li), and the warrantor, sign the loan contract, the transaction can be complete. The warrantors are all local people who are familiar with the borrower and are also known by Li. The risk is controlled through this kind of warranty, which is the magic weapon for Li.

Li's modes of lending are very flexible, and his procedures for obtaining a loan are simpler than those of formal finance. If a person borrows from Rural Credit Cooperatives (the main mode of formal finance in rural area), it requires at least 10 days. But if an individual borrows from Li, 10 min is enough.

Li's repayment terms and modes are also very unique. Most of the repayment terms do not exceed half a year. Early repayment and repayment in stages are encouraged. This way, the interest income is less, but the principal is safer.

The three-party contracting policy, flexible lending methods, unique repayment terms and modes, and interest rates are scrupulously abided by Li, which is the secret of his success.

According to Xuzhao Jiang's analysis, Yuncheng Li cannot supply long-term capital for local enterprises due to the limits of one individual's capital and the lack of business inspiration of the local people. However, many local people do escape from poverty through the use of Li's lending. This kind of informal finance is based on regional and familial relationships and therefore a high level of information symmetry, so it has its unique advantage, but it cannot achieve a large volume for the same reasons.

As people's income is increasing and risk consciousness has been enhanced, private lending has gained the following new characteristics:

1. The aim of using private lending has shifted from using it mainly for living and consumption to using it mainly for production and business (Xiang 2005).
2. The ratio of friendship lending as a percentage of private lending as a whole is decreasing. There are two reasons for this. The first is that small-scale finance for living is decreasing because people's income is increasing. The second is that the aim of using private lending has shifted from using it mainly for living and consumption to using it mainly for production and business. As a result, the purpose of lending for mutual assistance is weakened, and the risk associated with money lending is increasing. Therefore, the interest rate is higher.
3. People's risk consciousness has been enhanced and the procedures associated with private lending are becoming more formal. In the

past, private lending could be accomplished using verbal promises, broker relationships, or rough contracts. Now, it requires formal contracts in which the volume of money, terms, interest rates, and defaults are all listed in detail. For large-volume private lending, a home mortgage, land deed, or shop mortgage is often needed (Xiang 2005).
4. The broker system has also evolved. With the help of broker web sites, the two parties of private lending can meet with each other more efficiently.

Compared with other types of informal finance, private lending is different in that it is between individuals. The capital one individual can supply is relatively less than the capital of many persons in other types of informal lending. Private lending does not require a developed credit system. The lender faces only one borrower and simply needs to know the borrower's credit history. Therefore the credit relationship is simple.

Enterprise fundraising is a form of informal finance in which enterprises raise money from the public for the purpose of production or other affairs without the permission of financial supervisors (Li Jianjun 2005). Fundraising is different from obtaining capital through issuing stocks. It is a type of low-level direct informal finance.

Fundraising, especially within the enterprise, is an important form of informal finance in northern China. The reasons are as follows. The first is that the residents in northern China are generally more financially conservative and at the same time the credit system is not perfect. The suppliers are always inclined to lend the money to those they are familiar with. In the situation in which the credit system is not perfect, people are more familiar with the enterprise they serve than with other forms of informal finance. The second is that compared with the more developed areas in southern China, the labor force in northern China lacks fluidity and the workers are very afraid of being fired. When the enterprise wants to raise funds within, the workers feel obligated to supply the money, lest they be fired. But in the more developed areas in southern China, things are different. The credit system is better and the labor force more fluid. Therefore, fundraising is more serious in northern China than in southern China.

The Illegal Public Fundraising of Yingkou Donghua Group

In June of 2005, Liaoning Police uncovered the illegal[2] social fundraising organization of Yingkou Donghua Group.[3] According to the inquisition of the court, from April 2004 on, the board chairman of Yingkou Donghua Group, Zhendong Wang, illegally raised funds of more than RMB 3 billion from more than 30,000 residents through 13 branch companies. He told the residents that the money would be used to breed ants, but this was not the case. He lured the residents by promising especially high interest rates of 35% to 60%. In February 2007, he was sentenced to death. Others were sentenced to set terms of imprisonment.

According to the relationship between the initiator and the money suppliers, enterprise fundraising can be divided into inside fundraising and social fundraising. Inside fundraising means that the initiator raises money inside the area the initiator controls. Social fundraising means that the initiator raises money from the public.

For inside fundraising, the interest rate is commonly lower than that of other informal finance, but higher than the bank deposit rate since the demanding party has some authority over the suppliers. The suppliers are familiar with the demanding parties; that is, the suppliers are part of the local government, enterprise, or national department; therefore, the risk is lower and the suppliers are willing to accept lower interest rates. For inside fundraising, the scale of funds is limited by the number of workers and the wealth accumulation.

But there are also some special situations in which the interest rate is higher than that of other informal finance. One reason is that the distribution of income for local governments, enterprises, or national departments is usually restricted by law. If they have high profits, they can adopt this kind of informal finance with high interest rates. A part of the profits can be obtained by the employee through receiving high interest rates.

For social fundraising, the risk is high, even higher than with most other kinds of informal finance, because the suppliers of money know very little about the fundraisers. In order to attract money, the fundraisers have to set high interest rates.

Generally, the reasons that the main kinds of informal finance are lower-level, such as private lending and fundraising, are that in northern China, the nongovernmental economy and the credit system are not developed, and most people are more financially conservative.

The Main Types of Informal Financial Organizations in Southern China

Hehui

In southern China, *hehui*, money houses, and nongovernmental investment alliances are the main types of informal finance.

Hehui is usually called a ROSCA, and this type of informal financial organization is very active in Zhejiang, Fujian, and Guangdong. *Hehui* is a lower-level informal financial organization, although it has existed for thousands of years. It adopts a form of cooperation and mutual aid based on regional and familial relationships. Since the opening-up policy was actualized, this age-old form of informal finance began to resuscitate and became fashionable. *Hehui* mainly exists in rural areas. In general, farmers live in the same village for generations. The regional and consanguinity relationships, which are an important basis for *hehui* mainly located in rural areas, are easily formed.

The general rules of *hehui* are as follows: A person who serves as the "head" of *hehui* organizes a certain number of persons who comprise the "foot" of *hehui*. Every person (including the head) supplies promissory money every period which may be every month, every other month, every quarter, every half year, or every year. In each period, one member can be financed by using the collected money from all the members. The ways to determine who can use the money collected by *hehui* are drawing cuts or bidding on the interest rate. The member who uses the money in the first several rounds needs to pay back the same amount of money to one member each time in subsequent rounds. These are in fact "installments" and for the person who uses the money later, he or she gets an amount of money that nearly equals the total number of "installments" he or she lent in previous rounds; this is similar to small savings for a lump-sum withdrawal. *Hehui* is a temporary organization and after every member is financed by the ROSCA, the *hehui* is ended.

There are many names for *hehui*, such as *biaohui, bahui, lunhui, yaohui, taihui,* and so on. In a *biaohui*, the person who can obtain the money in each period is decided by bidding on the interest rate after the first period (the first period's money is used by the "head"). The person who offers the highest interest rate will get the right to use the money. The characteristic of *bahui* is that only the head uses the money in the first round. The head invites some relatives of friends as "feet" to organize a *bahui*. The feet supply some money equally or unequally in the first round. In the following rounds, nobody supplies money again except the head who pays the principle and the interest to the feet according to the sequence set up in the first period, by drawing cuts. In a *lunhui*, the sequence of who uses the money is decided by the "feet" in advance. There are 6 to 10 members in a *lunhui*. The sustaining period of *lunhui* is usually one year or half a year. The member who is most anxious to obtain the money can ask to be in front of the sequence; otherwise, he or she can ask to be in the back of the sequence. In a *yaohui*, the person who can obtain the money in every round is decided by drawing cuts after the first period. In a *shouyuanhui*, members save money every period and as a member dies, the money is paid back for his or her funeral. The members may be elderly individuals or the elderly individual's relatives. *Shouyuanhui* is a kind of life insurance. *Taihui* is a new form built up on the old forms. For a *taihui*, there are many small *hehui*'s in a big *hehui*, that is, the bigger *hehui* is supported by many smaller *hehuis*. Smaller *hehuis* comprise the "feet" of a bigger one. *Tai*, in Chinese, means support. The whole form looks like a pyramid (see Figure 4.1).

According to the "Notice to Ban Money Houses and Usury" issued by People's Bank of China in 2002, the interest rate of informal finance between individuals can be determined by the lender and the borrower. But the money of the lender must be his or her own money and cannot be comprised of deposits of other persons. In addition, the interest rate cannot exceed four times more than that of a loan of the same period from banks.

In recent years, *hehui* appeared with some new characteristics.

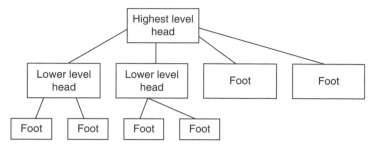

Figure 4.1 The structure of *Taihui*.

Firstly, the objective of *hehui* changed from serving as a mutual aid to chasing profits in part. When the whole national economy is more developed, people have more deposits than those needed only to satisfy living needs, and therefore redundant deposits can be used to chase profits. With the development of commodity production and circulation, farmers demanded much more capital. *Hehui*, which appears in such conditions, aims more at chasing profits.

Secondly, *biaohui* is the main form of *hehui*. In *biaohui*, the person who offers the highest interest rate can obtain the right to use the money in each round after the first round. This embodies the *hehui*'s characteristic of chasing profits (Li Jianjun 2006). The scale of money of *hehui* is increasing.

Thirdly, the possibility of bankruptcy for *hehui* is much higher, which may bring more damage to social stability. The total volume of money is bigger, and the possibility of failing to return the money is higher. The interest rate is higher because of the aim of chasing profits. The members may use the money for high-risk items, such as gambling, in order to pay for the larger volume of interest. And therefore the possibility for this member to default is even higher and the *hehui* may be in danger of breaking down. In general, the bigger *hehui* is supported by the smaller *hehui*s so that the risk may be transferred to a wide range of individuals.

In 2002, in Shatian County of Fujian Province, the capital raised by the *biaohui* reached about RMB 520–580 million. Some youths who planned to marry or study abroad may borrow money from *biaohui*. The capital of *biaohui* took up more than one third of the income of local residents in Ningde city of Fujian Province (Cui Lijin and Li Jiang 2002).

The money house is also one of the main kinds of informal finance, and the money house has many different Chinese names in different areas, such as *yinhao* in old-time southern China, and *qian zhuang* usually used in northern China. China's money houses might have appeared as early as the Ming Dynasty. In the 1840s, the early years of the Qianlong emperor in the Qing Dynasty, the main function of the money house was currency exchange. In the late years of the Qianlong emperor, the business of the money house was changed from currency exchange to credit business, such as making loans and taking deposits.

Since the reform and the opening-up of China, money houses have also been reconstructed. But after the People's Republic of China Provisional Regulations of Banking Administration was issued, private money houses were forbidden.

Three Authorized Money Houses Appeared and Were Closed

Qianku Money House appeared in Qianku Town, Cangnan County, WenZhou City. In the 1980s, it was under the sole proprietorship of Peilin Fang. The registered persons were Peilin Fang, his wife, and his father. Fang was a worker in a local hospital with unpaid leave. His wife was a worker in a local shop also with unpaid leave. His father was retired. The total enrolled money was RMB 540,000. According to an investigation that took place between July and August 1985, Qianku Money House accepted deposits of RMB 6,521,900 and lent out RMB 7,387,800 in total. The interest rate for a deposit of three months was 1% or 1.2% per month and the rate of lending for three month was between 1.8% and 2.1% per month. Lecheng Money House and Jinxiang Money House in Cangnan County and Wenzhou City were private money houses that appeared at the same time. The three houses were permitted to operate by the PBC when they opened, but then, a settlement crisis happened, and they were closed by the PBC.

The Illegal Money House of the Du Family

On June 26, 2007, the Shenzhen Branch of the State Administration of Foreign Exchange together with the Shenzhen Branch of the Public Security Bureau successfully destroyed a large and well-organized illegal money house, capturing 6 criminal suspects including the boss Ling Du, and freezing RMB 4.2 million in 55 accounts. The Du money house had existed in Shenzhen for 7 or 8 years. From the beginning of 2006 to May 2007, the trading volume in the Shenzhen Branch of the Du money house was more than RMB 4.3 billion. The trading mainly included foreign exchange and a great deal of illegal capital which had flowed into China's stock market and real estate market. The trading volume flowing into real estate reached RMB 0.13 billion and the volume flowing into the stock market had reached RMB 0.105 billion. Including the amount of RMB 2.2 billion in its Guanzhou branch, there was more than RMB 6.5 billion of illegal capital flow through this money house in one and a half years. Different from the traditional money house, the Du money house did not use cash, but only transferred money among companies on the bank's network. In addition, the branches in Shenzhen and Guangdong connected tightly with the headquarters in Hong Kong and had an effective and secret way of exchanging foreign exchange.

Compared with *hehui* and private lending, money houses have several distinct characteristics. The money house can supply much more money than *hehui* and private lending because it absorbs deposits from the public. Money houses usually have a scale advantage and some management experience. Therefore they have many more advantages in reducing transaction costs, correcting for information asymmetry, and securing credit standing. Money houses have no time restriction for borrowing and depositing as *hehui* has. The borrower can obtain the loan almost whenever he or she wants, and the depositor also can deposit whenever he or she wants. But the money house is a financial broker, and it will obtain profits through the spread between the deposit interest and the loan interest. Therefore, the supplier of money will obtain less interest income and the demanding party will pay more interest costs compared with *hehui* and private lending.

With the increasing scale of money houses, the business scope is also extended. It manages not only traditional deposits and loans, but also foreign exchange and money laundering.

Money houses usually exist in some southern provinces in China, such as Jiangsu, Zhejiang, Fujian, and Guangzhou, where China's market economy is well developed. The reasons are as follows. First, since the reform of the economy, China's commodity economy has developed very rapidly in southern China, especially in Wenzhou, Zhejiang Province. Individuals' and private enterprises' demand for capital has increased rapidly. Since formal finance cannot supply enough funds, these enterprises must borrow from money houses, so the money houses continue to exist and develop. Second, individuals and private enterprises are inclined to use cash. The volume of cash demanded is very large, but the bank or credit cooperatives, which are both considered formal finance, cannot meet the demand so that the money houses join the financing through deposits. Third, from the viewpoint of capital supply, the commodity economy in Wenzhou, Zhejiang Province, developed faster and residents' income increased. The residents with surplus capital would surely pursue profit. But the interest rate in banks is lower than the profit rate of the local economy; therefore, a part of the surplus capital is attracted to money houses.

In northern China, by contrast, money houses are fewer. The first reason is that the money house can survive only when demanding parties and suppliers coexist in a relatively small area. In northern China, the commodity economy is not as developed as it is in southern China, and the demanding parties of capital are fewer so that single capital demand is relatively less. The second reason is that capital supply is much less abundant in northern China than in southern China. The third reason is that the residents in northern China have a "government-run" complex and do not dare to take risks. Most of the residents prefer deposits in government-run banks with lower risk but lower interest rates than deposits in money houses. The money houses in Jiangsu and Zhejiang Provinces mainly carry out traditional business, that is, deposits and loans, while in Fujian, Guangdong, and Yunnan Provinces, they mainly manage foreign exchange and money laundering (Jiang Xuzhao and Changfeng Ding 2004; Li Jianjun 2006).

When the money house carries out the business of foreign exchange or money laundering, it needs to settle with money houses abroad. Because it is illegal, the settlement has to be accomplished using cash. Therefore, the geographic area near the coastal regions with easy access to international markets is the best location for these money houses. Fujian Province, Yunnan

Province and especially Shenzhen city are such areas. Large volumes of RMB and foreign exchange (especially HKD) are exchanged through the money houses in these areas,[4] weakening the effect of China's restrictions on the capital account. HKD and other foreign exchange are exchanged for RMB for consumption or investment in China. And at the same time, RMB is exchanged for HKD or other foreign exchange to consume or invest in Hong Kong or other areas. Some money is illegally transferred abroad through these money banks. According to related data, there are at least 100 sites of money banks. Every year, they can accomplish more than RMB 100 billion in exchange or capital flow (Xi Xiumei and Lin Wang 2004).

Nongovernmental investment alliances mainly exist in Jiangsu and Zhejiang Provinces.

Jiangsu Investment Alliance

When Yurui Group, Hongdou Group, Yuandong Group, Yide Group, Yuexing Furniture Group and Lianda Group signed the Jiangsu Investment Alliance Cooperation Agreement on June 15, 2004, the Jiangsu nongovernmental investment alliance was set up. The agreement defines the "investment alliance" as a "profit community that is set up according to our country's code in the cooperation among juridical persons, using the agreement to restrict member enterprises' behavior, with the aim of fastening the development of the member enterprises." Through this alliance, the members can share information, invest together, finance each other, train together, and purchase together by combining resources.

Since 2003, some kinds of nongovernmental investment alliances have appeared in Jiangsu and Zhejiang Provinces. Several money suppliers constitute an alliance to collect the money and invest together, and the profit or the loss is attributed according to rules made in advance. Most of the alliances are not authorized by industrial and commercial administrative department, except the well-known Wenzhou Real Estate Speculation Group. There are still other alliances, such as Cixi[5] Culture Relic Speculation Group, Lishui[6] Water and Electricity Speculation Group, Wenzhou Car Speculation Group, Wenzhou Trade Mark Speculation Group, Wenzhou Cotton Speculation Group, Wenzhou Coal Speculation Group, and Yongkang[7] Building Real Estate Group. Even some famous private enterprises have also built up investment alliances since 2003, such as the Zhongrui Consortium, Zhongchi Consortium, and the Jiangsu Nongovernment Enterprise Investment Alliance. The nongovernmental investment alliances develop fast, and the investment directions are turned to petroleum, finance, and public utilities. Nongovernmental investment alliances have become an increasingly important way to enlarge private capital.

All of these nongovernmental investment alliances have restricted access. They are built up based on regional and familial relationships. They only accept their relatives, friends, or fellow villagers. They seldom accept persons with whom they are not familiar. Every member has a certain number of shares in the alliance.

The nongovernmental investment alliance is a new form of informal finance which reflects the development of nongovernmental enterprises' organization styles in Jiangsu and Zhejiang Provinces. Since the policy of reform and opening-up, the nongovernmental enterprises' organization style has changed from a family workshop to a limited company, to a joint stock limited corporation, and to a Nongovernmental Investment Alliance (Yu 2004; Zhu Guodong 2005).

The economies of Jiangsu and Zhejiang Provinces have developed faster than in other areas, due to the characteristics of the residents. Residents are inclined to be enterprising and risk-loving, while the residents in northern China "would be satisfied when they are rich to a low extent" and therefore are not as enterprising. Even residents in Guangdong are less enterprising and risk-loving than residents in Jiangsu and Zhejiang Provinces. Nongovernmental enterprises in Guangdong Province lack the desire to expand (He Zhaohui 2005). These spirits of residents in Jiangsu and Zhejiang Provinces provide the impetus for the enterprises there to upgrade.

Other Types of Informal Finance in China

Other types of informal finance, such as enterprise inner lending, pawnbroking, informal note discounting, and private placement funds, exist in both southern China and northern China,

Enterprise inner lending is financing among enterprises. It is a lower-level type of informal finance. The scale of enterprise inner lending is bigger than the scale of individual lending. Enterprise lending is usually done through the commerce association or union of enterprises, in which the enterprises can borrow money from other enterprises in the same association, which solves the problem of information asymmetry. Sometimes, mortgage and security are necessary in enterprise lending if the lenders are not familiar with the borrowers, so credit guaranty companies may act as guarantors. In 2004, there were more than 1000 guaranty companies in Zhejiang Province.

Pawnbroking means the money-demanding party pawns goods which he or she owns and gets money from the pawnbroker, redeeming the goods when the principal and interest are paid off in the agreed period. Pawnbroking is a type of higher-level direct informal finance.

In 1988, the first pawnbroker was set up in Chengdu, Sichuan Province, and then the same company appeared in Beijing, Shanghai, Wenzhou, Taiyuan, Kaifeng, and Jinan successively. Pawnbroking is more important in undeveloped areas than in developed areas, but the volume is much larger in developed areas than in undeveloped areas. Beijing Baoruitong Pawnbroker Co. Ltd. was established in 1997 and is one of the four earliest pawnbrokers in Beijing. The enrolled capital is RMB 0.17 billion. It mainly manages real estate, automobiles, securities, jewelry, famous watches, high-quality cameras, high-quality music instruments, electric instruments, electronic IT products, pawning of goods, mortgage loans, the auction of dead pawns, appraisals, evaluations, and consultation services.

Compared with the old pawnbrokers in history, the modern pawnbroker has some new characteristics. The customers of the old-time pawnbrokers were mainly poor persons who with difficulty made a living, and the interest rate was typically high. The new pawnbroker is different. The customers include individuals and enterprises and the latter are the main customers. Pawnbroking is not used for day-to-day consumption, but mainly for production financing. The interest is relatively more reasonable because the pressure of financing for production is much less than that for living.

Pawnbroking resolves the problem of information asymmetry by pawning goods. This way it offers less risk to the lender compared with individual lending, *hehui*, money houses, and so on. But the ownership of goods pawned must be transferred to the pawnbroker, which needs to be evaluated and preserved. When a dead pawn occurs, the pawnbrokers need to auction the goods, and the price of the goods and whether or not the goods can be auctioned are uncertain. All these factors increase the cost of financing through pawnbrokers and partly counteract the advantage of reducing risk. If the credit system is less developed, pawnbrokers have a relatively greater advantage in reducing risk and therefore develop quickly. In Jiangsu and Zhejiang Provinces, pawnbrokers are not important for the nongovernmental enterprises.

Informal note discounting means that a nonfinancial unit (the supplier of the note discounting service) buys the undue commercial notes from enterprises and collects money from the drawers when the notes mature. The supplier of the note discounting service can be an individual or an organization, such as an informal note discounting institution or enterprise.

There are two reasons for the existence of informal note discounting. The first is that the supplier of note discounting services from formal finance is not sufficient. The People's Bank of China does not supply the rediscount on commercial acceptance notes, and some national commercial banks prefer the discount inside their own system, and reduce and even refuse discounting notes from other middle-size or small banks. So some notes cannot be discounted through formal finance. The second reason is that the supply of note discounting services from formal finance is slow and the procedures are trivial, while the supplier of informal note discounting does not require that the enterprise supply documents. And as long as the notes are real, the suppliers will pay cash at once. In 2002, there were 4701 nongovernmental enterprises that had accounts in financial institutions, and 300 of them participated in informal note discounting.

The supplier of informal note discounting services needs not know too much about the credit of the note holders; he just needs to look at whether the note is valid. In fact, he needs to know more about the credit of the payer and the acceptance institution. If the note is one of bank acceptance, the risk of supplying money through informal note discounting is much less than forms in which the supplier gives money directly to the demanding party. Even if the note is of commercial acceptance, if the payer or the acceptance enterprise is powerful or well known to the supplier of the informal note discounting service, the risk is less. Even if the payer and the acceptance enterprise are not powerful, the risk of many enterprises defaulting at the same time is less than the risk of one enterprise defaulting.

Informal note discounting mainly existed in Shandong and Jiangxi Provinces in the past, where the formal discounting market is not developed. But in recent years, it has developed more rapidly in Zhejiang, Jiangsu, Fujian, Guangdong, and other southern provinces.

A **private placement fund** is a kind of investment fund that is not permitted by the government. It collects funds from specified investors privately. Its sales and redemptions are accomplished through the private consultation between the administrator of the fund and the investors. It is a kind of financing for clients and a type of higher-level informal finance. According to People's Republic of China Security Investment Fund Law actualized in 2004, the "fund" under restriction is the public placement fund, and there are no rules on the private placement fund. Therefore, the private placement fund is an illegal way of raising money. Its public status may be "investment consultancy," "investment management company," "financing consultancy," and so on. Private placement funds mainly speculate in the stock market or in the futures market.

The private placement fund has some specific characteristics. It usually promises the investor a higher interest rate than the banks, thereby attracting much money. It is unstable and usually changes with the market. When the market is active and is ascending, it will also be active and have a large scale. Private placement funds are not supervised by the law and are illegal. Therefore the risk to invest in such funds is high. Once there is dissension, the rights of the investor cannot be protected by law and may cause societal instability. The scale of private placement funds is typically large. According to a survey of Central University of Finance and Economics (2004), the money invested in the private placement funds occupied 30%–35% of the total money invested in security markets directly or indirectly, and double that of the public placement fund.

Private placement funds mainly exist in Beijing, Shanghai, Guangzhou, and Jiangsu where the capital is plenty and residents are more inclined to invest.

Underground Insurance Markets in Southern and Northwestern China

Illegal insurance business is conducted when insurance companies abroad sell insurance products to domestic residents through branches in Hong Kong or Macau. These kinds of insurance policies are illegal. Therefore they are referred to as underground insurance products. Underground insurance products offend regulations on domestic and foreign insurance companies and evade taxes.

The illegal insurance business appeared in 1999. Many people regard purchasing underground insurance products as fashionable. Underground insurance products were very rampant in some cities in the Pearl River Delta where the economy is better developed. Because the underground insurance products mainly come from Hong Kong and Macau, they are rampant in areas where the residents are richer and more adjacent to Hong Kong and Macau. But in recent years, underground insurance policies have flowed from Guangdong and Fujian Provinces to Shanghai, Zhejiang, Jiangsu Provinces, and even to Urumqi, Sinkiang Autonomous Region. According to an investigation by the Zhejiang Insurance Supervising Association in May 2005, the premium of underground insurance products reached at least USD 30 million in Wenzhou. According to the investigation of Hong Kong and Domestic institutions, there is HKD 12 billion that flows into Hong Kong from the domestic insurance market through underground insurance products every year.

The illegal insurance business lures customers by advertising a high rate of return. We choose common life insurance as an example. The rates paid by domestic companies are only half of that of the underground insurance policies; as far as connection insurance is concerned, the difference is much larger. The rate of domestic connection insurance is about 3%–7%, but the underground insurance policies may promise 20%.

The underground insurance policies bring profits to the insurance companies abroad, but the domestic policyholder's benefits cannot be protected and the holder may even be presented with a lawsuit. Any country's regulations about insurance request signing the financial product should happen in the place where the company is enrolled and any insurance products contracted otherwise are invalid. And the influence of this invalidity is great. The customer cannot obtain normal claims on compensation and may meet with a series of lawsuits. If a domestic customer buys a Hong Kong insurance policy, but does not sign in Hong Kong, then he needs a false certification, which not only makes the insurance policy invalid but also encounters a lawsuit, because in Hong Kong and Macau, it is a crime to make up false documents.

The commission of the agent who sells underground insurance products is typically high. The commission can reach up to 100% of the first year's insurance premium. This is the reason why so many agents scramble to enter underground insurance business, although they know it is illegal.

Trader's Credit, Micro Nongovernmental Loans, and Rural Mutual Savings Funds: Transitional Forms from Informal Finance to Formal Finance

Trader's credit means that business enterprises offer loans to their customers, and the customers repay the loans with their products. This is a lower-level type of direct informal finance. Trader's credit combines the credit relationship and the business relationship. Because the information asymmetry is lower, this kind of finance is very effective. Trader's credit exists in Southeast Asian countries and other developing countries. In recent years, the Chinese government continued to encourage "contract farming," especially in the "company plus farmer" mode. The typical mode is that the company signs an agreement with the farmer and supplies the farmer with seeds, technology, loans, or guarantees support, and the farmer will pay the loan principle and interest with products in the future. For example, Lanshan Group in Gaotang County, Shangdong Province, offers loans in advance to farmers to raise cattle. Every farmer can obtain RMB 1000 in advance each year after signing an agreement with Lanshan Group. According to the agreement, when young cattle grow up, they will be sold to Lanshan Group with a price of RMB 6 per kilogram. Mengniu Milk Co, Ltd., a famous milk producer in Inner Mongolia also uses this model for offering loans to farmers in advance, and the farmers pay the loans back with milk.[8]

Through this model, farmers can obtain loans to produce, and at the same time they need not be worried about selling the products. This is quite beneficial to building a harmonious society and solving agricultural problems, so the trader's credit model is supported by the Chinese government. But this financing model is not based on law, and once a dissension between the two sides of agreement occurs, there is no suitable law to resolve the problem.

Micro nongovernmental loan companies are one kind of nongovernmental organization. In July 2005, the People's Bank of China carried out the **nongovernmental microcredit company** trial in Shanxi, Shaanxi, Guizhou, and Sichuan Provinces (which are located in midwestern China). This kind of informal finance is not important because it is in the trial phase. The investors of microcredit companies are local rich individuals or private entrepreneurs. This kind of informal finance adopts a model of "only lending but not accepting deposits." The money supply includes the initiators' supply, entrustment funds, and transferred loans. By December 22, 2006, there were seven nongovernmental microcredit companies in China. Figure 4.2 shows the outside of one of these microcredit companies, Rishenglong.

Micro nongovernmental loan companies serve the needs of farmers, the countryside, and agriculture and are important in making the market exert its function of resource allocation, inducting financial innovation in countryside, increasing the supply of rural finance, solving financing issues for farmers, and building the new socialism spirit in the countryside.

The methods to appraise customers' credit and the technique to manage loans for micro nongovernmental loans are entirely different from those used for formal banking loans. The historical experience of China's financial reform shows that rural formal finance lacks enough impetus and innovation to engage in microlending. Micro nongovernmental lending, however, can make use of its advantage in the way of having customers' information, and then develop special techniques to manage microloans.

There is much private capital outside the banking system that wants to find a suitable way to formal financial institutions in China. But several years

Figure 4.2 Rishenglong: the first private microcredit company built in 2005 in Pingyao County, Shanxi Province.

ago, some financial institutions, for example the rural cooperative fund associations, set up during the financial reform, caused tremendous financial risk and damaged social stability. So the supervising authority is concerned with the risk caused by private capital which invests in formal financial institutions, and the authority does not permit microcredit companies to do deposit business. Micro nongovernmental credit companies are a kind of transitional informal organization. This is a compromise between the private capital investors who are eager to enter the formal financial system and the supervising authority that is prudent on opening the formal financial market. For the supervising authority, it is easy to control and solve the problems if they appear in this model (Jiao 2006).

But now, the micro nongovernmental loan company is on trial and there is no complete set of laws to decide the status of the microcredit company, nor is there a supervisory system for it (Wang 2006). Both the People's Bank of China and the China Banking Regulatory Commission slide toward the problems of its validity and supervision. And the development of the micro nongovernmental loan organization is greatly limited because it lacks legal status (Kang 2005).

The rural mutual saving fund is an autonomous, self-serving, and mutual informal financial organization based on members' voluntary fund-raising, and it exists in the poor countryside in northern China. The money is collected from the local residents. The aim is to rescue and prepare for famine and help residents eliminate poverty. Therefore the interest rate is almost zero. The rural mutual saving fund is a type of lower-level informal finance. It is similar to the rural cooperative association.

According to its function, the rural mutual saving fund can be divided into the rescue mutual fund, the antipoverty fund, and the business cooperative fund.

The rescue fund is set up by the residents to rescue or prepare for the risks in areas where natural disasters occur frequently. It is a lower-level cooperative financial organization with the characteristics of a social welfare organization.

The antipoverty fund collects money from public finance and endowments of societies or enterprises. This fund supports poor people by lending them microloans. Its aim is not to gain profits, so the interest rate is very low.

The business cooperative fund is a new type of mutual organization. In July 2006, the farmers of Puyang City, Henan Province, set up a rural loan cooperative. It adopts the model of a Headquarters plus Branches plus a Mutual Center. The center is built in each village. Farmers can get the loans from the center in their village and repay the center when the loans mature. The farmer should first become a member of the center after he or she pays RMB 50 as a membership fee. Then, if the member wants to borrow from the center, he or she must buy shares from the center. One share is sold at RMB 1000. After that, the members can borrow RMB 5000 each year, and the interest rate is a bit higher than the formal banking rate.

This type of mutual fund appeared also in cities. The employers of an enterprise or an institution and the residents of a district can organize a mutual fund spontaneously to collect savings to help each other. Every member of the organization saves a certain volume of money monthly, and all the money from the members is managed by some persons chosen by the members. The collected money is mostly deposited in the bank and the interest is dispensed to the members according to their savings. When the members face difficulties, they can apply for a certain amount of loan money and repay according to the agreement. The loan's interest rate is zero. At the end of year, if some members want to withdraw from the organization, their savings are repaid. In the 1980s, the early years of reform, this kind of organization was popular in some areas, but now it is rare.

Usury, Illegal Underlying Capital Companies, and Money Brokers

Usury exists all over the country, especially in poor areas and inshore, port, and frontier areas where the economy is well developed. In poor areas, although the per capita income is low, the consumer conception is influenced by outside information. People may resort to usury to pursue a lifestyle of overconsumption. For example, the costly marriage depends on usury. Besides, the conditions of living and production are poor and the ability to resist hazards is not strong. Once natural or manmade disasters happen, residents have to borrow from usury. In some inshore, port, and frontier areas, illegal economic activities, such as smuggling, drug trafficking, and ammunition trafficking are more active and usury is also more rampant. There are two characteristics for these activities. One is that these illegal businesses may bring sudden, huge profits in a short time, so entities will dare to borrow money from usury. The other is that the risk of these businesses is much higher and therefore lender must ask for a higher interest to compensate for the potential loss.

The **illegal underlying capital company** sprang up in Shanghai after the policy named "mortgage transfer in a year" was enacted to restrain the short-term real estate speculation that was carried out in April 2005. From then on, if people want to sell their houses purchased from the developers with mortgages, they must pay off all the loans to the banks, and then the banks may offer a mortgage transfer. But the illegal underlying capital companies appear and offer mortgage transfers for real estate speculators. The illegal underlying capital companies can lend money for 30 days to speculators as long as the borrowers pay a 10% capital fee. These companies are often disguised as "real estate consultation companies." These companies collect some capital through several kinds of channels, such as through relatives and friends. There are more than 100 such companies in Shanghai, and some companies can transact more than ten mortgage transfer dealings in about 10 days. Illegal underlying capital companies appear as the result of the short-term speculators coping with real estate policy. This type of informal finance weakens the effect of real estate policy whose original goal was to restrain short-term housing speculation and control price bubbles. The illegal underlying capital company is a direct form of informal finance and mainly exists in Shanghai (Xu Shou Song 2005).

Money brokers in the northeastern area are called *dui feng zhe* and can obtain loans from formal financial institutions and then lend the money to people who need loans but cannot get it from banks (Li Jianjun 2006). Normally banks lend money to large enterprises, but these operating sound enterprises do not need many loans. By contrast, there are many small enterprises that need money but banks do not support them. So the *dui feng zhe* appeared, and they built relations with big enterprises and banks in the form of a club. *Dui feng zhe* is the boss of the club. The boss lends the money borrowed from banks by big enterprises to small enterprises, which pay a higher interest than the big enterprises pay to banks. For example, if the broker gains a 2% interest profit, he would pay 1% to big enterprises. If some enterprises want to be a member of the club, they will need an introduction of acquaintance and will be observed for some time. According to the knowledge about the members, the boss will request the interest rate one or two times that of banks. The loan is usually lent for a short time to solve the enterprises' liquidity problem.

Conclusion

To sum up, different types of informal finance in different areas of China are distinguished here. These include both the resuscitation of the old forms of informal finance and the appearance of entirely new forms. There are both reasonable forms of informal finance (such as private lending) and unreasonable types that should be banned (such as the illegal insurance business). There are both informal finance types that can be included in formal finance (such as the money house) and informal finance types that can never be included.

From a geographical perspective, as a whole, in southern China, especially in southeastern China, the scale of informal finance is bigger and the categories are more numerous than in northern China. Specifically, in northern China, the main kinds of informal finance are private lending and enterprise fundraising. *Hehui* or ROSCAs, money houses, and nongovernmental investment alliance mainly lie in southern China. Enterprise lending, pawnbroking, informal note discounting, and private placement funds lie in both southern and northern China, but the southern part does a larger volume of business in these informal finance types than northern China. The illegal insurance business mainly exists in some cities in southern China because of their geographical location. Micro nongovernmental credit and trader's credit are promoted by the government. Micro nongovernmental credit mainly exists in some provinces in the center and the west of China. Trader's credit lies in many rural areas both in northern and southern China. Rural mutual saving funds mainly lie in the poor rural areas of northern China. Usury exists in some poor areas and some inshore, port, and frontier areas where the economy is well developed (mainly in the southeast inshore area, as well as in the southwestern and northwestern areas). Shanghai is the typical area for the illegal underlying capital companies since the real estate industry developed quickly. A special kind of broker called *dui feng zhe* exists in the northeast of China. These various types of informal finance are a reflection of the social, historical, and economic factors present in the diverse regions of China.

Notes

1. See Fang Hua and Wen Yue (2005).
2. Not authorized by relative supervisor.
3. http://www.gov.cn/jrzg/2007-07/27/content_698746.htm
4. Money houses in frontier of Yunnan mainly realize the exchange between RMB and VND.
5. Cixi is a city in Zhejiang Province.
6. Lishui is a city in Zhejiang Province.
7. Yongkang is a city in Zhejiang Province.
8. See Village Development Research Institute of China Social Sciences Academy, Village Social and Economic Investigation Team of National Bureau of Statistics of China (2005).

References

Central University of Finance of Economics. 2004. The legalization of private placement fund—the direction of market development Online. Available: http://finance.sina.com.cn/jjzj/20040729/0957909556.shtml. July 29.

China Academy of Social Sciences, Village Development Research Institute, Village Social and Economic Investigation Team of National Bureau of Statistics of China. 2005. *Green book of agriculture economy—analysis and forecast of China countryside economy.* Beijing: Social Science Literature Press.

Cui, Lijin and Li Jiang, 2002. The investigation of the informal finance of Zhejiang, Fujian, and Guandong provinces. *Manager Reference* March: 8–10.

Fang, Hua and Wen Yue. 2005. How does the legend appear? Online. Available: http://yndt.bank.cnfol.com/051011/137,1410,1479279,00.shtml. October 11.

He, Zhaohui. 2005. Why the scale of enterprises in Guangdong is difficult to enlarge?, Online. Available: http://gov.finance.sina.com.cn/zsyz/2005-06-24/63173.html. June 24.

———— and Changfeng Ding. 2004. The theoretical analysis of informal finance: the definition, comparative, and system flux. *Journal of Financial Research* August: 100–111.

Jiao, Jinpu. 2006. How to develop low-volume financing institution. Online. Available: http://www.qzwb.com/gb/content/2006-10/23/content_2266040.htm. October 23.

Kang, Ning. 2005. The non-governmental financing companies begin with the transition model of lending only and not accepting deposits. Online. Available: http://news.xinhuanet.com/fortune/2005-12/29/content_3982955.htm. December 29.

Li, Jianjun. 2005. *The Study of the Scale of Informal Finance and Macroeconomy in China.* Beijing: China Financial Publishing House.

————. 2006. *The Investigation of Informal Finance of China.* Shanghai: Shanghai People's Publishing House.

Wang, Shuguang. 2006. The system environment for low-volume loan. *New Finance & Economics Monthly* December.

Xi, Xiumei and Lin Wang, 2004. The way for informal finance in Zhejiang. *Business World* November: 44–48.

Xiang, Ke. 2005. The investigation of informal finance in Shandong province. *Jinan Finance* January: 56–57.

Xu, Shou Song. 2005. Mortgage transfer in a year is abandoned to restrain the short-term real estate speculation. Online. Available: http://news3.xinhuanet.com/house/2005-04/21/content_2858781.htm. April 21.

Yu, Li. 2004. Famous Wenzhou enterprises began to build up syndicate. Online. Available: http://www.nanfangdaily.com.cn/ZM/20040617/jj/qs/200406170037.asp. June 17.

Zhu, Guodong. 2005. Non-governmental investment alliance spring up. Online. Available: http://news.sina.com.cn/c/2005-03-31/14176252511.shtml. March 31.

Chapter 5

Beyond Banks: The Local Logic of Informal Finance and Private Sector Development in China

Kellee S. Tsai

The most vibrant sector of the Chinese economy lacks access to formal sources of credit. Over 30 million private businesses have been established during the first three decades of reform; yet, as of year-end 2007, only 1.3% of the loans extended by state banks went to private enterprises.[1] Although some scholars have described China as a growth-promoting "developmental state," following in the footsteps of its East Asian neighbors, private entrepreneurs in China have not directly benefited from allocated credits or centrally mandated preferential treatment by state banks (White 1988; Blecher 1991; Xia 2000). How, then, has the "miracle" of China's private sector development been financed? Drawing on fieldwork conducted in Fujian, Zhejiang, and Henan, this chapter offers three explanations.[2]

First, the vast majority of private businesses in China rely on informal finance, or what economists call the "curb market," for their start-up and working capital needs. These informal financing mechanisms range from interest-free loans between friends and relatives, to sophisticated financing arrangements that circumvent national banking laws in creative ways.

Second and relatedly, a certain degree of leakage from state banks into the private sector has occurred. The consolidated balance sheets of state banks underreport the amount of formal credit that is actually going into the private sector because local entrepreneurs and officials have devised strategies to obtain credit through state and collective enterprises.

Third, local political and economic conditions fundamentally mediate the emergence of informal financing mechanisms. Local governments are not equally protective or tolerant of curb market practices—even within a particular province.[3] Some localities harbor a tremendous array of informal financial institutions, while others have a much more limited scope of informal financial activity. The causal logic underlying the production of informal finance lies at the local rather than national level. More specifically, I attribute the local variation in informal finance to the orientation of the local government toward private sector development, which reflects in part structural legacies inherited from the Mao era.

To clarify these propositions, this chapter proceeds as follows. The first part reviews the main forms of informal finance used by private entrepreneurs and the extent to which they are considered legitimate and legal fundraising activities (most are not). The second section demonstrates the wide range of local variation in informal finance within China by presenting examples of four different developmental contexts. The cases suggest that the more institutionalized forms of private sector finance depend on political bargains struck between financial entrepreneurs and regulators at the local level. This is not to say that centrally mandated policies are ineffectual or irrelevant, but rather that local actors creatively interpret existing state policies to serve their particular objectives—in this context, the provision of financial services to private entrepreneurs through mutually profitable arrangements. The third part analyzes why substantial local variation exists in the scope and scale of informal finance. I argue that the contours of curb market activity at the grassroots level reflect a certain degree of path dependence in local developmental trajectories.

The conclusion considers the broader implications of this contention for our understanding of China's transitional political economy. In particular, the differential patterns of local development and informal finance suggest that financial authorities will continue to face challenges in standardizing and commercializing the state banking system. Furthermore, even if formal financial institutions become more accessible to private entrepreneurs, the segmentation of local credit markets suggests that informal finance will continue to thrive with considerable local variation rather than with national homogeneity. Classifying China as a whole into a single developmental category would obscure the differing realities that private business owners and aspiring entrepreneurs face at the ground level.

Financing the Private Sector Informally (and Illegally) in China

The Party School of the Central Committee of the Chinese Communist Party reported at the beginning of 1999, "Self-employed individuals, private business owners, and entertainers have gained the most benefit from China's [first] twenty years of reform" (Xinhua 1/27/1999). What the report did not mention was that during the previous year, only 0.4% of official bank credit went to the private sector. Indeed, 88% of the entrepreneurs that I surveyed during 1996–97 indicated they had never borrowed from the formal financial system.[4] Instead, business owners have relied on a wide range of informal financing mechanisms and institutions, most of which are not sanctioned by the state-controlled banking system. Entrepreneurs have been operating in a transitional policy environment where private businesses are legal, but most of their financing mechanisms are not.[5] Table 5.1 summarizes private entrepreneurs' primary sources of credit according to their relative legality (Zhu and Hu 1997; Li 2006).

The extremes of "legal" versus "illegal" forms of financing are distinguished by whether or not they are sanctioned by the People's Bank of China (PBC) and Central Banking Regulatory Commission, which depends largely on whether they mobilize savings from the general public and offer/charge interest rates above the repressed interest rate ceilings. Interpersonal lending and trade credit, for example, are among the most basic strategies that entrepreneurs use to deal with short-term liquidity requirements. Business

Table 5.1
Summary of Financing Mechanisms Employed by Private Entrepreneurs in China

Legal	Quasi-Legal	Illegal
Interpersonal lending (*minjian jiedai,* 民间借贷)	Rural cooperative foundations (*nongcun hezuo jijinhui,* 农村合作基金会) [until 1999]	Professional brokers and money lenders (loan sharks) (*yinbei, gaoli dai,* 银背, 高利贷)
Trade Credit (*hangye xinyong,* 行业信用)	Fake collectives, red hats, hang-on enterprises (*jia jiti qiye, dai hongmaozi, guahu qiye,* 假集体企业, 带红帽子, 挂户企业)	Private money houses (*siren qianzhuang,* 私人钱庄)
Rotating credit associations [in some areas] (*lunhui, biaohui, hehui,* 轮会, 标会, 合会)	Mutual assistance societies/cooperative savings foundations (*huzhu hui, hezuo chu jijinhui,* 互助会, 合作储基金会)	Rotating credit associations [in some areas] (*lunhui, biaohui, hehui,* 轮会, 标会, 合会)
Pawnshops [in some areas] (*diandang ye, dangpu,* 典当业, 当铺)	Pawnshops [in some areas] (*diandang ye, dangpu,* 典当业, 当铺)	Pyramidal investment associations (ponzi schemes) (*taihui, paihui,* 抬会, 排会)

Note: None of the practices/institutions in the second and third columns are sanctioned by the People's Bank of China. Those in the first column are only "legal" if they do not entail the use of high interest rates. "Quasi-legal" practices are those that are registered by a bureaucracy outside of the financial hierarchy.

owners frequently borrow money from friends, relatives, and neighboring shopkeepers. Wholesalers may deliver goods to retailers on 10-day or even 30-day credit if they have an established relationship. Such practices are not illegal to the extent that they do not entail interest above the rates of state banks,[6] in contrast to those charged by the proverbial loan shark or private money houses. The latter are clearly illegal by PBC standards because they reflect the higher market cost of capital in a financially repressed environment. Moreover, with the exception of Minsheng Bank, private commercial banks are prohibited in China.

Rotating credit associations (*hui*), however, have contradictory legal standing in different localities. When *hui* involve relatively small groups of people (five to ten members on average) who pool set monthly contributions and rotate the disbursal of the collective pot of money to each member, they are usually considered a productive form of mutual assistance among ordinary people, that is, "popular finance" (*minjian jinrong*). But if a member runs off with the collective pot early in the life of an association, the members who have not had their turn in collecting money are cheated out of their contributions. In the coastal south, a handful of high-profile cases have accumulated where various types of *hui* were exposed as fraudulent schemes organized by con artists (*pianzi*). The discussion of Wenzhou in the next section illustrates an extreme example of how basic rotating credit associations degenerated into ponzi schemes, which are illegal.

Pawnshops straddle a finer line between being legal and not quite legal. Their reemergence during the reform era has been uneven and ambiguously been regulated due to their usurious connotation. Communist-era references to pawnshops in imperial China condemn them as an expression of class-based exploitation (Xin 1993). After the first one opened up during the reform era in Chengdu in 1987, however, they developed rapidly, with particular intensity in Chengdu, Shanxi (Taiyuan), Shanghai, Wenzhou, and other cities in the coastal south. By 1993, there were 3013 documented pawnshops throughout the country. Most were operated by various branches of government agencies, including state banks, policy departments, tax bureaus, customs bureaus, and finance and insurance companies, though some simply registered as ordinary private businesses with the Industrial and Commercial Management Bureau (ICMB) (Li 2000). It became increasingly apparent that many were (illegally) mobilizing savings deposits from the public and offering loans at high rates of interest (China Online 9/9/99).[7] As a result, throughout the mid- to late-1990s, the PBC issued various regulations to circumscribe financial malfeasance of pawnshops. In August 2000 they were reclassified from being "financial institutions" under the PBC's authority to "a special kind of industrial and commercial enterprise" regulated by the State Economic and Trade Commission (SETC), which was folded into the Ministry of Commerce in 2003. In short, over the course of the reform-era, pawnshops have been legally registered in some cases, registered with the incorrect local agency in others, and engaged in practices that are clearly illegal. Yet in many cities, they have filled an important gap in providing credit to ordinary people, including private entrepreneurs.

The ambiguous and shifting legal status of other curb market practices listed in the second column of Table 5.1 shares the attribute of being legal according to certain governmental agencies, but not sanctioned by the PBC. The establishment of rural cooperative foundations (RCFs) by the Ministry of Agriculture (MOA) in the mid-1980s exemplifies this phenomenon (Cheng, Findlay, and Watson 1998; Du 1998). The PBC never recognized them as legitimate "financial institutions" (*jinrong jigou*) because another ministerial bureaucracy created them. Nonetheless, by the early 1990s RCFs had been established in approximately one-third of all townships, and by 1998 there were over 18,000 RCFs with over 5 million depositors (Holz 2001). Since RCFs were not permitted to mobilize deposits or extend loans like formal financial institutions, they used euphemistic terms for comparable transactions; instead of paying interest on deposits, for example, they sold "shares" (*rugu*) and extended "capital use fees" (*zijin zhan feiyong*). Like pawnshops and other forms of informal finance, RCFs had a variety of governance structures and were more central to rural finance in some provinces than others. Their quasi-legal status proved to be short-lived, however. As part of broader national efforts to rectify the financial system, in March 1999, the State Council announced the closure of poorly performing RCFs, and the takeover of better performing RCFs by Rural Credit Cooperatives. These actions triggered farmers' protests in at least six provinces and cities, including Sichuan, Hubei, Hunan, Henan, Guangxi, and Chongqing (Associated Press 3/22/99; Agence France Presse 3/23/99).

Apart from RCFs, some de facto nongovernmental financial institutions have managed to operate above ground and serve private businesses by registering as "social organizations" (*shehui tuanti*), which are administered by the Ministry of Civil Affairs. These go by a variety of names, including "mutual assistance societies" and "cooperative savings foundations," but they essentially operate like RCFs or private money houses.

And finally, among the most common strategies that larger private entrepreneurs (*siying qiyejia*) have used to enhance their access to credit is by registering as a collective enterprise ("wearing a red hat") or affiliating with a state-owned enterprise (SOE). Especially during the earlier years of reform when the political legitimacy of the private sector was still uncertain, aspiring business owners chose a less conspicuous registration status, which also enhanced the likelihood that they could access credit from formal financial institutions and state banks. While state bank lending to the private sector has been miniscule, by the end of the 1990s, nearly 10% of official bank credit was going to "collective" enterprises, some of which were actually private (Jinrong nianjian 2000).

It is difficult to specify the aggregate scale and volume of private entrepreneurs' financing practices precisely because they are informal; by definition, they occur outside the official banking system and do not seek to be counted.

A conservative estimate would be that during the first two decades of reform, curb market activities accounted for at least one-quarter of all financial trans-actions,[8] but as the next section shows in more detail, not all of the financing arrangements can be found in every city or village, and the relative popularity of certain curb market practices has fluctuated over time. Ultimately, this variation is not only a reflection of macroeconomic conditions and the national policy environment, but also a product of the changing nature of interaction between local governmental officials and private entrepreneurs.

The Political Economy of Local Variation in Informal Finance

Considerable variation is apparent in the extent to which particular areas possess a diversity of financing options versus absence of private finance. For heuristic purposes, four development contexts may be identified. First, at one extreme are impoverished localities in remote areas that have stagnated or further deteriorated during the reform era. In such places, government and party cells have atrophied, sometimes to the point of abandonment; the local economy consists primarily of subsistence farming; and not surprisingly, private commerce and informal finance is virtually nonexistent. Second, local governments in areas with a strong legacy of commune and brigade institutions during the Mao era have systematically allocated credit to larger collective enterprises, while small business owners have relied primarily on unregistered forms of informal finance, such as trade credit and rotating credit associations (e.g., Quanzhou). Third, in areas that had an earlier start on decollectivization and private sector development, the local governments are more lenient toward local curb market activities (e.g., Wenzhou). Fourth, localities that have large concentrations of SOEs are more likely to comply with financial rectification campaigns in curbing informal finance, while subsidizing local SOEs (and restructured SOEs) with bank loans (e.g., Zhengzhou).

Governmental Flight from Extremely Impoverished Rural Areas

Although the standard of living for the average Chinese citizen has certainly increased since the commencement of economic reform, according to the World Bank, nearly 130 million people continue to live in poverty (World Bank 2007). Most of the poverty is concentrated in the southwest and northern-central hinterlands. But even within increasingly prosperous provinces in the coastal south, large pockets of poverty remain due to geographical isolation and/or ecological conditions (Lyons 1992). In such areas, people capable of becoming private entrepreneurs generally leave town rather than attempting to stimulate commerce in their hometowns. The mountainous villages surrounding Chang Le in Fujian are good examples of this phenomenon. Because the town of Chang

Le is bustling with overseas remittances and commercial growth,[9] able-bodied people from the surrounding rural villages have been abandoning their shoddy homes in the mountains in hopes of making a better living in the city. Even village chiefs are willing to leave their political positions behind. Only the elderly and children are left to remain, though in many cases the entire family moves away. Dilapidated mud and thatch buildings are the only visual indication that these villages were once well populated. Under such circumstances, it is not surprising that even interpersonal lending, the most basic form of informal finance, is virtually nonexistent. When asked whether villagers sometimes pool their cash to help each other, the typical response is that they rarely have the chance to receive cash, much less lend it out. Many villages continue to rely on barter trade to meet the bare necessities for subsistence.

In such an impoverished situation, local officials are not actively supportive of private sector development because the local government is not physically present for all practical purposes. It is worth pointing out that there are also officially designated impoverished counties that receive national and/ or provincial assistance from the Poverty Alleviation Bureau. One of the developmental tools employed by the official poverty alleviation strategy takes the form of low-interest "poverty alleviation loans," which are distributed to impoverished households for private income-generating activities.[10] These projects rely on the cooperation of local cadres, but local governments in these targeted counties are not explicitly "supportive" of the private sector because their developmental strategies are typically shaped by particular poverty alleviation policy requirements rather than the other way around.

Choosing Collective Rural Industrialization Over the Private Sector

In contrast to remote areas where scant hope exists for economic development, rural counties that fall within the jurisdiction of growing urban centers have been better positioned to engage in private (or collective) income-generating activities. Given that state banks have not been geared toward serving the non-state sector at the subcounty level, there is also greater demand for credit at both the grassroots and local governmental levels in these areas. In addition to interpersonal lending, local entrepreneurs organize rotating savings and credit associations (ROSCAs) and throughout the 1980s and 1990s, local governments operated RCFs. As discussed below through the case of Hui'an County, ROSCAs and RCFs serve different parts of the local population. Both operate primarily in rural and peri-urban areas, but ROSCA participants organize credit societies among themselves to finance small private businesses, while RCFs reflect in part the economic priorities of the local government, which is to promote the collective sector.

The reform era experience of Hui'an County in southern Fujian is typical in some ways of the model of rural industrialization that has transformed the standard of living for formerly impoverished counties in Fujian—and spawned financial institutions to fuel this transformation. Before reform, Hui'an's economy depended primarily on fishing, agriculture, and a smattering of stone-carving factories. During the 1990s, however, Township and Village Enterprises (TVEs) developed under the active guidance of local governments (Fei 1989; Oi 1999; Whiting 2001); some villages attracted substantial infusions of Taiwanese investment, and the construction of new roads and bridges increased the accessibility of Hui'an to the nearest urban center, Quanzhou municipality. A demographic result of this transformation in Hui'an's local economy is male out-migration and the feminization of agriculture. The Hui'an County Women's Federation estimates that women account for 70% of the local industrial labor force, 80% of agricultural labor, and over 90% of small-scale entrepreneurs (Interviews No. 22, 24). Not surprisingly, women also dominate participation in rotating credit associations, a staple in the world of informal finance.

While a wide range of variation exists in the actual mechanics of rotating savings and credit associations or "peer lending circles," most entail a group of people who come together for the express purpose of mutual financial assistance. Typically, ROSCA members contribute a fixed amount of money each month to a collective pot and each month one member takes her or his turn in collecting the entire pool of cash. In China ROSCAs *(hui)* reemerged in places such as Hui'an during the early years of reform as a community-based strategy to provide rural households with a source of savings and credit (Tsai 2000). As more and more households turned to petty commodity production in southern coastal areas like Guangdong, Fujian, and Zhejiang, the *hui* not only retained their social nature in recruitment, but also became an important source of capital for investing in fixed assets, mass purchasing of raw materials, and other production-related costs.[11]

Generally speaking, local governments have maintained a hands-off attitude toward rotating credit associations since they are viewed as a popular (*minjian*) form of grassroots credit.[12]

Aside from ROSCAs, RCFs represent an additional source of credit in rural and peri-urban areas like Hui'an (Deng 1994). Unlike ROSCAs, which are clearly informal and organized by private individuals, RCFs fell into the gray area of quasi-legality as financial institutions until the PBC shut them down in 1999. As discussed earlier, most were managed by township or village governments and registered with the local Agricultural Office and/or the Civil Affairs Bureau. RCFs generally offered higher rates of interest on savings deposits and charged higher interest rates on loans than the permissible level stipulated by the PBC. In addition to financing local agricultural activities, they also represented a key source of funds for rural industrial development in the form of TVEs. Technically, the RCFs' official mandate was to promote agricultural projects, not industrial undertakings. But since local governments governed them, the lending portfolios of RCFs predictably reflected the developmental priorities of their immediate administrative agents.

There are two striking characteristics of the local financial institutional environment in places like Hui'an. First, state banks are not physically accessible to most people. To the extent that rural residents interact with state banks, it tends to be in a depository rather than borrowing capacity. Most rural entrepreneurs do not even attempt to apply for loans from state banks. The second defining feature of these rural areas is the bifurcation within the unoffficial financial sector between governmental and nongovernmental mechanisms that provide credit for the non-state sector. RCFs generally extend credit to small and medium-sized businesses that conform with the local governments' developmental agenda. ROSCAs, on the other hand, comprise individual entrepreneurs who lack access to state banks and RCFs. A related implication of this is that women are more likely to organize ROSCAs, while men are more likely to receive loans from RCFs—even in areas where the year-round population is predominantly female (Tsai 2000).

Promoting Private Enterprise and Private Finance

In contrast to the collective sector orientation of the local government in places like Hui'an, other local governments have openly promoted private sector development throughout the reform era—and implicitly permitted the emergence of a colorful range of nonbanking financial institutions. These financial institutions not only compete with one another, but have drawn the formal financial sector into their competitive dynamics as well. This phenomenon is exemplified by the case of Wenzhou during the 1980s.

For the first 30 years of PRC governance, Wenzhou's economy was stagnant and the standard of living was poor in relative and absolute terms. As with other southern coastal cities, Wenzhou's proximity to Taiwan made it a high-risk district geostrategically speaking. Hence, neither the central nor provincial government was inclined to devote its limited resources to Wenzhou's industrial development. Although Wenzhou accounted for 11% of the province's land mass and 15% of its population, it received only one percent of Zhejiang's fixed capital investment throughout the Mao era. Adding to the disadvantage of official neglect, only 2% of Wenzhou's total surface area is arable due to its mountainous terrain; as a result, nearly half of its rural labor force was de facto unemployed or underemployed at the beginning of reform.

Given this developmental legacy, local officials are proud of the fact that Wenzhou was early relative to the rest of China in developing a de facto private economy of petty commodity producers and retail vendors.[13] Private enterprise in Wenzhou flourished to publicity proportions in tandem with the development of nongovernmental financing mechanisms, which defied and competed with the formal financial sector. When private finance in Wenzhou attracted the most domestic attention in the mid-1980s, the capital-raising strategies employed by entrepreneurs spanned from ad hoc, interest-free lending among relatives, neighbors, and local merchants to more institutionalized and controversial arrangements, such as private money houses that operated around the clock. If the early 1980s was about nongovernmental financial innovation in Wenzhou, a decade later, the original innovations were being curbed, incorporated, or redirected by financial system reform promulgated by higher administrative levels. This is not to say that official reform policies thwarted the development of additional innovations. Rather, both the local market and financial institutional environments in which economic actors were operating had changed; and the net effect of that change was to redefine the terms of the economic playing field. The rise, fall, and transformation of private money houses are a good example of this.

During the post-Mao era, private money houses first reappeared in Wenzhou in 1984 (Zhang and Mao 1993). By registering with the local ICMB rather than with the PBC, the first money house set a controversial precedent: an administrative bureaucracy in charge of commerce had approved the operations of an institution whose activities technically fell under the jurisdiction of the financial bureaucracy. Money houses appealed to a client base whose financing needs were not being met by the state banks. They operated 24 hours a day, seven days a week, and offered savings rates slightly higher than those of banks, and borrowing rates substantially higher than those of other forms of nongovernmental finance.

Two years after the first money house opened up, the Director of the central PBC at the time, Chen Muhua, visited Wenzhou in May 1986 and admonished the Wenzhou PBC for not keeping a tighter rein on illegal financing activities (Zhang and Mao 1993, 8). He also publicly announced that national banking laws do not allow governments, enterprises, and private individuals to run financial institutions (Zhang 1989). Despite this warning, private money houses continued to conduct their businesses openly. The elimination of the money houses was not implemented locally until 1989 when the national political crisis triggered a period of economic retrenchment and uncertainty about the future of reform. By the time that money houses were effectively banned in Wenzhou, there were 26 others that people openly referred to as "private banks" (Wenzhou City Communist Party Propaganda Department 1989, 65–6).

In addition to the money houses, which flagrantly violated national banking regulations, the popularity of rotating credit associations *(hui)* in Wenzhou also reached problematic proportions. It is estimated that by 1986, over 95% of the households in Wenzhou were participating in *hui* (with the exception of those in two small counties) (Li 1989). Several cases accumulated where a single *hui* organizer would default, thereby affecting hundreds, even thousands of households (Ma 1995, 414). The most serious cases of domino-style financial collapse involved "escalating financial associations," which mutated from the traditional *hui*, a community-centered, institutional expression of mutual assistance to a more insidious, destabilizing form: the pyramidal investment scam. Official banking statistics for Wenzhou during the mid-1980s exhibited a dramatic decline in savings deposits since cash was being funneled into higher-interest-yielding opportunities in the informal financial sector. In response, local banks and officially sanctioned credit cooperatives started offering higher interest rates to capture their share of business. This move pushed up the interest rates in the underground financial markets even higher and seemed to fuel participation in *hui*—even as they were collapsing. Wenzhou subsequently received a steady stream of upper-level cadres and economists from Beijing, Hangzhou, and Shanghai who sought to eradicate the practice of *hui*, as well as to understand how an informal financing mechanism could snowball into such chaotic proportions.[14]

Due to the national spotlight on Wenzhou's pyramidal schemes and the official banks' opposition to money houses, financial entrepreneurs who would have established private money houses turned to a less controversial option for engaging in financial brokering. Rather than directly confronting officials in the financial hierarchy with a corporate institution of questionable legality, they chose an organizational form that was more palatable to the formal financial sector: the credit cooperative. Just as privately owned businesses found it more convenient politically to register as collectives ("wearing a red hat"), would-be managers of money houses organized their operations as credit cooperatives. Because they were structured as stock-issuing financial institutions, credit cooperatives provided the institutional appearance of being collectively held even if the actual distribution of shares was dominated by only two or three people.

Like the private money houses, urban credit cooperatives (UCCs) were also first established in Wenzhou in 1984. By 1989 there were 43 UCCs, including fourteen "rural financial service cooperatives," accounting for one-third of the total UCCs in Zhejiang province (Zhang and Mao 1993, 124). Like the money houses, they worked extended hours to serve the financing needs of private businesses. Moreover, they offered rates that were as competitive as that of the money houses, even though they should have been subject to the interest rate limits defined by the state banking system. Bankers, officials, and merchants all understood that while the UCCs were registered as collective financial organizations, they were basically privately owned.

In 1990 the Wenzhou PBC investigated the UCCs and discovered a number of cases where managers were being overcompensated or dividends were not being distributed to shareholders properly. One year later, the Wenzhou PBC issued a policy ruling that placed UCCs and rural financial service societies under the management of the PBC. Yet local officials openly admit that UCCs continued to act independently of the PBC. Their interest rates remained higher than those of the state banks. They retained autonomy in personnel appointments and lending decisions, and essentially continued to operate business as usual. In early 1997 the financial hierarchy attempted once again to govern UCCs more stringently by forcing them to convert into

Urban Cooperative Banks (UCBs), which are considered stock-issuing commercial banks. The stated rationale for creating UCBs was to increase the efficiency of UCCs by consolidating them into standardized commercial banks (Liu 1996, 6). At the time that UCBs were being established, both bankers and local officials believed that the de facto privately run UCCs, an outgrowth of the private money houses, would finally have to relinquish their majority stakes and operational autonomy (Interview No. 160, 161, 162, 163, 164). Furthermore, since UCBs were formed by merging all the UCCs in Wenzhou, the UCB branches now report to a UCB central office that monitors their management and business practices. In effect, the red hat that the would-be managers of money houses wore to evade official interference turned into a hard one. Figure 5.1 below summarizes the organizational progression of money houses over time.

The center's repeated efforts at disciplining unconventional financial institutions further underscores the point that Wenzhou's reform era growth has clearly been driven by local initiative on the part of its entrepreneurs in collaboration with local officials (Parris 1993). Wenzhou did not have the benefit of state-invested industry or the financial infrastructure that came with it. Hence, the competitiveness of the local financial market was driven by private suppliers of capital and only later spilled over into the formal financial sector. The Central Banking Regulatory Commission's reaction has been to centralize the regulation of nonbanking financial institutions. Judging by the result of earlier efforts at financial repression, to the extent that private entrepreneurs face restricted access to legitimate financial institutions and need credit, informal finance will continue to flourish.

Ambivalence: The Changing Face of Market Socialism

While Wenzhou started with a relatively clean slate at the beginning of reform in terms of local industry, other localities are burdened by underperforming (SOEs). For example, the capital of Henan, Zhengzhou, received substantial capital infusions from the center during the Mao years to build an industrial base, but in the reform era the apparent benefits of heavy industrialization became developmental dilemmas. With most of the labor force employed by the state at the outset of reform, the local government must sustain employment for hundreds of thousands of industrial workers. Adding to this pre-existing challenge, agricultural decollectivization flooded the streets of Zhengzhou with surplus labor from the countryside, without the structural creation of new employment opportunities for them by central policy (Xinhua, 6/20/98).[15] The earliest migrants from the countryside were essentially vegetable vendors, peddlers, and sometimes, criminals. Private businesses have been viewed with some suspicion even though private sector development is one of the practical solutions for alleviating unemployment. In short, the local government is factionalized by competing developmental needs and therefore "ambivalent" about the range of permissible financial

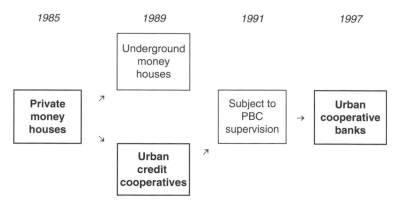

Figure 5.1 No hat → red hat → hard hat: the fate of private money houses in Wenzhou.

institutions in their territories. As a consequence, private financial institutions have had to wear a variety of hats that disguise their true nature and they often bear the brunt of political campaigns against corruption and illicit financial activities.

As in other parts of China, state banks continue primarily to serve the ailing (SOEs) in Zhengzhou.[16] Of the private entrepreneurs surveyed in Henan, 93% reported that they had never received loans from official financial institutions, while nearly 60% of the business owners had borrowed money from non-state sources. Although financial entrepreneurs in Henan have not operated private banks as openly as those in Wenzhou, throughout the 1990s an increasing number of nongovernmental financial institutions appeared in the legal form of nonprofit financial "societies." Their registration status as societies comes with the condition that they aim to "assist the poor and supply private businesses with capital . . . [thereby] promoting the values of material and spiritual civilization" (Henan Economic System Reform Committee 1993). Yet their lending portfolios reveal that most, if not all, of their debtors are private entrepreneurs who have substantial savings deposits with the societies (Interviews No. 94,101, 104, 105, 107, 108, 109, 111, 184). The commercial nature of their operations is further evidenced by the fact that the PBC is responsible for some of them. Technically, the PBC possesses authority over all financial institutions. In the case of financial societies, however, many are simply managed by the Civil Affairs Bureau. In short, registering as a "social organization" provides private financial entrepreneurs with a more politically acceptable guise for engaging in their de facto for-profit financial activities.[17]

Another legally sanctioned institutional cloak for privately run banks takes the form of "people-run enterprises capital mutual assistance associations" (CMA). They, too, are registered as societies and provide private businesses in Henan with short-term commercial loans. But the CMAs are actually overseen by the ICMB rather than by the PBC. This means that they possess more operational leeway than societies because the CMAs are legally permitted to operate as for-profit businesses—even if it happens to be the business of retail savings and loans. In essence, the CMAs are similar to the private money houses in Wenzhou. They operate as private banks that serve the local market of private entrepreneurs and do not make much of an effort to veil their private sector-oriented, for-profit mission.

While financial societies and CMA's were springing up all over the city during the 1995 to 1997 period, the Zhengzhou PBC was already in the process of "rationalizing" UCCs by forcing them to merge into UCBs. By mid-1996, there were already a total of 59 UCBs in 23 cities in Henan (Interview No. 101). The takeover of the UCCs in Zhengzhou reflected the PBC's growing concern about the ability of the formal financial system to keep up with the ambitious economic reform strategy set forth at the 15th National Party Congress in 1997, coupled with an attempt to prevent China from slipping into the Asian financial crisis. Given the dual pressures of reforming the state sector and rationalizing the financial sector, Henan's nonbanking financial institutions became a target of PBC investigations.

The first victim of the crackdown on illicit financial businesses was the Three Star Holding Company, an industrial conglomerate founded in 1992 by a former farmer from the suburbs of Zhengzhou. When the business ran into financial difficulties in 1995, the owner started a "flexi-sales" scheme to "honorary employees" who would invest in the company and sell products from home on consignment. By promising a 20% to 30% return on its shares to "gold card" and "silver card" members/employees, who contributed 20,000 and 10,000 yuan respectively, the company managed to attract 899 million yuan ($109.6 million) in deposits from the public (Wang 1998). When the PBC and the ICB conducted a joint investigation into its operations in March 1998, the investors/depositors got nervous and made a run on Three Star. Two months later, the city government forced it to close down and a large portion of its 30,000 depositors took to the streets in protest. They were enraged that a small, private financial institution had been investigated, while larger state banks continued to make bad loans on the scale of four to 5 billion yuan. The Henan provincial government issued an Emergency Notice to all state units (*danwei*), instructing them to keep their workers from protesting in the streets. Shortly after the Three Star incident, the owners of another private financial institution, the White Flower Company, suddenly closed the operation down and fled to the US with all their depositors' money (People's Daily 3/31/01).[18] White Flower's closure triggered a citywide bank run and all 16 of the privately owned finance companies in Zhengzhou became illiquid.

The newly established UCBs (formerly UCCs) were not spared from the panic. By July 1998, the 46 UCBs were operating under emergency conditions; they had not been shut down since the government feared additional public displays of the local financial distress in the streets. Instead, they had capped the maximum daily withdrawal at 40,000 yuan with the condition that only 20,000 yuan could be withdrawn in a single bank visit. Nonetheless, sporadic protests by depositors continued in front of the Provincial Government and Party buildings, the commercial center of Zhengzhou, and even the along the Beijing–Guangzhou railway line through September and November 1998 (Chan 1998; Rennie 1998).

In some ways, the financial mayhem in Zhengzhou at the end of the 1990s mirrored the turbulence in Wenzhou's financial markets during the mid-1980s. The life savings of average citizens were lost and the local government tried desperately to contain the damage. A defining difference, however, is the proximate cause of the financial turmoil. In Wenzhou, people were caught up in complex networks of pyramidal investment schemes (similar to those in Albania in 1997), while the bank runs in Zhengzhou were triggered by official investigations into high interest yielding private financial companies. Living in a provincial capital, residents of Zhengzhou have always been more attuned to shifts in state policy (whether at the national, provincial, or city level) since they tend to witness its implementation in a more immediate manner than say, farmers in remote rural areas do. As such, the closure of a single finance company was sufficient to evince a crisis of confidence in the viability of the city's private financial institutions. Another related contrast between Wenzhou and Zhengzhou is the fact that private sector development occurred much earlier in the former, while Zhengzhou has been more constrained by its SOEs and associated political ambivalence about capitalist profit. In light of these structural differences, it is striking that Zhengzhou's entrepreneurs have gone as far as they have in finding creative ways to engage in private finance. The 1998 crackdown on these very institutions was certainly unexpected, but to those who came of age before the reform era, it was not surprising. While Wenzhou's private entrepreneurs were able to co-opt the local staff of the state during the early reform years, in Zhengzhou the reverse has been the case.

Explaining Local Variation in Informal Finance

To clarify how the developmental cases discussed above contrast with one another, the Table 5.2 below summarizes them according to their structural legacy from the Mao era, political orientation toward the local economy (i.e., in relation to the private sector), and resulting curb market environment.

It is also important to note that the four "types" are by no means representative of the full range of developmental contexts within China. Depending on the level of detail, many more patterns of political economic interaction may be discerned.[19] The key here lies in appreciating the diverse ways in which different areas have developed or not developed curb market institutions that tread on the territory of state banks. Although state banks still are not well positioned to engage in commercial lending (as opposed to

Table 5.2
Summary of Developmental Paths and Informal Finance in China

Condition at Outset of Reform	Orientation of Local Government Toward Private Sector	Examples discussed	Local Supply of Informal Finance
Extreme poverty; neglected due to geographical remoteness	**Absent** Local government is absent	Impoverished mountainous villages (Changle, Fujian)	None
Strong development of commune and brigade structures	**Not Supportive** Supportive of collectives and larger private enterprises	Hui'an County (Fujian)	Low (ROSCAs & RCFs)
Deliberately deprived of capital for geostrategic reasons; low level of industrial development	**Supportive** Supportive of private business and financial innovations	Wenzhou City (Zhejiang)	High (ROSCAs, RCFs, loan sharks, private money houses, UCCs/UCBs, pawnshops)
High level of urban SOE industrial development	**Ambivalent** Bureaucratic factionalism over developmental priorities	Zhengzhou City (Henan)	Medium (Financial societies, people-run CMAs, UCCs/ UCBs)

Source: Adopted from Back-Alley Banking (2002).

policy driven lending), they would at least prefer to maintain a monopoly on savings mobilization. This objective has proved to be difficult not only because official interest rate levels have been artificially repressed, but also because private financial institutions possess the flexibility to provide a wider range of services and have a financial incentive (hard budget constraint) to do so. Furthermore, as suggested above, there are two main political reasons why curb market mechanisms have managed to flourish in certain areas.

First, local government officials entrusted with the responsibility for carrying out central policies have their own understanding of how to implement the letter if not the spirit of certain regulations. Lower level officials may seek to foster local economic growth, enhance their skimpy salaries, foil higher level administrators, or all of the above. The Weberian bureaucrat is an ideal-type, not a reality. Analytically speaking, the complexity of the multidimensional bureaucrat may be reduced somewhat by assuming that bureaucrats will be more loyal to the mandates of their particular ministry when confronted with a situation where jurisdictional territories overlap (Lieberthal and Lampton 1992;

Perry 1994). For example, financial regulators dispatched by the central banks are more likely to uphold national banking laws than to concede to another agency's policies. With this in mind, local financial entrepreneurs choose their battles carefully. Until there are truly low barriers to entry in the financial market (in which case it would not be a financially repressed environment), financial entrepreneurs will cultivate ties with key bureaucratic patrons to insulate them from official interference. As shown in the above cases, the choice of bureaucratic patron—if one or more are indeed chosen—has implications for the institutional form of nongovernmental financial intermediation. Those operating with a commercial retail storefront, for example, are registered with some agency, while less visible, underground curb market activities are not formally registered and generally avoid official attention.

Second, in addition to inter-bureaucratic conflicts over the governance of private entrepreneurs and their financial institutions, the orientation of the local government toward the economy represents a baseline from which the interpretation of central policies may be derived. The relatively decentralized nature of policy implementation in China means that policy mandates emanating from the center may be interpreted liberally and adjusted to fit perceived local conditions (Yang and Wei 1996; O'Brien and Li 1999; Wang and Hu 1999). This local interpretation thus provides a more accurate gauge of how various economic needs are defined and addressed. The above cases demonstrated that the attitude of the local government toward the private sector may be divided broadly into four categories: absent, nonsupportive, supportive, and ambivalent.[20]

This raises the question of why local governments have different attitudes toward the private sector in the first place.[21] I suggest that the differential attitudes toward the private sector reflect a certain degree of path dependence based on structural legacies of the Mao era.[22] Just as former socialist countries in central and eastern Europe started with varying degrees of industrialization, which have influenced the course of their political and economic development since 1989–1990, the same could be said of subnational units in China.

First, local governments that have not been supportive of the private sector derive from two developmental paths. In particularly impoverished and ecologically disadvantaged areas, the government may not be opposed to private income-generating activities, but both the local cadres and inhabitants tend to view permanent out-migration as the most expedient means to escape poverty. In areas with a stronger collective tradition, however, the government has a preference for developing the "collective" sector, which may be de facto privately owned in some cases, but entails a close relationship between business and local government.

Then there are localities that had minimal industrial development at the outset of reform, but were readily able to build their non-state sectors with the rural surplus labor unleashed by decollectivization. Such governments have been relatively "supportive" of private sector development in the sense that local officials may overlook the infractions of national laws by private entrepreneurs or even actively devise legal loopholes to facilitate novel business practices.

In the last developmental category are localities that inherited mammoth SOEs. Local governments in such areas are willing to foster economic growth through any means possible but are simultaneously restrained by the challenge of maintaining the payrolls of state sector employees. This represents the case of an "ambivalent" governmental stance toward private sector development; the developmental preferences of local officials are constrained by the hands that they were dealt, so private entrepreneurs may pay a high fiscal cost for existing alongside fledgling SOEs. But in the absence of exogenous pressure from higher administrative levels or local crisis, such local governments have maintained a more hands-off approach toward private financial institutions.

Note that although the initial economic conditions of a locality represent the proximate starting point of the developmental paths outlined above, the overarching logic of this argument is not purely "economic" for two reasons. First, the developmental condition of various localities is very much a reflection of state policies from the pre-reform era. The economic unevenness of the country derived from political and strategic considerations, which often defied conventional economic notions of comparative advantage (e.g., forcing areas to produce crops that were ill-suited to local ecological conditions, building heavy industrial plants in remote areas, prohibiting port cities from engaging in external trade, etc.). Second and more importantly, I argue that the local government's attitude toward the private sector plays a critical role in either enabling or limiting curb market activities.

Conclusion

Financial institutions do not magically appear even when the market demand for credit clearly exists. They have to be created. And in the case of reform-era China, financial entrepreneurs have created financial institutions despite state efforts to monopolize the supply of credit in the economy. Private entrepreneurs cannot simply mind their own businesses and raise capital through the most expedient means. They have to deal with the staff of the regulatory state on a day-to-day basis. Yet the "state" is not a single entity that devises policies and implements them consistently. The state consists of multiple administrative levels and functional bureaucracies across geographically defined areas. This chapter has therefore argued that the orientation of the local government toward the private sector is a key indicator in determining the density of informal financial institutions in any given locality. Ultimately, the implementers of "state" policy decide how to carry out their assigned tasks.

The differing developmental orientations of local governments may be rooted in economic legacies from the Mao era, but they are not static. By the mid-1990s, areas known for their large collective sectors, for example, were starting to privatize collective assets (Sargeson and Zhang 1999; Whiting 2001). Furthermore, the broader policy environment also influences the viability of informal financial institutions over time. During permissive political economic periods, novel forms of financial intermediation may have less difficulty in registering as legitimate corporate entities, but once they are registered, they are also more easily identified for disciplinary "rectification" when the PBC is instructed to clamp down on curb market activities. Regardless of their color, hats are still visible. The forced conversion of UCCs into UCBs might suggest to some observers that the days of free-wheeling financial creativity are over. Attempting to learn from the apparent mistakes of its neighbors, Beijing sees the downside of unregulated financial companies in Thailand, patronage-driven development in Indonesia, and overly networked corporate governance structures in Japan. Nonetheless, China's reform experience thus far also demonstrates that the rationalization of state banks and nonbanking financial institutions cannot simply be imposed from above. Even in an authoritarian regime with a unitary political system, local bureaucrats and entrepreneurs are continuously redefining the institutional space for private sector finance.

Ultimately, the economic and political realities discussed above complicate the decision-making calculus of reformers in Beijing. On the one hand, informal finance has played an important role in facilitating private sector growth; on the other hand, curb market activities may have destabilizing effects because they fall beyond the regulatory scope of the state banking system. In addition to violating interest rates ceilings, informal financial intermediaries may compete with formal financial institutions banks in savings mobilization and contribute to local financial crises when they are involved in fundamentally unsustainable speculative activities. Generally speaking, banking authorities have attempted to ban rather than to legalize and regulate informal finance. These efforts have not been that effective, however, because local officials and bureaucrats may collaborate with private entrepreneurs in disguising (or ignoring) curb market institutions that enhance personal financial compensation and local economic development. Yet local governments are not equally protective of curb market operators—even within a particular province. Some localities harbor a tremendous array of informal financial institutions, while others have a much more limited scope of informal financial activity. Given such local variation, it would be misleading to conclude more broadly that China is evolving toward a coherent, preexisting model of political economy, such as a "developmental state," an "entrepreneurial state," or a "predatory state" (Evans 1989; Blecher 1991; Duckett 1998). In the first three decades of reform, we have seen local governments quietly channel bank credit to the non-state sector; we have also seen local governments engage in income-generating activities, including arbitrary collection of rents from private businesses.

By the same token, increasing segmentation within the private sector is also apparent. Entrepreneurs operating in the same locality at a similar scale of business may use vastly different types of financing mechanisms because they have different social and political resources at their disposal. While it is reasonable to expect that private entrepreneurs will rely on more formal sources of credit as China's financial system becomes more commercialized and capital markets become more developed, informal finance is not merely a transitional phenomenon. Formal and informal finance are not perfect substitutes because in practice, some portion of the population will remain excluded from conventional sources of credit. Indeed, substantial pockets of curb market activity can be found even in advanced industrialized countries with liberalized financial systems. In short, informal finance facilitated the initial spurt of private sector growth not only during China's reform era, but it may be expected to remain significant in the economy—to varying degrees around the country—for years to come as well.

Notes

1. This was calculated based on the percentage of "loans to private and urban collective enterprises" to total loans. *China Statistical Yearbook 2008.*

2. The field research entailed a survey of private entrepreneurs ($n = 374$) and interviews with bankers, government officials, street-level bureaucrats, academics, and journalists ($n = 186$) in 18 localities in Fujian, Zhejiang, and Henan over the course of 1994 to 2001. A complete list of the surveys and interviews is available in Tsai (2002).

3. In this chapter, "local governments" and "localities" refer to sub-provincial administrative levels, that is, city, county, township, and village.

4. This finding is consistent with the results of a 1999 survey conducted by the International Finance Commission and the State Economic and Trade Commission, which found that 90.5% of private businesses rely on "self-financing." The sample ($n = 628$) included private entrepreneurs (*siying qiye*) in Beijing, Chengdu, Shunde, and Wenzhou (Gregory, Tenev, and Wagle 2000).

5. In brief, the reasons why private entrepreneurs have been excluded from formal bank credit are as follows. First, despite efforts at separating commercial from policy lending, state banks face political pressure to extend loans to state-owned enterprises. Second, state banks lack experience in lending on a commercially viable basis. Third, state banks lack the incentive to lend to creditworthy clients because they do not face hard budget constraints. Fourth, especially during the early years of reform, the legal (and ideological) status of private enterprises remained ambiguous and subject to change, so state banks have been hesitant to engage in private sector lending.

6. They are "legal" to the extent that they have not been banned explicitly.

7. For example, pawnshops in Xingtai, Hebei offered annual interest of 40% to its depositors in 1991 (China Online 9/9/99). Another study found that some pawnshops charge monthly interest rates between 5% and 8% (i.e., up to 72% interest annually).

8. Based on a 2004 national survey ($n = 7000$ in 20 provincial-level units), Li Jianjun estimated that in 2003 curb market lending ranged from RMB 740.5 to 816.4

billion, which on average represents 28.07% of the total scale of lending by formal financial institutions (Li 2005).

9. Technically, Chang Le is classified as a "city." Until 1996, it was a "county." Chang Le represents the primary port of departure for illegal Fujianese immigration to the United States and elsewhere.

10. A number of internationally sponsored microfinance projects have also appeared since the mid-1990s. An annotated listing is provided in *China Development Briefing* 3, October 1996. Their relative performance is discussed in Park and Ren (2001).

11. In some areas, the monetary scale of the *hui* also increased dramatically and became a profit-making end in itself. Both Wenzhou (Zhejiang) and Quanzhou (Fujian) experienced periods where the scale of *hui* became extremely large and unsustainable (i.e., one defaulter would bring down entire networks of *hui*s).

12. The exception to governmental noninterference is when the ROSCAs have collapsed en masse and affected substantial portions of the population.

13. By the official commencement of rural reform at the beginning of 1979, there were already an estimated 1844 microentrepreneurs in the Wenzhou area; three years later, the number multiplied eleven times to 20,363 entrepreneurs.

14. The aggregate scale of *hui* reached 1 billion yuan (over $330 million).

15. Zhengzhou comprises six "districts" in the city and six rural "counties." Nearly 70% of Zhengzhou's population of 6 million people is registered as residing in rural areas. The 6 million does not include an additional estimated 600,000 migrant workers on any given day (Xinhua, 6/20/1998).

16. In 1997, only 0.10% of the state banks' lending portfolio in Henan were loans to private commercial businesses. *Henan tongji nianjian 1997* (Henan Statistical Yearbook 1997), Table 16.10, 497.

17. Some disguises are quite ingenious. For example, one "nonprofit" society operates as a magazine reading club that offers its readers an annual 15% to 20% "reading bonus" on their book deposit money. The second floor of the reading club consists of trading desks, where employees are busy trading futures to generate high returns on members' deposits. Interview No. 100.

18. In March 2001, the Intermediate People's Court of Zhengzhou found that between May 1996 and May 1998, Baihua illegally mobilized 336 million yuan ($40.6 million) and $120,000 in deposits from 12,295 individuals. The former general manager, Li Jian, was sentenced to death and six of his accomplices were sentenced to prison terms ranging from 18 months to 15 years (*Renmin ribao* March 31, 2001).

19. By the same token, additional factors could be identified that affect dynamics in the local political economy, including the relative availability of overseas Chinese capital/foreign investment, the local structure of kinship networks (e.g., single surname vs. multi-surname villages), and ethnic composition. This chapter, however, aims primarily at emphasizing the relative importance of local governments in mediating curb market activity.

20. In each of the research sites, I evaluated the extent to which the local government is "supportive" of the private economy according to the presence/absence of an active Industrial and Commercial Management Bureau and the mass organization representing microentrepreneurs, the Individual Laborer's Association, de facto rates of taxation (including various fees and surcharges), internal policy documents regarding the private sector, as well as the public rhetoric on related reform issues.

21. As suggested previously, the "local government" is not a monolithic whole, but for the present purposes, I categorize the attitude of the aggregate entity according to the overall direction of its policies and practices vis-à-vis the private sector.

22. My use of path dependence is consistent with that of David Stark and László Bruszt, who "see that the past can provide institutional resources for change in the present," in contrast to the involutionist approach to path dependence, which sees "in the present the dead weight of the past" (Stark and Bruszt 1998, 7; cf. Pierson [2004]).

References

Blecher, Marc. 1991. Developmental state, entrepreneurial state: the political economy of socialist reform in Xinju Municipality and Guanghan County. In *The Chinese State in the Era of Economic Reform*, ed. Gordon White, pp. 265–91, Armonk: M.E. Sharpe.

Chan, Yee Hon. 1998. Investors take to streets over billion-dollar scams. *South China Morning Post*, September 27.

Cheng, Enjiang, Christopher Findlay, and Andrew Watson. 1998. "We're not financial organizations!": financial innovation without regulation in China's rural co-operative funds. *MOCT-MOST: Economic Policy in Transition Economies* 8(3): 41–55.

China closes credit coops. 1999. Associated Press, March 22; and Over 1,000 investors protest closure of credit cooperative in Hubei. 1999. Agence France Presse, March 23.

Chinese Experts Evaluate China's Pawnshop Industry. 1999. China Online (http://www.chinaonline.com), September 9.

Deng, Yingtao. 1994. *Development and Reform of Rural Finance in China*. Tianjin: Tianjin daxue chubanshe.

Duckett, Jane. 1998. *The Entrepreneurial State in China: Real Estate and Commerce Departments in Reform Era Tianjin*. London: Routeledge.

Du, Zhixiong. 1998. The dynamics and impact of the development of rural cooperative funds (RCFs) in China. Chinese Economies Research Centre Working Paper No. 98/2, The University of Adelaide, March.

Evans, Peter. 1989. Predatory, developmental and other apparatuses: a comparative political economy perspective on the Third World State. *Sociological Forum* 4(4): 561–87.

Fei, Hsiao-Tung. 1989. *Rural Development in China: Prospect and Retrospect*. Chicago: University of Chicago Press.

Gregory, Neil, Stoyan Tenev, and Dileep Wagle. 2000. *China's Emerging Private Enterprises: Prospects for the New Century*. Washington, DC: International Finance Corporation.

Henan provincial economic system reform committee and PBC. 1993. Policy Document No. 134.

Holz, Carsten A. 2001. China's monetary reform: the counterrevolution from the countryside. *Journal of Contemporary China* 20(27): 189–217.

Li, Jianjun. 2005. *Research on the Scale of Underground Financing and Its Economic Effects*. Beijing: Zhongguo jinrong chubanshe.

————. 2006. *China Informal Finance Survey.* Shanghai: Shanghai People's Press.

Li, Mingyu. 2000. Pawnshops: future after removing the "gold store sign." *Homeway Financial News,* October.

Li, Yu. 1989. Financial kaleidoscope. In *New Reflections on Wenzhou's Reform Model,* ed. Yu Shizhang. Wenzhou: Zhonggong wenzhoushi wixuanchuangu.

Liu, Qingfen. 1996. An elementary introduction to the developing strategy of urban cooperative banks. *Zhengzhou Late Edition News,* June 21.

Lyons, Thomas P. 1992. *China's War on Poverty: A Case Study of Fujian Province, 1985–1990.* Hong Kong: Chinese University of Hong Kong.

Ma, Jinlong. 1995. *Wenzhou's Financial Market. In Wenzhou's Market.* Beijing: Zhonggong dangshi chubanshe.

Oi, Jean C. 1999. *Rural China Takes Off: Institutional Foundations of Economic Reform.* Berkeley: University of California Press.

Park, Albert and Ren Changqing. 2001. Microfinance with Chinese characteristics. *World Development* 29(1): 3–62.

Parris, Kristen. 1993. Local initiative and national reform: the Wenzhou model of development. *The China Quarterly* 134: 242–63.

Lieberthal, Kenneth and David M. Lampton, eds. 1992. *Bureaucracy, Politics and Decision Making in Post-Mao China.* Berkeley: University of California Press.

Man Sentenced to Death for Financial Fraud. 2001. *Renmin ribao,* March 31.

Ming, Xia. 2000. *The Dual Developmental State.* Brookfield: Ashgate Publishing.

O'Brien, Kevin and Lianjiang Li. 1999. Selective policy implementation in rural China. *Comparative Politics* 31: 167–86.

Perry, Elizabeth J. 1994. Trends in the study of Chinese politics: state-society relation. *The China Quarterly* 139: 704–13.

Pierson, Paul. 2004. *Politics in Time: History, Institutions, and Social Analysis.* Princeton: Princeton University Press.

Rennie, David. 1998. Street protests as Chinese are bled of their savings; banks face a run as deposits vanish into the black hole of state-run enterprises. *The Daily Telegraph,* November 19.

Sargeson, Sally and Jian Zhang. 1999. Reassessing the role of the local state: a case study of local government interventions in property rights reform in a Hangzhou district. *The China Journal* 42: 77–99.

Stark, David and László Bruszt. 1998. *Postsocialist Pathways: Transforming Politics and Property in East Central Europe.* New York: Cambridge University Press.

Survey: 20 years of reform benefits private sector most. 1999. *Xinhua News Agency,* January 27.

Tsai, Kellee S. 2000. Banquet banking: gender and rotating savings and credit associations in South China. *The China Quarterly* 161: 143–70.

————. 2002. *Back-Alley Banking: Private Entrepreneurs in China.* Ithaca: Cornell University Press.

Wang, Fashen. 1998. The myth of 'San Xing' is over—a record of how the criminal case of Li Guofa illegally accepting savings deposits from the public was resolved. *Dahebao,* September 6: 4–5.

Wang, Shaoguang and Angang Hu. 1999. *The Political Economy of Uneven Development: The Case of China.* Armonk: M.E. Sharpe.

Wenzhou City Communist Party Propaganda Department. 1989. Wenzhou people run the first private banks in China. In *Examination and Reflections on Wenzhou's*

Reform Model. Wenzhou: Wenzhou City Communist Party Propaganda Department.

White, Gordon, ed. 1988. *Developmental States in East Asia*. New York: St. Martin's Press.

Whiting, Susan H. 2001. *Power and Wealth in Rural China: The Political Economy of Institutional Change*. New York: Cambridge University Press.

World Bank. 2007. *World Development Report 2008: Agriculture for Development*. Washington D.C.: IBRD/The World Bank.

Xin, Jin. 1993. *History of Pawnshops*. Shanghai: Shanghai wenyi chubanshe.

Yang, Dali and Houkai Wei. 1996. Rising sectionalism in China? *Journal of International Affairs* 49(2): 456–77.

Zhang, Heping. 1989. The money house "boss," Fang Peilin. In *Wenzhou Tide*, ed. Zhiren Zhang. Beijing: Wenhua yishu chubanshe.

Zhang, Zhenning and Chunhua Mao. 1993. *Perspectives on the Phenomenon of Finance in Wenzhou*. Hangzhou: Zhejiang daxue chubanshe.

Zhengzhou becomes a regional commercial center. 1998. *Xinhua News Agency*, June 20.

Zhongguo jinrong nianjian (Almanac of China's Finance and Banking). 2000. F Yearbook. Beijing: Zhongguo jinrong chubanshe.

Zhu, Delin and Meiou Hu. 1997. *China's Grey Black Finance—Market Trends and Reflections on Improvements*. Shanghai: Lixin huiji chubanshe.

Chapter 6

New Venture Financing: An Empirical Investigation of Chinese Entrepreneurs

Jianwen Liao, Qian Ye, David Pistrui,
and Harold P. Welsch

In this chapter, we turn to the makeup and role of venture capital (VC) in Chinese business, including the relative importance of informal finance. Given the role that entrepreneurial ventures play in job creation, employment growth, innovation, and export potential, venture financing has important implications for the economy at the macro level (Ács, Carlsson, and Karlsson 1999; Wennekers and Thurik 1999; Cassar 2004; Wong, Ho, and Autio 2005; Drucker 2006) and also serves as the lifeblood of entrepreneurial new ventures at the micro level. With adequate capitalization, entrepreneurs can pursue market opportunities, hire qualified personnel, and continue product development (Gompers and Lerner 1999; Timmons 1999). Indeed, inadequate financial resources are often viewed as a primary reason for the failure of emerging businesses (Rujoub, Cook, and Hay 1995).

The bulk of research on venture financing so far has been devoted to the practices in developed countries with only limited attention given to emerging economies, especially with regard to China. Given the differences in Chinese institutional factors as well as the emergence of a new generation of entrepreneurs, it calls for research in uncovering unique patterns of venture financing.

This research is aimed to fill this gap by reporting a survey conducted in the city of Wuhan, located in Hubei province. The paper is organized as follows. We first review the existing research in venture financing by looking into the effects of venture financing and the various predictors of venture financing. Next, we highlight the unique operating and institutional environments Chinese entrepreneurs face, providing the context under which venture financing, from both formal and informal sources, takes place. It is followed by our empirical results from our survey. The paper is concluded with implications and future research directions.

Existing Research in Venture Financing

The Effects of Venture Financing

Research has documented the importance of venture financing and its effects on business survival, growth aspiration, and strategy. For example, Bates (1990) investigated the relationship between small business longevity and entrepreneurs' human and financial capital. Utilizing a nationwide random sample of males who entered self-employment between 1976 and 1982, he found that both human capital and financial capital were strongly linked to business viability. In a similar vein, Holtz-Eakin, Joulfaian and Rosen (1994) examined the role of entrepreneurs' access to capital in the likelihood of entrepreneurial failure. Based on a data set that consisted of the 1981 and 1985 federal individual income tax returns of a group of people who received inheritances, they found that liquidity constraints have a noticeable influence on the viability of entrepreneurial firms. Their results suggest that the effect of entrepreneur's inheritance on the probability of surviving is small but noticeable. However, if enterprises do survive, inheritances have a substantial impact on their performance.

Venture financing also plays a role in affecting a venture's initial strategy. For example, in their longitudinal research of 1053 entrepreneurs, Cooper et al. (1994) examined the impacts of human and financial capital on the performance of start-ups. In terms of financial capital, they argued that the amount of capital raised was related to the initial strategy that might be pursued by a firm through both direct and indirect effects. With direct effects, they found that more initial capital provides the possibility of carrying a broader mix of merchandise or undertaking more ambitious projects. More initial capital buys time when entrepreneurs learn and overcome problems at the start-up stage. With the indirect effects, capital accumulation may reflect better training and more extensive planning, which can afford ventures to be more promising propositions and pass the screening of lenders and investors.

Finally, venture financing is viewed to be related to entrepreneurial growth aspiration. For example, Wiklund and Shepherd (2003) employed the theory of planned behavior to develop a model of small business managers' growth aspirations and the level of growth achieved. Using a sample of 603 CEOs of small business participated in the survey of 1996 and a subsequent follow-up survey of 552 in 1999, they found that access to financial capital had direct and positive effect on growth, which suggests that small businesses with access to more financial capital grow more.

The Predictors of Venture Financing

Broadly speaking, there are two theoretical frameworks that describe a firm's capital structure and financing choices: static trade-off choice or pecking-order framework. Both frameworks predict differences in financing costs and the use of financing for different firms (Cassar 2004). These theories explain why some start-ups borrow more than others, why some borrow with short-maturity and others with long-maturity debt, and so on.

Within static trade-off choice framework, one determinant of a firm's financing choices is the exposure of the firm to bankruptcy and agency costs against the tax benefits associated with debt use. Bankruptcy costs are the transaction costs of liquidation or reorganization (Myers 1977). A firm will incur bankruptcy costs when its perceived probability of a default on financing is greater than zero (Cassar 2004). Agency costs arise when firms are financed by debt and other external sources (Myers 1977). Debt-holders set up costly monitoring devices or make contracts to restrict and monitor the firm's behavior, which will increase the cost of capital offered to the firm.

From a pecking-order theory perspective, capital structure choices are created by the presence of information asymmetries between the firm and its potential financier (Myers and Majluf 1983). The greater the risk associated with the information asymmetries, the higher the demanded return of capital by financing source. Thus, the exposure to the risks leads the firm to prefer inside finance to debt, short-term debt to long-term debt, and so on.

Around these two theoretical frameworks, studies have examined both firm-level and individual-level characteristics that may explain the differences in the choices of venture financing options.

Firm Level Characteristics

The nature of a firm's assets. Firm assets include tangible and intangible assets. The role of asset structure in the start-up financing demonstrates the importance of tangibility of assets. Gompers and Lerner (1999) pointed out that with tangible assets, entrepreneurs are easier to obtain financial support or obtain more favorable terms. When their most important assets are intangible, raising outside financing from traditional sources is a great challenge and those firms that lack tangible assets tend to be financed through less traditional means. Such loans come from individuals who play an important role in capital structure of start-ups, which emphasizes the importance of network resources in these types of ventures.

Firm Size. Utilizing a survey, Cassar (2004) investigated the determinants of capital structure and types of financing used across business start-ups. His results empirically supported the theoretical financing life cycle model. In this study, Cassar hypothesized that firm start-up size, asset structure, start-up incorporation, start-up growth intentions, and decision-makers' characteristics significantly influence the capital structure and financing of firm. He found that firm size appears to be an important factor in the financing of new business. The results of this study highlight the importance of scale and market access to the capital structure of start-ups. The larger the start-up, the greater the proportion of debt, long-term debt, outside financing, and bank financing, which is consistent with the theoretical arguments of financing life cycle.

Market conditions. Because the capital and product markets are subject to substantial variations, the supply and the price of capital may vary remarkably. Similarly, when great uncertainty or intensive competition characterizes the nature of product markets, entrepreneurial firms may encounter difficulties to raise capital from traditional sources (Gompers and Lerner 1999).

Liquidity Constraints. From the financing life cycle perspective, new firms' unique characteristics, such as low-scale potential and early reliance on internal capital, may lead to limited venture capital use (Cassar 2004). This point is consistent with the literature dealing with liquidity constraints and market imperfections faced by the small firms. When entrepreneurs want to see their ideas to fruition, they suffer from the liabilities of newness and smallness. Some traditional financing options are not available to them; therefore, they always have capital constrains. Thus, new firms face unique financing problems. Evans and Jovanovic (1989) developed a model for entrepreneurial activity under liquidity constraints. The results show that entrepreneurs do face liquidity constraints and rely heavily on their own assets to finance new firms. This finding is consistently echoed by research in Hall (1992), Holtz-Eakin et al. (1994), Fazzari et al. (1988), Berger and Udell (1998), and Huyghebaert (2001) etc. In general, the conclusion from new venture and financing structure research is that personal savings remain the most important source of start-up funding, with venture capital playing a greater role in the early growth phase rather than start-up phase (Bruno and Tyebjee 1985; Van Auken and Carter 1989; Manigart and Struyf 1997; Cassar 2004).

Individual-Level Characteristics

In addition to firm characteristics and market access that may influence entrepreneur's financial choices, the entrepreneur himself or herself may also influence financing and capital structure choices.

Gender of the owner. Studies have investigated the role of gender difference in access to loan finance (Akoten, Sawada, and Otsuka 2006; Treichel and Scott 2006; Carter, Shaw, Lam, and Wilson 2007). For example, using the National Survey of Small Business Finance, Haynes and Haynes (1999) examined the financial structure of women-owned businesses in 1987 and 1993. They hypothesized that women-owned small business borrowers have a lower probability and a smaller share of total debt held in line-of-credit loans from commercial banks than men-owned small business borrowers. The results of analysis of the 1987 data support these two hypotheses, but those of analysis of the 1993 data do not. Women-owned small businesses appear to have gained access to line-on-credit loans from commercial banks similar to the access gained by men-owned small business. The authors also gave several possible explanations for this change such as the reduced education and business experience gaps between men and women from 1987 to 1993, the changed risk preference and aggressive behavior of women owners, the increased experience of lenders with women borrowers, etc. Similarly, Coleman (2004) reported that women are significantly less likely than men to take out a loan, including a line of credit. Chaganti et al. (1995) documented that women entrepreneurs tended to use internal sources of equity rather than external sources. In another study of Norwegian women entrepreneurs, Alsos et al. (2006) found few gender differences existing in funding perceptions and behaviors, but the results of their study show that women obtain significantly less financial capital to develop their new businesses. Moreover, the results indicated that the lower levels of financial capital that women business founders achieve are associated with lower early business growth compared with their male counterparts.

Educational background. Bates (1990) investigated small business longevity. He analyzed a sample drawn from the 1982 Characteristics of Business Owners (CBO) survey. His results show that years of education is the strongest human capital variable for identifying business continuance. Specifically, Bates attempted to estimate how debt capital obtained by entrepreneurs affects the viability of their enterprises. Over 98% of the businesses among his sample received no equity capital from organized financial markets at the point of start-up, but most of them did have access to debt capital. Two dominant sources of debt—commercial bank loans (most frequent) and debt from family and friends (second most frequent)—accounted for 83.1% of the loans received by the nonminority male sample. Debt from former business owners ranked a distant third, accounting for 8.7% of the loans received. Those who have access to debt capital are usually those that have strong educational background. His results also indicated that a college education directly improved access to debt capital for the commercial bank borrowers; however, education variables were statistically insignificant determinants of debt levels for nonbank borrowers.

Years of experience. Knowledgeable practitioners seem to consider entrepreneur's experience as an important criterion to evaluate their behaviors (Macmillan, Siegel, and Narashima 2002). It has been found that founder's stock of experience has a better predictive ability of performance of new venture than other outcomes (Reuber and Fischer 1999). Using a sample of small Hungarian private sector firms in 1991, Hersch et al. (1997) found that characteristics of the owner are important in determining the perceived difficulty of obtaining loans. Owners without business experience perceived getting a loan to be more difficult than did experienced owners. Chandler and Hanks (1998) shed light on the factors that determine the amount of money needed to start a business, and the factors that drive the decisions of whether such funding should come from founder savings or from outside sources. They used a sample of 102 manufacturing and service firms between 3 and 7 years of age. The results of this study also suggest that founders with strong background experience may be able to start businesses that survive and thrive with less financial capital than their less experienced counterparts.

Venture Financing in China

China's economic transition from planned economy to a market-oriented economy began in rural area and was instituted in the late 1970s. At that time, Chinese leaders encouraged the formation of rural enterprises and private businesses, liberalized foreign trade and investment, relaxed state control over some prices, and invested in industrial production and the education of its work force (Hu and Khan 1997). During the 1980s, the private sector was the fastest growing part of the Chinese economy (Dana 1999; Starr 2001). In the next decade, the scale of privatization in China was grand. By the end of the 1990s, it was estimated that more than 12 million private enterprises were operating in China (Quanyu, Leonard, and Tong 1997). In the meantime, Chinese leaders deepened the fundamental reform among state-owned enterprises (SOEs). In 1994, China had about 1,022,000 SOEs producing about 34% of national GDP and employed 43.49 million employees. While in 2001, the number of SOEs had been reduced to 345,000 producing about 18.1% of national GDP with 18.1 million employees (Lu 2006). Currently, the private sector now has become a critical component in terms of its contribution to the nation's GDP. Recently, Fung et al. (2006) reported that the non-state sectors contributed to more than 60% of production, 90% of employment, and 70% of tax revenue.

With the development of the private sector, researchers have documented that there is an increasing need for private enterprise in Asian transitional economies (Scheela and Van Dinh 2004). Similar to other transitional-economy countries, China has underdeveloped capital markets. The financial system of China is still tightly controlled to avoid instability (Hitt, Ahlstrom, Dacin, Levitas, and Svobodina 2004). Under these circumstances, the banking system and capital markets are underdeveloped, which limits firms' financing options (Hitt et al. 2004). Private new firms in these economies are facing significant challenges in accessing financial capitals (Scheela and Van Dinh 2004).

Internal and Informal Financing Sources

Internal financing sources include founders' equity investment and retained earnings. Founders' equity investment includes founders' own equity as well as informal financing funds from friends and family.

Family savings are the primary resources used to establish private enterprises. Extended family networks represented two of the top five sources of start-up capital (Pistrui, Huang, Welsch, and Jing 2006). Chinese entrepreneurs get their ventures started with the help of close friends, partners, and trusted colleagues who provide financial resources. Therefore, Chinese entrepreneurs' seed capital is likely to be obtained from informal and family networks rather than public institutions. This finding is supported by the work of Davis (2000), which demonstrated that Chinese entrepreneurs rely much less on formal institutions, such as banks and government assistance, to get started.

However, personal savings are not adequate for financing fast-growing business, such as capital-intensive industries. Retained earnings are also a limited source for new ventures. Internal financing is typically a good source for starting up, but cannot provide adequate capital for growth needs (Fung, Liu, and Yau 2007).

External Sources

Bank loans. In China, it is not easy for new ventures to obtain loans from the state-owned banks. One of the major obstacles to obtaining bank finance is the fact that banks perceive new ventures as more prone to high default risk than larger firms (Fung et al. 2007). In order to solve this problem, the central government set up a network of more than 200 guarantee agencies nationwide to guarantee approximately $120 million a year. Thirty percent of this amount went to high-tech start-ups. More than 100 cities established credit guarantee institutions that were expected to help guarantee $4.8 billion in bank loans for the SMEs (Pei 2002). However, the criteria were too high, since only 1% of SMEs could qualify for their services. Lending decisions were made by guarantee agencies, which prefer supporting larger enterprises to smaller and new ones.

Venture capital. Until very recently, venture capital (VC) in China was still a state-controlled business. Since the mid-1990s, many government-sponsored VC funds have been established to provide financial support for SMEs. In the meantime, the Chinese government adopted a series of policy to foster the development of the VC industry. Since then, China has become one of the fastest growing markets for VC investment in the world (Ahlstrom, Bruton, and Yeh 2007). In the year 2005, it was estimated that $1.17 billion was raised by VC firms to invest in China, up from $325 million in 2002 (Balfour 2006). However, VCs' venture investing in a transition economy faces significant challenges. China, like most Asian economies, is characterized by the underdeveloped institutions that are needed to support a VC industry, in which VC plays a significantly different role than it does in the West (Aylward 1998).

Compared to Western-based venture capitalists, venture capitalists (VCs) operating in China monitor their investee companies much more closely, by evaluating the networks developed by their investee entrepreneurs (Scheela and Van Dinh 2004). In addition, these VCs also developed a networking strategy to maintain the relationships built with local Chinese government officials (Bruton and Ahlstrom 2003), which is very important to VCs' operating in China. On the other hand, in the context of China, science parks and universities provide important sources for potential high-tech growth ventures (Phan, Siegel, and Wright 2005); however, it is also noted that VCs have difficulties in locating and building relationships with such individuals (Wright 2007).

Operating in China, VCs face the problems of the lack of institutional stability, poor property rights, and weak rule of law (Ahlstrom et al. 2007). Asymmetric information may be especially problematic in a transitional economy such as China (Wright 2007). In this institutional context, VCs adapt their due diligence approaches and information sources. Wright et al. (2004) provided empirical evidence that VC firms in Asia are less likely to use information from interviews with entrepreneurs or business plan data than their counterparts in the West. Their own due diligence is especially import-ant for their decision to invest.

Batjargal and Liu (2004) examined the effect of entrepreneur's social capital on VCs' decisions about investments. They used different data sources creating a list of 158 domestic VC firms. They found that direct ties moderate the effects of the growth potential of the project on VCs' investment selection. Their results also show that strong relations lead to fewer contractual coven-ants that directly protect the investor's interests. The reverse effects of strong ties on investment delivery speed and the effects of friendly relationships with investors on getting higher valuation for their firms are also reported by this study.

Stock Market. Since the establishment of the stock exchange in the early 1990s, Chinese SMEs have been trying to gain access to the market for capital. Since 1978, China has adopted a different approach toward entrepreneurship and private optioning for the development of a mixed "socialist market economy." At the very beginning of its reform, China began to realize some of the advantages of mixing state and private enterprise. In an effort to stimulate economic growth and development, Chinese leaders encouraged the formation of township and village enterprises (TVEs) and private busi-nesses, liberalized foreign trade and investment, relaxed state control over some prices, and invested in industrial production and the education of its work force (Hu and Khan 1997).

China provides a unique living laboratory to explore entrepreneurship and small business development. Although there has been an emerging body of knowledge about entrepreneurship and private enterprise development in the Chinese context, few in-depth empirical investigations have been made to date. Siu and Kirby (1999) pointed out that the opening of the Chinese economy provides an opportunity for extended research into Mainland China where small and medium sized enterprises have begun to play an increasingly import-ant role in the development of the economy. Consequently, researchers have a unique opportunity to identify, probe, and analyze the characteristics of both Chinese entrepreneurs and the enterprises they are developing, especially with regard to their financing options.

Overall, it is noted that China has a relatively weak formal system in supporting venture development. If this institutional process fails to come about, an alternative method of financing is left to the individual or his or her family. This is the informal and family network which, through years of savings, offers financial support to individual family members who embark upon their entrepreneurial journeys. While family financing has become known to be a significant source of capital, as a field it has largely been overlooked and there remains very little theory or evidence relating to factors determining family financing. Basu and Parker (2001) proposed a new model interpreted in terms of family equity financing. They suggest a mix of altruistic and selfish motives underlying family lending. Altruism often appears in the form of gifts or lower-than-market interest rates. Thus it becomes an interesting empirical question: how are new businesses financed in a transition economy, through an institutional (government) program or through the social network of family relationships? Also, how do Chinese entrepreneurs finance their start-ups, and to what extent do these patterns differ across a number of demographic variables such as age, gender, education, and experience?

Research Methodology

Sampling Procedures

Researchers usually face a number of challenges when it comes to collecting data in developing countries. These well-documented challenges include low response rates and low percentages of useable questionnaires. To improve response rates, we adopted a focused method of investigation by choosing Wuhan—a major urban area and the provincial capital of Hubei, China. Located on both the Yangtze and Hanshui Rivers, Wuhan serves as a major transportation hub in central China. Wuhan has two international harbors, two airports, and a major railway network. With a population of 7.3 million and an area of 8467 square kilometers, Wuhan serves as the largest financial and commercial center in central China (Wuhan Huaye Information Development Co. 2000) and was one of the earliest cities to be industrialized. Metallurgy, automobiles, machinery, and high-tech industry are the key economic sectors of Wuhan. In recent years, the Wuhan region has established a number of major joint ventures with foreign multinationals, including Citroen (based in France), Budweiser and Coca-Cola (based in the US), NEC (based in Japan), and Philips (based in Holland).

China is a huge country with a diverse local culture and uneven economic development across different regions. Even though conducting research in one location would not be sufficient to grasp the complexity of Chinese entrepreneurship development in general and venture financing issue in particular, Wuhan has a unique vantage point in this regard. On the one hand, Chinese coastal cities such as Shanghai, Qingdao, and Guangzhou are among the first few cities opened to the outside world during the early stage of economic reform. Historically, people in these cities are more entrepreneurial than those in inner cities such as Wuhan. On the other hand, compared with those in the western areas of China such as Gansu and Chongqing, people in Wuhan are more entrepreneurial. Therefore, by sampling Wuhan entrepreneurs, we expect to have a nominal view of Chinese entrepreneurs in terms of their demographics, financing, personal attributes, growth aspirations, and motivations, among other dimensions.

Survey Instrument and Data Collection

The Entrepreneurial Profile Questionnaire (EPQ) was utilized as a data collection instrument. The EPQ was designed to survey the effect of individual, societal, and environmental factors on entrepreneurship by collecting a combination of demographic information and extensive details related to characteristics and orientations. A five-point Likert scale ranging from "strongly agree" (5) to "strongly disagree" (1) was provided next to each statement.

The EPQ was successfully piloted and validated through a series of studies in Romania, Turkey, Russia, Poland, the Czech Republic, Hungary, Lithuania, Estonia, Germany, Venezuela as well as South Africa, Mexico, and the United States. The EPQ was professionally edited, translated into Mandarin, pretested, and then translated back to clear up ambiguities or idiosyncratic terminology.

With the assistance of the local chamber of commerce, we randomly selected 500 firms from a firm registration database. In China, the Chamber of Commerce is a government agency with tremendous political influence. The introduction by the Chamber of Commerce provides us great access to local small businesses and entrepreneurs in a way that we would not have had otherwise. During early 2000, MBA students from a local university, where the researchers taught, were trained to conduct interviews based on the questionnaires. This is a way to ensure a reasonable response rate. All interviewees were assured anonymity. Out of 500, we received 222 usable EPQ questionnaires. Many questionnaires were disqualified due to incomplete data and missing information.

Variable Operationalization

Venture Financing. Each respondent was asked to provide a percentage of each source of financing they secured during the start-up stages, including personal savings, mortgage of own assets, corporate stock (IPO), partners contribution, personal loans, loans from parents/relatives/friends, VC, customer advances, grants from the government or private sources, and other debt sources. The sum of these percentages should amount to 100%. Those who failed to report sources of financing and those whose percentage did not add up to 100% were eliminated from our sample. Consequently, 57 responses were eliminated from the sample and the final sample consisted of 165 entrepreneurs, of which 40 are females and 125 males.

For the purpose of comparing different patterns of financing across demographic variables, we created groups based on age, gender, education, experience, and gestation time. The median age of 37 was used as a cutoff point to create two groups—old and young entrepreneurs. Based on gender, we segregated the respondents into male and female entrepreneurs. Based on educational background, we created one group of entrepreneurs with high school or less education (less than 13 years) and the other group of entrepreneurs with college or higher education (greater than or equal to 13 years). Based on the median experience level of 8 years, we created a group of entrepreneurs with less working experience (less than 8 years) and the other group of entrepreneurs with more years of working experience (greater than 8 years). Gestation time is measured by the difference between the year when the entrepreneur first thought about creating a business and the year when she or he actually created a business. Based on the median of 2 years, for entrepreneurs who spent less than 2 years in firm gestation, we called them "doers" and the rest we called "thinkers."

Analysis of Variance

We used Analysis of Variance (ANOVA) to test different financing methods across different groups. ANOVA would uncover the difference between venture financing methods across age, gender, education, experience, and gestation group and indicates the statistical significance of the difference.

Results

Sources of Venture Financing

As indicated in Figure 6.1, informal finance in the form of personal savings and financial support from parents, relatives, and friends accounted for 68% of venture financing, followed by mortgage of own assets (9.667%). In total, the first three sources of financing accounted for 77.7% of all financing alternatives. By contrast, financial support from the government (1.576%), VC (1.321), customer advance (0.897%), and the equity market (0.424%) were marginal.

Table 6.1 provides descriptive statistics of the sampled entrepreneurs. On average, these entrepreneurs received a junior college education (14 years), with a median age of 37 and 8 years of professional experience. The median gestation time is 2 years, from the year they first thought about a business idea to the year when the business was established.

Entrepreneurs' Demographics and Sources of Financing

Age. As noted in Table 6.2, younger Chinese entrepreneurs use significantly fewer personal saving (42.690%) than older entrepreneurs (57.144%).

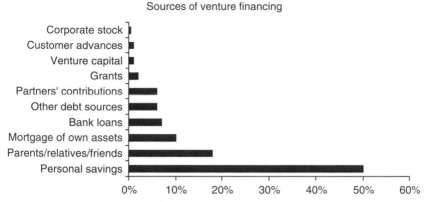

Figure 6.1 Sources of venture financing.

Meanwhile, younger ones received significantly more support from the informal sources of parents, relatives, and friends (25.036%) than their older counterparts (11.243%). The differences in other categories of financing across the two groups of entrepreneurs are statistically insignificant. However, one item worthy of note is that older entrepreneurs do seem to receive more government support (2.720%) than younger ones (0.667%).

Gender. Chinese female entrepreneurs used significantly more personal saving by a way of financing their business (60%) as compared to their male counterparts (47.054%). By contrast, Chinese male entrepreneurs received significantly more loans from banks (7.624%) than female entrepreneurs (3.125%). Chinese female entrepreneurs also relied more on parents, relatives, and friends (20.9%) than male entrepreneurs (16.922%), even though the difference was not statistically significant.

Years of Education. Entrepreneurs who received a college or higher education tended to use less personal savings (44.402%)—they received contributions from partners (8.374%), were able to secure more loans from banks (8.011%), and sought more support from the government

Table 6.1
Descriptive Statistics

Statistic	N	Minimum	Maximum	Mean
Age	159.000	18.000	60.000	36.849
Gender*	165.000	1.000	2.000	1.758
Years of Education	163.000	6.000	18.000	13.074
Total years of experience	153.000	0.000	40.000	10.588
Gestation time	146.000	0.000	24.000	3.150

Note: *1—female; 2—male.

Table 6.2
ANOVA Results

Entrepreneurs' Age and Sources of Financing

Financing Source	Young (<=37)	Old (>37)	F-test	Sig.
Personal savings %	42.690	57.144	8.274	0.005***
Mortgage of own assets %	9.607	8.973	0.047	0.829
Corporate stock "IPO" "%"	0.238	0.667	1.028	0.312
Partners contributions(s) %	6.560	4.763	0.530	0.467
Personal loan (bank) %	7.536	5.467	1.169	0.281
Parents/relatives/friends %	25.036	11.243	12.872	0.000***
Venture capital %	1.643	1.000	0.240	0.625
Customer advances %	0.452	1.333	2.162	0.144
Grants (government or private) %	0.667	2.720	1.698	0.195
Other debt sources %	5.571	6.691	0.159	0.691

Gender and Sources of Financing

Financing Source	Female	Male	F	Sig.
Personal savings %	60.000	47.054	5.048	0.026**
Mortgage of own assets %	5.875	10.880	2.273	0.134
Corporate stock "IPO" "%"	0.250	0.480	0.234	0.630
Partners contributions(s) %	4.675	5.810	0.167	0.683
Personal loan (bank) %	3.125	7.624	4.413	0.037**
Parents/relatives/friends %	20.900	16.922	0.775	0.380
Venture capital %	1.500	1.264	0.026	0.873
Customer advances %	0.700	0.960	0.142	0.707
Grants (government or private) %	0.125	2.040	1.167	0.282
Other debt sources %	2.850	6.966	1.715	0.192

Years of Education and Sources of Financing

Financing Source	High school or less	College or above	F	Sig.
Personal savings %	58.812	44.402	8.404	0.004***
Mortgage of own assets %	9.391	9.968	0.039	0.844
Corporate stock "IPO" "%"	0.145	0.638	1.405	0.238
Partners contributions(s) %	1.536	8.374	8.311	0.004***
Personal loan (bank) %	4.565	8.011	3.344	0.069*
Parents/relatives/friends %	18.365	16.851	0.156	0.693

Venture capital %	0.217	2.160	2.284	0.133
Customer advances %	0.580	1.149	0.888	0.347
Grants (government or private) %	0.058	2.723	2.966	0.087*
Other debt sources %	6.330	5.723	0.048	0.827

Entrepreneurs' working experience and Sources of Financing

Financing Source	Less working experience (<=8)	More working experience (>8)	F	Sig.
Personal savings %	43.862	55.750	8.274	0.005***
Mortgage of own assets %	8.481	11.222	0.047	0.829
Corporate stock "IPO" "%"	0.494	0.278	1.028	0.312
Partners contributions(s) %	7.311	4.389	0.530	0.467
Personal loan (bank) %	6.519	6.389	1.169	0.281
Parents/relatives/friends %	22.506	12.669	12.872	0.000***
Venture capital %	1.296	1.500	0.240	0.625
Customer advances %	0.469	1.042	2.162	0.144
Grants (government or private) %	1.617	1.736	1.698	0.195
Other debt sources %	7.444	5.025	0.159	0.691

Entrepreneurs' Gestation Time and Sources of Financing

Financing Source	Doers (<=2)	Thinkers (>2)	F	Sig.
Personal savings %	47.478	54.256	1.559	0.214
Mortgage of own assets %	10.565	9.722	0.067	0.796
Corporate stock "IPO" "%"	0.326	0.741	0.759	0.385
Partners contributions(s) %	6.076	6.078	0.000	1.000
Personal loan (bank) %	5.185	8.907	3.288	0.072*
Parents/relatives/friends %	19.315	11.911	3.355	0.069*
Venture capital %	1.902	0.463	0.980	0.324
Customer advances %	0.815	1.352	0.607	0.437
Grants (government or private) %	1.348	2.519	0.432	0.512
Other debt sources %	6.989	4.052	1.027	0.313

(2.723%)—than those who only had a high school education or less. Chinese entrepreneurs who had fewer years of education tended to rely on more personal savings than other alternative ways of financing. Additionally, we also found that the impact of educational background on sources of financing was greater for female entrepreneurs than for male entrepreneurs. In other words, the financing differences between the two educational groups for female entrepreneurs were significantly greater than those for male entrepreneurs. For example, female entrepreneurs who had high school or less education relied upon 71.5% of their financing from personal savings, as compared to 51.05% for those with college or higher education. By contrast, male entrepreneurs with high school or less education had 53.63% of their financing from personal savings, as compared to 42.72% for those with college or more education.

Work Experience. Chinese entrepreneurs with more work experience tended to have more financing from personal savings (55.750%) and less from parents, relatives, and friends (12.669%). Comparatively, those with less work experience had 43.862% of financing from personal savings and 22.506% from parents, relatives, and friends. In both financing categories, the differences between experienced and less experienced entrepreneurs were statistically significant.

Gestation Time. On average "thinkers" have 8.907% of money in the form of bank loans, which is significantly higher than 5.185% for "doers." On average, the combined sources of financing from personal savings and parents, relatives, and friends were 66.79% for "doers" as compared to 66.16% for "thinkers." It seems that both groups were equally committed to their business and were willing to commit financing resources to ventures. However, "doers" had a significantly higher percentage of investment from parents, relatives, and friends (19.315%) than "thinkers" (11.911%). For the remaining sources of financing, we failed to find any significance between the two groups.

Discussion

This study examined the sources of financing by Chinese entrepreneurs and the extent to which the sources of financing vary across age, gender, educational background, work experience, and gestation time. Overall, a few interesting patterns emerge from our study.

Overall Financing Patterns

Our results indicate that Chinese entrepreneurs heavily rely on financial sources of their own or parties that are within the close circle of their social network. By contrast, external and formal sources of financing such as banks, the government, and the equity market are notably missing and significantly underutilized. There are a few explanations for such patterns. First, the pattern reflects Chinese culture of family values and informal networks. Members of a family and relatives have the obligation to support each other not only emotionally but also financially when necessary. Very often a Chinese entrepreneur would first seek financial support from the inner circle of his or her social network (family members, relatives) before looking into the circle of friends. The external and formal support sources are usually the last resort.

Second, the pattern may also suggest the fact that the formal sector support for entrepreneurial development is inadequate and underdeveloped. There may be limited financial support available for Chinese entrepreneurs. Historically, China has been a planned economy and almost all governmental resources have been devoted to support SOEs. In recent years, money-losing SOEs have become increasingly more dependent on financial support from state-controlled banks to get loans to survive. There is mounting pressure to save these nonperforming SOEs to maintain employment and social stability. As a result, few financial resources have been allocated to promote the creation of private free enterprises. To a certain extent, the Chinese government's strong commitment to entrepreneurial development as a key economic policy has not yet materialized.

Additionally, VC is still an emerging industry in China. The late nineties' dot-com frenzy creates a momentum for the development of the Chinese VC industry. The majority of VC investment has been concentrated in a few big cities such as Beijing and Shanghai with a focus on technology-based sectors. Such a source of financing is still off-limits to entrepreneurs in other cities and in other sectors. Additionally, the Chinese equity market has such very stringent listing criteria that only well established and large companies can meet. This source of financing is still not on the radar screen of Chinese entrepreneurs. In more recent years, the Chinese government is developing a "secondary board" for the listing of small startups. We believe that this is certainly a step in the right direction for the economic development of China.

Overall, our findings suggest that there is a great room for the growth of formal financial support for entrepreneurial development in China. More government loans are needed and more support from banks is needed.

Demographics and Sources of Financing

The differences in sources of financing between the two age groups are not surprising. Older entrepreneurs tend to have more savings and would probably rely more on their personal savings before seeking support from parents, relatives, and friends. For younger entrepreneurs, the fact that they seek greater support from parents, relatives, and friends may be due to low personal savings. Additionally, older entrepreneurs may have worked in government agencies or (SOEs) for a long time before they decided to create their own businesses. They probably have more *guanxi*, or connections, in the government. As a result, they are more likely to seek and receive grants from the Chinese government.

There are two plausible explanations for the financing differences between Chinese male and female entrepreneurs. First, in Chinese society, women are traditionally confined to family and supportive roles. As a result, they tend to have smaller social networks than men, and their social network mainly consists of close family members, relatives, and classmates. It is not surprising that Chinese female entrepreneurs are more likely to rely on personal savings more than on external sources of support. Second, Chinese female entrepreneurs may be hesitant to seek loans from banks. At the same time, banks may be reluctant to provide loans to female entrepreneurs. The differences in bank loans point to the idea that there may be a certain degree of gender bias against female entrepreneurs in China.

The differences in venture financing across the two educational groups are interesting. Traditionally, Chinese culture places great value on education; the more years of education a person has, the more respect and trust she or he may receive. In essence, education is a form of human capital as well as social capital. For entrepreneurs with college or higher education, educational background would bestow a certain degree of legitimacy on their business establishment. Consequently, they are able to tap into a broader range of social networks and receive more financial support from external sources such as the government and banks.

The results from entrepreneurs' working experience and financing suggest that the more experience an entrepreneur has, the more she or he utilizes personal savings, and the less she or he uses money from parents, relatives, and friends. This may be due to the fact that entrepreneurs with longer working experience would be more likely to have personal savings, which can be subsequently used to finance start-up activities.

The differences in venture financing across the "doers and the "thinkers" suggest that the "doers" are more apt to tap into resources in their close social network. By contrast, the "thinkers" are more independent and rely on personal savings and loans. The "doers" are action-oriented and have a relatively short gestation period. As a result, they have to rely more on immediately available financial resources from sources such as parents, relatives, and friends, rather than on sources such as bank loans which take a long time to secure.

Conclusion

In terms of venture financing, this study found that Chinese entrepreneurs in Wuhan mainly rely on their own funding or informal funding from parties that are within their close social networks such as parents, relatives, and friends. External and formal financing sources are notably missing. We also found that entrepreneurs who use significantly more personal savings in venture financing are older (>37 years), female, with high school education or less, and have longer working experience. Entrepreneurs who are male with college or higher education and who take time to build their business (more than 2 years) tend to receive significantly more bank loans. Young male entrepreneurs who have less working experience and who intend to create a business quickly tend to rely more on financial support from their inner social network such as parents, relatives, and friends.

This study generates a few important implications for policy makers and for banks as well. From a policy standpoint, this study indicates a low degree of venture financing from the Chinese government. It therefore highlights the urgent need for the Chinese government to channel financial resources into creating innovative programs to support entrepreneurial endeavors. Historically, the Chinese government has devoted much of its attention to (SOEs) and scant attention has been paid to the development of privately owned enterprises. Not until after 1992, did the Chinese government start to accept and realize entrepreneurs as the engine of economic development. However, our findings show that there is still a disparity between governmental intention and actions. For banks that are interested in providing loans for start-ups, this study yields the profile of entrepreneurs who are most likely to seek bank loans. These are male entrepreneurs who are college educated. Banks should also recognize that there is a group of underserved entrepreneurs who are female and have no college degrees.

We note that no attempt is made here to generalize findings from this study to other areas of China. This study represents an initial effort in identifying sources of venture financing of Chinese entrepreneurs. Future research could be focused on the following two areas. First, researchers can explore the antecedents of the choices of sources of financing. For example, what are the relationships between entrepreneurs' personal attributes such as self-efficacy, motivations, and venture financing? Second, studies can also be devoted to the consequences of financing patterns. For example, what are the relationships between venture financing and growth aspirations? To what extent may the type of venture financing affect a firm's survival?

References

Ács, Zoltan J., Bo Carlsson, and Charlie Karlsson. 1999. *Entrepreneurship, Small and Medium-Sized Enterprises, and the Macroeconomy.* New York: Cambridge University Press.

Ahlstrom, David, Garry D. Bruton, and Kuang S. Yeh. 2007. Venture capital in China: past, present, and future. *Asia Pacific Journal of Management* 24: 247–68.

Akoten, John E., Yasuyuki Sawada, and Keijiro Otsuka. 2006. The determinants of credit access and its impacts on micro and small enterprises: the case of garment producers in Kenya. *Economic Development and Cultural Change* 54: 927–44.

Alsos, Gry Agnete., Espen John Isaksen, and Elisabet Ljunggren. 2006. New venture financing and subsequent business growth in men- and women-led businesses. *Entrepreneurship: Theory and Practice*, 30(5): 667–86.

Aylward, Anthony H. 1998. *Trends in Capital Finance in Developing Countries.* Washington, D.C.: World Bank Publications.

Balfour, Frederik. 2006. Venture capital's new promised land. *Business Week* 3967: 44.

Basu and Parker. 2001. Family finance and new business start-ups. *Oxford Bulletin of Economics & Statistics*, 63: 551–59.

Bates, Timothy. 1990. Entrepreneur human capital inputs and small business longevity. *Review of Economics and Statistics* 72: 551–59.

Batjargal, Bat, and Manhong Liu. 2004. Entrepreneurs' access to private equity in China: the role of social capital. *Organization Science*. 15(2): 159–72.

Berger, Allen N. and Gregory Udell. 1998. The economics of small business finance: the roles of private equity and debt markets in the financial growth cycle. *Journal of Financial Economics* 50: 187–229.

Bruno, Albert V. and Tyzoon T. Tyebjee. 1985. The entrepreneur's search for capital, *Journal of Business Venturing* 1: 61–74.

Bruton, Garry D. and David Ahlstrom. 2003. An institutional view of China's venture capital industry Explaining the differences between China and the West. *Journal of Business Venturing* 18: 233–59.

Carter, Sara, Eleanor Shaw, Wing Lam, and Fiona Wilson. 2007. Gender, entrepreneurship, and bank lending: the criteria and processes used by bank loan officers in assessing applications. *Entrepreneurship Theory and Practice* 31(3): 427.

Cassar, Gavin. 2004. The financing of business start-ups. *Journal of Business Venturing* 19: 261–83.

Chaganti, Radha, Dona Decarolis, and David Deeds. 1995. Predictors of capital structure in small ventures. *Entrepreneurship: Theory and Practice* 20: 7–18.

Chandler, Gaylen N. and Steven H. Hanks. 1998. An examination of the substitutability of founders human and financial capital in emerging business ventures. *Journal of Business Venturing* 13(5): 353–69.

Coleman, Susan. 2004. Access to debt capital for women-and minority-owned small firms: Does educational attainment have an impact? *Journal of Developmental Entrepreneurship* 9: 127–43.

Cooper, Arnold C., F. Javier Gimeno-Gascon, and Carolyn Y. Woo. 1994. Initial human and financial capital as predictors of new venture performance. *Journal of Business Venturing* 9: 371–95.

Dana, Leo Paul. 1999. Small business as a supplement in the People's Republic of China (PRC). *Journal of Small Business Management* 37: 76–81.

Davis, Deborah. 2000. *The consumer Revolution in Urban China*. Berkeley: University of California Press.

Drucker, Peter F. 2006. *Innovation and Entrepreneurship*. New York: Collins Business.

Evans, David S. and Boyan Jovanovic. 1989. An estimated model of entrepreneurial choice under liquidity constraints. *The Journal of Political Economy* 97: 808.

Fazzari, Steven M., R. Glenn Hubbard, and Bruce C. Petersen. 1988. Financing constraints and corporate investment. *Brookings Papers on Economic Activity* 1: 141–95.

Fung, Hung-Gay, Donald Kummer, and Jinjian Shen. 2006. China's privatization reforms: progress and challenges. *Chinese Economy* 39: 5–25.

Fung, Hung-Gay, Qingfeng Liu, and Jot Yau. 2007. Financing alternatives for Chinese small and medium enterprises: the case for a small and medium enterprise stock market. *China and World Economy* 15: 26.

Gompers, Paul A. and Josh Lerner. 1999. *The Venture Capital Cycle*. Cambridge: The MIT Press.

Hall, Bronwyn H. 1992. *Investment and Research and Development at the Firm Level: Does the Source of Financing Matter?* Cambridge: National Bureau of Economic Research.

Haynes, George W. and Deborah C. Haynes. 1999. The debt structure of small businesses owned by women in 1987 and 1993. *Journal of Small Business Management* 37: 1–2.

Hersch, Philip, David Kemme, and Jeffry Netter. 1997. Access to bank loans in a transition economy: the case of Hungary. *Journal of Comparative Economics* 24: 79–89.

Hitt, Michael A., David Ahlstrom, M. Tina Dacin, Edward Levitas, and Lilia Svobodina. 2004. The institutional effects on strategic alliance partner selection in transition economies: China vs. Russia. *Organization Science* 15(2): 173–85.

Holtz-Eakin, Douglas, David Joulfaian, and Harvey S. Rosen. 1994. Sticking it out: entrepreneurial survival and liquidity constraints. *Journal of Political Economy* 102: 53.

Hu, Zuliu and Mohsin S. Khan. 1997. Why is China growing so fast? *International Monetary Fund* 44: 101–31.

Huyghebaert, Nancy. 2001. The capital structure of business start-ups: determinants of initial financial structure. *Revue Bancaire et Financière* 2: 83–87.

Lu, Ting. 2006. *Three essays on corporate governance and entrepreneurial finance.* Unpublished Ph.D., University of California, Berkeley.

Macmillan, Ian C., Robin Siegel, and P. N. Subba Narashima. 2002. Criteria used by venture capitalists to evaluate new venture proposals. *Journal of Business Venturing* 1: 119–28.

Manigart, Sophie and Carol Struyf. 1997. Financing high technology startups in Belgium: an explorative study. *Small Business Economics* 9: 125–35.

Myers, Stewart C. 1977. Determinants of corporate borrowing. *Journal of Financial Economics* 5: 147–75.

———— and Nicholas S. Majluf. 1983. *Corporate Financing and Investment Decisions When Firms Have Information that Investors Do Not Have.* Cambridge: Massachusetts Institute of Technology Press.

Pei, N. 2002. Let weakness become strength. *Zhongguo chuangxinwang* 22.

Phan, Phillip H., Donald Siegel, and Michael Wright. 2005. Science parks and incubators: observations, synthesis and future research. *Journal of Business Venturing* 20: 165–182.

Pistrui, David, Wilfred V. Huang, Harold P. Welsch, and Zhao Jing. 2006. 25 Family and cultural forces: shaping entrepreneurship and SME development in China. In *Handbook of Research on Family Business,* ed. Panikkos Poutziouris, Kosmas Smyrnios, Sabine Klein.

Quanyu, Huang, Joseph W. Leonard, and Chen Tong. 1997. *Business Decision Making in China.* New York: International Business Press.

Reuber, A. Rebecca and Eileen Fischer. 1999. Understanding the consequences of founders' experience. *Journal of Small Business Management* 37: 30–31.

Rujoub, Mohamed A., Doris M. Cook, and Leon E. Hay. 1995. Using cash flow ratios to predict business failures. *Journal of Managerial Issues* 7: 75–91.

Scheela, William and Nguyen Van Dinh. 2004. Venture capital in a transition economy: the case of Vietnam. *Venture Capital* 6: 333–50.

Siu, Wai-Sum and David Kirby. 1999. Small firm marketing in China: a comparative study of Chinese and British marketing practices. Research Into Entrepreneurship (RENT) Proceedings of The Thirteenth RENT Conference. London, England: November 25–26th.

Starr, John B. 2001. *Understanding China: A Guide to China's Economy, History and Political Structure.* New York: Farrar, Straus and Giroux.

Timmons, Jeffry A. 1999. *New Venture Creation.* Boston: Irwin/McGraw-Hill.

Treichel, Monica Zimmerman and Jonathan A. Scott. 2006. Women-owned businesses and access to bank credit: evidence from three surveys since 1987. *Venture Capital* 8: 51–67.

Van Auken, Howard E. and Richard B. Carter. 1989. Acquisition of capital by small business. *Journal of Small Business Management* 27: 1–9.

Wennekers, Sander and Roy Thurik. 1999. Linking entrepreneurship and economic growth. *Small Business Economics* 13: 27–56.

Wiklund, Johan and Dean Shepherd. 2003. Aspiring for, and achieving growth: the moderating role of resources and opportunities. *Journal of Management Studies* 40(8): 1919–41.

Wong, Poh K., Yuen P. Ho, and Erkko Autio. 2005. Entrepreneurship, innovation and economic growth: evidence from GEM data. *Small Business Economics* 24: 335–50.

Wright, Michael. 2007. Venture capital in China: a view from Europe, Asia Pacific. *Journal of Management* 24: 269–81.

―――― Jonathan Kissane, and A.ndrew Burrows. 2004. Private equity and the EU accession countries of Central and Eastern Europe. *Journal of Private Equity* 7: 32–46.

Wuhan Huaye Information Development Co. *Wuhan city.* 2000. Online. Available: http://www.chinapages.com/hubei/wuhan.bak/wuhan_s.htm#wuhan.

Chapter 7

Is Informal Finance Faster, Cheaper, and Better than Formal Finance? A Study of Small and Medium Enterprises in Shanghai and Nanjing

Sara Hsu

In this chapter we discuss whether or not informal finance is faster, cheaper, and better for small and medium enterprises (SMEs) than formal finance.

Informal, or nonbank finance, is used frequently by most SMEs. This is not necessarily because it is better than formal, or bank, finance (although we want to find out if this is the case), but often because it is the only means of financing available since the formal sector remains plagued by lending constraints. We compare informal and formal finance here in terms of transactions costs, financial costs, and physical costs, basing this comparison on a study performed in the cities of Shanghai and Nanjing.[1]

Transactions costs include the amount of time it takes, as well as the process one has to go through (such as wining and dining the lender), to obtain a loan. Financial costs associated with the loan include the interest rate and value of collateral used to guarantee the loan. And physical costs refer to the potential for physical or social harm done to the borrower by the lender when loan payments are late.

China's Financial Market Segmentation

China's financial markets suffer from a great degree of market segmentation. The separation between formal and informal finance has resulted in different transactions, financial, and physical costs to firms borrowing from banks or nonbank parties. Greater constraints in the formal market lead to an increased demand for informal finance. There is a crossover in the demand for both types of financing, but demand at very high and very low interest rates is constrained, since the formal sector generally does not make these types of loans.

The problem of segmentation between formal and informal finance in China was created by both policy lending and huge information costs in the formal sector, in contrast with very low information costs yet lower risk diversity within single loan products in the informal sector. Capital cannot reach its competitive equilibrium interest rate, and there is a disparity in rates of return due to dysfunction in the lending market.

The separation between formal and informal finance is a reflection of this financial repression in China. Banks, with artificially low interest rates, are in a difficult position since policy lending has been formally abolished but is still expected by SOEs. Informal lenders can offer loans to small businesses but are unregulated with an array of interest rates, some being markedly high. Both types of lending hold constraints that threaten the viability of China as a competitor in the international economy.

Typically, higher interest rates charged by the informal sector are not due to monopoly profits but rather due to outright or implicit interest rate ceilings, credit rationing in the formal sector as opposed to increase in interest rates, limitation in the informal sector to own capital (therefore necessitating a higher risk premium), and higher opportunity costs to informal financiers (Bisat, Johnston, and Sundararajan 1992). In other words, excess demand flowing from the formal sector causes a rise in interest rates in the informal sector, whose capacity is constrained to begin with.

Financial repression has limited the banking sector to lending to particular sectors or for certain activities (Steel, Aryeetey, Hettige, and Nissanke 1997). The extreme information asymmetries in Chinese commerce have led to a wide variety of costs of assessing and enforcing the viability of loans. Together, these difficulties have divided Chinese financial markets not only into formal and informal markets, but into the formal market and many very specifically focused informal markets as well, which make up for information asymmetries across the Chinese economy. The same information asymmetries that allow informal financiers to thrive also prevent them from diversifying into full-scale financial intermediaries, reinforcing the segmentation problem.

The role of finance at its best, whether formal or informal, should be to bridge gaps that were formerly too wide, reducing information and transactions costs (Levine 1997). China's potential lies in its ability to improve its formal financing system, to legalize or emulate the gap-bridging nature of informal finance as it exists today, and to allow the entrepreneurial spirit to imbue itself in the formal sector as well. Otherwise, a lack of financial development can hinder growth by maintaining segmented financial industries, in which some have artificially high rates of return, and some have artificially low rates of return due to restrictions on financing availability (McKinnon 1973). This prevents the efficient allocation of capital.

Due to constraints on formal financing, some regions of China have elevated informal financing to an art form, while others have made do with small savings from income. The areas that are well known for informal financing include, but are not limited to, Zhejiang Province, particularly in the city of Wenzhou, Nanhai in Guangdong Province, and Jiangsu Province, while larger, more established cities like Beijing carry out a somewhat smaller level of informal financing. Less well known areas of intense informal financing include Henan Province and Fujian Province (Tsai 2002).

Market segmentation has perpetuated differences, between the formal and informal sector, in transactions, financial, and physical costs associated with obtaining a loan. Below, we describe a model to illustrate these differences.

Transactions, Financial, and Physical Cost Model

In this model, there are two lenders each contributing one input, that is, x_1 and x_2; x_1 is known as an informal loans; x_2 is known as a formal loan. x_1 and x_2 are differentiated inputs that are imperfect substitutes since the businessperson has different access to each of them and the terms are somewhat different as well. Both types of inputs can be used to create the same product.

A businessperson has a utility function that reflects his position on the loan(s) as a borrower. His utility (shown here as a vector) will be a function of W, wealth, C, collateral, I, interest, and D, loss of future earnings from default (Christensen 1993). Here we also add P, which are physical costs in the event of default, and T, which are transactions costs that are the function of each loan. Each businessperson has the following utility function:

$$\text{Maximize } U[W - x(1+i) - T(x)] \text{ where } U[W - x(1+i) - T(x)]$$
$$> U[W - D - C - P] \tag{7.1}$$

Both the informal and the formal lenders have expected utilities or expected return function from the loan(s). For each lender or x the following function is

$$\text{Maximize } E[U] = E(R(x)$$
$$= [x \bullet (1+i) - x] \bullet (1 - \pi + [C - L] \bullet \pi$$
$$= x \bullet i \bullet (1 - \pi + (C - x) \bullet \pi, \tag{7.2}$$

where π is the probability of failure of the vector of loans.

The main difference between the formal lender and the informal lender is that the informal lender knows better what the value of π is for a range of borrowers, which allows his or her to lend to this range of borrowers. The formal lender knows the value of π only for a selected group of borrowers with very low π; therefore, the formal lender tends to lend only to the low-risk borrowers. For the informal lender, the risk of firm failure is offset by the lender's knowledge that the firm obtains greater utility from the success of the loan than from a failed loan. Knowing π within a certain range helps minimize the time period mismatch implied by the difference between expected and known utility.

The utility of the borrower is determined by costs and benefits associated with the formal or the informal loan. If transactions costs and interest rate costs are lower in one area, the borrower will prefer that type of loan, while if he or she considers the possibility of default, he or she will also take into account the collateral and physical costs associated with the loan. This model provides us with a framework for thinking about the costs of formal and informal loans.

Survey Methodology

Our study is based on a survey which was conducted by the Central University of Finance and Economics (CUFE) in February and March of 2006. The Nanjing research group surveyed 183 privately owned companies, getting 172 qualified questionnaires, in 12 areas of Nanjing, especially in the Liuhe District and Economic and Technical Development Zone, which have large numbers of privately owned companies. The Shanghai group surveyed 199 privately owned companies in 16 districts of Shanghai, and got 187 qualified questionnaires.

The survey was conducted to determine transactions, financial, and physical costs for the businessperson. First, we were interested in collecting descriptive data on the business—size, gender of owner, and employees, and industry data was obtained in order to understand the most basic nature of the company. Secondly, we collected financial information on the business— liability-to-asset ratio, income to expenditure ratio, loan sources and proportion of total loans, average length and interest rate on each loan, and personal assessment of risk of life and livelihood. Data on the degree to which lenders were involved in the business was also collected.

Our survey took place during a time of monetary loosening, which had the effect of relaxing some constraints on bank lending and making formal loans more widely available to SME owners. During a time of credit tightening, however, interest rates in the informal sector are greatly heightened due to lack of available funds in the formal sector. The results of this survey show that interest rates in the informal sector are, as predicted, not much higher than interest rates set by banks since tightening had not occurred.

The survey is based on random sampling[2] of businessmen of mostly (84%) SMEs—firms with between 8 and 500 employees—within the city limits of Nanjing and Shanghai, China. A small number of *getihu*, or businesses with between 2 and 7 employees, (13%) and MLEs, medium and large enterprises, (3%) were also included in the survey. Elements of the survey include the individual business owner or a representative of a group of businessmen (such as a manager or co-owner) if there was more than one for a single business.

Nonresponse bias was curbed as surveyors attempted several times to return to absent respondents' firms to make up for nonresponse. We also framed the questions in such a way as to ensure maximum reliability while allowing respondents to divulge monetary ratios rather than exact numbers. The questions were made as clear and singly directed as possible. In addition, the survey instrument was framed in such a way as to maximize validity in the survey responses.

The Average Firm

The average businessperson in this study was male, oversaw 87 employees, and had been in business for 5 years. The majority of this businessman's contacts were also male, including those in SOBKs. Around 50% of his borrowings in the past year came from relatives and friends, while about 40% came from bank loans, and the rest were borrowed from private lenders or other channels. The loans he was able to borrow were for a term of just over a year, and he used the funding for working capital. His assets consisted mostly of office equipment and production machinery. His liability-to-asset ratio was around 50%, while his expenditure-to-income ratio was about 66%. There were variations within the data—the average businessperson is still just the average—but we can keep in mind this average business owner while considering costs incurred in obtaining a loan. Descriptive data averages can be found in Table 7.1.

Number of Informal and Formal Loans

We also looked at the types of firms that obtained more informal and formal loans. We ran stepwise regressions using SAS, with such independent variables as business type, industry, location, liability-to-asset ratio, expenditure-to-income ratio, age of firm, and the fact whether the firm had lent to others in the past years. Regression results can be found in Table 7.2.

We found that firms that had a higher number of informal loans had a higher liability-to-asset ratio, were likely to have lent to others in the past year, and were generally younger. City was also significant for borrowing informal loans, with business owners in Nanjing being more likely to have a higher number of informal loans.

Testing for characteristics that influence the number of formal loans obtained, we found that the expenditure-to-income ratio, the firm's age, and the fact whether the business owner had lent to others in the past year)

Table 7.1
Descriptive Data Results

Averages	Relatives	Friends	Private Lender	Private Financial Co.	Bank Loans
Average Percentage (per firm) of All Loans Borrowed in Past Year (%)	19.31	32.92	4.26	1.27	41.89
Average Percentage (per firm) of All Loans with Mortgage or Collateral Given (%)	0.79	8.86	34.48	100.00	97.80
Average Collateral Value as Percentage of Loan (%)	100	129	92	129	146
Average Working Capital to Total Capital Ratio, as Purpose of Loan (%)	88.11	90.96	90.91	92.31	85.19
Average Fear of Physical Violence by Lender (%)	2.44	15.66	58.82	20.00	0.97
Average Yearly Interest Rate (%)	8.44	10.41	15.30	13.91	8.02
Average Total Length of Loans (in months)	13.5	12.4	11.9	19.2	14.4
Average Days to Obtain Loan (in days)	6	5	6	25	27

Table 7.2
Stepwise Regression Results

Number of Informal Loans

Parameter	Parameter Estimate	T-value	P-Value
Constant	0.97856	7.31	<.0001
Years in business	−0.03783	−4.20	<.0001
City is Shanghai	−0.32909	−3.52	0.0005
Industry: Service	0.42017	3.72	0.0002
Industry: Retail or wholesale	0.37332	3.78	0.0002
Liability-to-asset ratio	0.50314	2.57	0.0107
Lent to others in past year	0.16884	1.94	0.0530
Location: Near shipping areas	−0.28545	−1.85	0.0650
Industry: Agriculture	−0.45899	−1.74	0.0825

F-Value	10.57		
P-Value	<.0001		
R^2	20%		
Adjusted r^2	18%		
N	342		

Number of Formal Loans

Parameter	Parameter Estimate	T-value	P-Value.
Constant	0.24588	1.94	0.0536
Years in business	0.02861	4.23	<.0001
Expenditure-to-income ratio	0.39519	2.36	0.0188
Lent to others in past year	−0.17178	−2.61	0.0095
Business type: Consumer services	−0.14948	−1.69	0.0916
Industry: Construction	0.37233	1.77	0.0782
Industry: Finance	4.27829	7.40	<.0001
Industry: Manufacturing	0.22920	3.15	0.0018
Industry: Transportation	0.93751	2.29	0.0228
Location: Residential area	−0.11407	−1.76	0.0799

F-Value	14.05		
P-Value	<.0001		
R^2	28%		
Adjusted r^2	26%		
N	342		

Determinants of the Probability of Assets Seized

Parameter	Parameter Estimate	T-value	P-Value
Constant	−0.07077	−1.76	0.0801
Number of formal loans	0.34296	14.34	<.0001
Ratio: Liability to asset	0.40482	6.44	<.0001

(Continued)

Table 7.2
(continued)

Determinants of the Probability of Assets Seized

Business type: Consumer services	−0.07187	−1.77	0.0770
Business type: Business good production (wholesale)	−0.09463	−2.53	0.0117
Industry: Finance	−1.07102	−3.66	0.0003
Location: Near many businesses	−0.05638	−1.89	0.0603
F-Value	45.42		
P-Value	<.0001		
R^2	45%		
Adjusted r^2	44%		
N	345		

were significant. The firm age, and whether the owner had lent to others in the past year were opposite in sign from the same variables that number of informal loans obtained were regressed upon. While the liability-to-asset ratio was not significant in the case of formal loans, the expenditure-to-income ratio was, with businesses that had a higher expenditure-to-income ratio being more likely to receive a bank loan.

So these are the types of firms that tend to obtain more informal or more formal loans. Anther research has found that Chinese banks prefer lending to older firms (Gao and Schaffer 2000) and a relationship between older firms and banks is apparent here as well. Also of note is that firms that were already part of the informal lending network, that is, those that had lent to others in the past year, were associated with having a higher number of informal loans, and those that had not lent to others in the past year were associated with having a higher number of formal loans. We will now move on to discussing transactions, financial, and physical costs associated with informal and formal loans.

Transactions, Financial, and Physical Costs

By looking at transactions, financial, and physical costs, we assessed the following: the number of loans obtained from formal and informal sources, interest rates, the time it took to obtain a loan, threat to life and livelihood, the presence and amount of collateral, and the possibility of assets being seized.

Number of Loans

In terms of number of transactions, borrowers often borrowed more from informal sources than from formal sources. In fact, most businesspeople used informal lending more than formal lending, especially in Nanjing. SME owners who were mainly informally financed had at least twice as many informal sources as formal sources. If transactions costs can again be conceived as a percentage of the total number of loans obtained, they were found to be higher in the informal sector.

Interest Rates

We found that informal sector interest rates were higher within each lending channel than formal sector interest rates due to market segmentation. This is an indication of market segmentation, in which some industries have artificially high rates of return, and some have artificially low rates of return due to restrictions on financing availability (McKinnon 1973).

Interest rates were lower, overall, than expected in the informal sector due to a central bank policy of credit loosening during the time of the survey. More available bank credit pushed down interest rates in both the formal and informal lending sectors. Interest rates for each lending channel in Nanjing and Shanghai combined were on average as follows: 8.4% for relative lenders, 10.4% for friend lenders, 15.3% for private lenders, 13.9% for nonbank private institutions, and 8% for SOBKs. While the interest rate of private lenders in China has been known at times to exceed 100% yearly interest (Tsai 2002), the highest found was 15.57% in Nanjing.

The 2002 average bank loan interest rate in Shanghai, and in China as a whole, was 5.31% and appeared to be part of a steadily declining trend (National Bureau of Statistics in China 2004; Shanghai Municipal Statistics Bureau 2004). But it is possible that the interest rates for smaller businesses were higher than the average. As a footnote in the *China Statistical Yearbook 2004* notes, interest rates on loans for small and medium businesses could be 30% higher than nominal interest rates as of September 1999.

The informal sector is able to charge a higher interest rate because firm owners cannot obtain bank loans to the extent necessary for business funding. Paying higher interest rates increases the costs of firms.

Time to Obtain Loan

Informal transactions were often significantly easier to obtain, in terms of time, than bank transactions. It took a considerably longer time to receive a loan from banks than from the informal sector—about 4 to 6 times as long, overall. Private lenders were similar to family and friends in terms of time to obtain a loan—roughly 5 days in both Nanjing and Shanghai. This means that transactions costs, in terms of time per lender, were lower in the informal sector. Reinforcing relationships through dining or bestowing other favors prior to receiving a loan was not prevalent. It was noted that "dining with friends" was a part of the loan application process in only 1% of total cases, and these cases were informal. The process for requesting a loan from most informal sources was as simple as contacting the lender and requesting a loan. As the lending institution became more formal, the time to obtain the loan increased steadily, jumping from an average of 5 days, in the most informal cases, to an average of 38 days, for particular banks.

Physical Costs—Threat to Life and Livelihood

In terms of perceived threat to life and livelihood, private money lenders were the biggest menace, presenting a threat in 59% of loan transactions, followed by nonbank private institutions at 20% of loan transactions, friends at 16% of loan transactions, and relatives at 2% of loan transactions. In some cases, businesspeople were even afraid of their contacts at the formal banking institution (1% of bank loan transactions).

What stands out in particular, is that although Shanghai businesspeople did not suffer threats from relatives or banking institutions, Nanjing businesspeople indeed did. Threats from relatives and banking institutions were low, but remain relatively unexpected, since the more repayment enforcement capacity the lender has (through shaming, as with relatives, or through seizing assets, as with banks), the less likely he is to introduce the threat of bodily harm.

Threat of physical violence or damage is not just a risk in and of itself, but it also brings with it increased financial damage, as the health and well-being of the business owner is called into question and the costs of protection against these threats increase.

Presence of Collateral

Family and friends did not typically request collateral, but when they did, the value of the collateral was comparable to the value of collateral for loans from money lenders. Nonbank private institutions requested collateral most frequently, with a value slightly less than that requested from banks. Private lenders in Shanghai were quite substantially[3] more likely to request collateral from borrowers, with an 80% rate of collateral requirement, than private lenders in Nanjing, with an 11% collateral requirement. Overall, 98% of banks required collateral, and this was even across both Shanghai and Nanjing.

Increased frequency and extent of collateral requirements, in turn, increase costs if the borrower defaults on the loan. Banks' uniform requirement of collateral increases the cost of borrowing from formal lenders.

Possibility of Assets Being Seized

On average, borrowers perceived that one-third of lenders were likely to seize assets if a default occurred. Assets consisted mainly of office equipment and secondarily of production machinery. The subjective likelihood of having assets seized (i.e., likelihood according to the borrower's estimates) spread rather evenly across businesses that were mainly informally financed, mainly formally financed, or equally informally and formally financed. In the next section, however, our discussion on the model reveals that while the number of informal loans obtained in the last year does not affect the borrower's perceived possibility that assets are seized, the number of formal loans does, no matter what type of loans the business holds in majority.

The Power to Seize Assets

Regression analysis also found that borrowers perceive that the power to seize assets lies in the formal sector; that is, banks have more power to seize assets than informal lenders. We found that while the number of informal loans obtained in the last year did not affect the possibility that assets are seized, the number of formal loans did. The number of formal loans and liability-to-asset ratio were the most relevant factors in determining whether assets would be seized in case of default.

This means that whether or not informal sources collect collateral, the determinant of whether or not the collateral assets are seized may really lie in the formal sector. This makes sense, since collectors in the formal sector have more legal power to seize assets. There are three kinds of laws in China that protect banks' rights to seize assets should business owners default on their loans. These include the Law of the People's Republic of China on Banking Regulation and Supervision, the Commercial Banking and Contract Law, and the Guarantee Law of the People's Republic of China. Banks are able to seize assets, as per these laws, without suing. Across the cities individually and together, despite the fact that informal lenders often threaten violence against loan defaulters, formal lenders hold the credibility that assets will be seized, since they are backed by law. The possibility that assets will be seized can be thought of as a risk, or transactions cost.

Implications of Study

To analyze these results, we go back to our model, in which firm utility (shown here as a vector) is a function of W, wealth, C, collateral, I, interest, D, loss of future earnings from default, P, which are physical costs in the event of a default, and T, which are transactions costs that are a function of each loan.

$$\text{Maximize } U[W - x(1 + i) - T(x)] \text{ where } U[W - x(1 + i) - T(x)]$$
$$> U[W - D - C - P] \tag{7.3}$$

Now suppose that the businessperson does not face the possibility of default, so that his or her only goal is to maximize $U[W-x(1 + i) - T(x)]$. Next, since the informal finance interest rate is always higher than the formal interest rate in our study, we shall subtract the interest rate in the formal market from that in the informal market to obtain the interest rate premium for obtaining finance in the informal market: $i_{for} - i_{infor} = i_{infprem}$.

Thus, we are comparing only transactions costs associated with informal versus formal loans. Since time to obtain a loan is longer in the formal sector, while the number of loans one must obtain is greater in the informal sector, we can make no general comment about the superiority of one type of loan to the other in terms of transactions costs.

$$U[W - x(1 + i_{infprem}) - T(x)] \text{ Informal Sector} \qquad [7.4]$$

$$U[W - x - T(x)] \text{ Formal Sector} \qquad [7.5]$$

If transactions costs are about the same, firms should prefer obtaining loans from the formal sector, in which they will not have to pay a premium for the interest rate.

However, if we account for the possibility of default, we must discuss collateral and physical costs as well. The constraint returns. Since, from the analysis above, physical costs in terms of the threat to life or livelihood lie mainly in the informal sector, and collateral costs in terms of assets being seized lie mainly in the formal sector, we obtain the following:

$$\text{Maximize } U[W - x(1 + i_{infprem}) - T(x)]$$
$$\text{where } U[W - x(1 + i_{infprem}) - T(x)] > U[W - D - P] \qquad [7.6]$$

(Informal sector)

$$\text{Maximize } U[W - x - T(x)] \text{ where } U[W - x - T(x)]$$
$$> U[W - D - C](\text{Formal sector}) \qquad [7.7]$$

Now we are comparing physical costs and collateral costs as well, given a default on the loan, and this comparison is not quantifiable. Therefore, if collateral costs are higher for obtaining a loan in the formal sector, they would have to be higher than the informal sector interest rate premium and the physical costs for one to prefer an informal loan. Alternatively, for the borrower to prefer a formal loan, collateral costs must be lower than the informal finance interest rate premium as well as the physical costs associated with the loan.

Those with the least amount of default should prefer the bank loan to the informal loan, since they will not default on the loan. For those who may or will default on the loan, the choice between obtaining a loan from the informal or from the formal sector is muddier. As the interest rate in the informal sector rises, preference for formal loans will also rise.

So we turn again to our original question: is informal finance faster, cheaper, and better than formal finance? Informal finance is usually faster in terms of time to obtain a loan, although if more informal loans are required to obtain sufficient financing, the time to obtain each loan adds up over several loans. Informal finance is, in other areas of China, cheaper in some circumstances, but in our study it is, on average, more expensive than formal finance. And although informal finance is associated with fewer collateral costs, it is associated with greater physical costs, so it cannot be considered necessarily better than formal finance.

The answer then is that for firms that do not default on their loans, informal finance is not faster, cheaper, and better than formal finance. For firms that may default on their loans, informal finance is not necessarily faster, cheaper, and better than formal finance. In many cases, formal finance is cheaper and better than informal finance.

Policy Recommendations

This turns us again to the question of why informal finance continues to be so pervasive. The answer is, of course, that formal finance is quite constrained, leading to the segmented markets described above. Businesspeople simply must turn to informal finance for sufficient financing. Formal financial institutions must expand their customer base, particularly to SMEs, and in order to do this it must first get rid of the constraints of implicit policy lending and nonperforming loans. This is much easier said than done.

The first thing to address in the reform of China's banking system is: what to do if banks fail? A deposit insurance system and more complete bankruptcy procedures must be implemented. Nonperforming loans must not be made. Measures taken in 2003 were a great improvement, with the creation of the China Banking Regulatory Commission to oversee regulations and the implementation of new systems of asset quality monitoring. The entrance of foreign investors into the banking system has also improved banking management (Berger, Hasan, and Zhou 2007). Without detailing a plan of action, further privatization of the mainly state-owned banking system would improve the efficiency of the formal financial system.

In addition, the formal sector can learn from the informal sector. Studies done in other countries have made note of some possibilities. P.B. Ghate (1992), looking at formal and informal financing in Asia, suggests that formal financing institutions rely upon informal financing channels to make loans to the informal loan consumers. He notes that this would promote competition in informal markets and push down interest rates.

Financial liberalization in Ghana has spurred the rise of institutions that formalize aspects of the informal sector. These "semiformal" institutions include savings and loans, *susu* companies, and mutual aid organizations and cater to populations that formerly used informal channels of financing (Awasu 1996). These institutions not only cater to populations that were previously not served by banks, but also use means earlier used in informal financing. Such organizations have, for example, adopted door-to-door services, short-term lending practices, and close-monitoring methods. These institutions have been critical in continuing to provide finance to groups who otherwise would have been left behind in the transition to a fully liberalized financial economy.

The biggest finding from past research on informal finance and the evolution of formal financing institutions has been that informal financing often provides extremely short loan cycles required by the smallest businesses, such as market vendors or food processors. Informal methods also involve the use of almost perfect information using personal networks, something that no formal institutions have yet been able to emulate.

Adel Varghese (2005) finds that linkage between the formal and informal sectors is more important to competition between the two sectors. He looks at the rural credit system in India and finds that due to transactions costs the cost of monitoring borrowers' incomes in rural areas is too high. The solution is to allow moneylenders to borrow from banks and lend to borrowers who are about to default on their bank loans. The borrowers repay a portion of their resulting profits to the moneylenders, who then repay the banks. The moneylenders take on extra risk in lending to borrowers who are essentially borrowing against expected returns, but then gain extra profits from borrowers whose businesses become viable.

In China, financial reform requires that the tax base be further broadened to ensure the government can obtain enough fiscal revenue during bank reform. Then, bank reform can be undertaken and extension of non-performing loans can be stopped. Finally, lending to small businesses and individuals can occur as banks adopt some informal financing practices.[4]

The informal sector must be allowed to continue and should be further legalized, so that businesses do not experience any drops in financing. As formal financing expands, informal financing may gradually diminish when it is a second-best solution.

We also recommend that the formal banking sector lend to smaller borrowers in shorter loan cycles by implementing closer-monitoring mechanisms. The formal sector can employ some former informal-sector moneylenders who already know individuals in their area, to collect deposits and make loans door-to-door, or it can launch a campaign to get to know individuals and businesses in the bank servicing area better.

Conclusion

We have found that informal finance is not necessarily faster, cheaper, and better than formal finance; in fact, for firms that are good credit risks, it is less attractive than formal finance due to its higher interest rates. However, due to the constraints of formal finance, informal finance plays a key role in providing capital to SMEs in particular. Further legalization of informal finance, along with continued reform of the formal sector, and incorporation into the formal sector of some informal finance practices would relax some of the constraints in lending that have led to market segmentation.

Notes

1. Shanghai and Nanjing were randomly selected since they are both large cities with many private enterprises.

2. Interviewers selected enterprises by randomly selecting firms from the enterprise directories at local business administrations in different districts of Shanghai and Nanjing.

3. The chi-squared was 14.7, with significance at the 5% level.

4. Microfinance can also adopt the same informal financing methods that we recommend for the banking sector, since these methods work well with Chinese culture. Of course, informal financing practices vary per region and therefore can be adapted by the formal sector or by microfinance enterprises.

References

Awasu, Charles. 1996. Savings Mobilization and Financial Market Development in Ghana. Ph.D. Dissertation, Syracuse University.

Berger, Allen N., Iftekhar Hasan, and Mingming Zhou. 2007. Bank ownership and efficiency in China: what will happen in the world's largest nation?" *Journal of Banking and Finance*: 119–44.

Bisat, Amer, R. Barry Johnston, and V. Sundararajan. 1992. Issues in managing and sequencing financial sector reforms: lessons from experiences in five developing countries. IMF Working Paper 92/83.

Christensen, Garry. 1993. The limits to informal financial intermediation. *World Development* 21(5): 721–31.

Gao, Shumei and Mark E. Schaffer. 2000. Financial discipline in the enterprise sector in transition countries: how does China compare? In *The Chinese Economy under Transition*, ed. Sarah Cook, Shujie Yao, Juzhong Zhuang. New York: St. Martin's Press.

Ghate, P.B. 1992. Interaction between the formal and informal financial sectors: the Asian experience. *World Development* 20(6): 859–72.

Levine, Ross. 1997. Financial development and economic growth: views and agenda. *Journal of Economic Literature* 35: 688–726.

McKinnon, R.I. 1973. *Money and Capital in Economics Development*. Washington, DC: Brookings Institution.

National Bureau of Statistics in China. 2004. *China Statistical Yearbook 2004*. Beijing: China Statistics Press.

Shanghai Municipal Statistics Bureau. 2004. *Shanghai Statistical Yearbook 2004*. Beijing: China Statistics Press.

Steel, William F., Ernest Aryeetey, Hemamala Hettige, and Machiko Nissanke. 1997. Informal financial markets under liberalization in four African countries. *World Development* 25(5): 817–30.

Tsai, Kellee S. 2002. *Back-Alley Banking: Private Entrepreneurs in China*. Ithaca, NY: Cornell University Press.

Varghese, Adel. 2005. Bank-moneylender linkage as an alternative to bank competition in rural credit markets. *Oxford Economic Papers* 57: 315–35.

Chapter 8

Conclusion: Regulating Informal
Finance in China

Jianjun Li

From a macroeconomic perspective, being part of the informal financial organization of *hehui* (rotating credit association), which is well designed for individuals in rural areas and for underground banks that provide services to the underground economy such as money-laundering and transformation of illegal income, private financial organizations are bound to split financial resources. This may cause more money go out of the financial system, weakening the function of the formal financial system, thereby impacting the balance of investment and savings, the external balance, monetary equilibrium, growth, changes in output, and economic efficiency. Informal finance may also cause macroeconomic imbalances and reduce the impact of regulation and control policies. However, from some local or individual perspectives, informal credit organizations certainly play a positive role. This chapter focuses on how to regulate the development of informal finance to improve its positive effect on social and economic development.

The Economic Effects of Informal Finance

The positive economic effects of informal financing are analyzed from the perspective of the enterprise life cycle. Informal finance provides start-up support to small and medium-sized enterprises (SMEs) and promotes local economic development. Using the analysis of the enterprise life cycle, it can be concluded that private enterprises and state-owned enterprises have distinct characteristics (Tan and Xia 2001), but their financing modes are the same (Tian 2004). The life cycle of private enterprises is generally divided into three phrases: the venture phase, the stability phase, and the decay period (Xu and Lu 2002).

In the early development period of the enterprise, the main source of financing is the entrepreneurs' own funds, as well as the funds of some affiliated investors. With the growth of the enterprise, the change in the proportion of financing through informal finance reveals a particular pattern: the proportion of informal finance to all finance systems is about 50% in the enterprise's infancy stage (0–2 years), which is reduced to 30%–40% in the enterprise's adolescence stage (3–4 years), but returns to 50% in the enterprise's middle-age stage (5–24 years), and finally increases to higher than 50% in the enterprise's old-age stage (above 25 years). The reason for this phenomenon is that small businesses face difficulties in meeting financing demands from formal channels in the start-up period, due to their lack of credit history; when enterprises enter the adolescent period and have a more established credit history, they can get a larger proportion of formal finance, and in their middle and old age, the entrepreneurs may prefer to invest additional resources in a second venture, also possibly using retained profits to purchase the company's stock from other internal owners in order to gain more control over the business. During the start-up phrase, venture capital comes mainly from stockholder's rights and from the debts from friends and family, which the company may repay in the later phase. Thus, for small businesses, informal finance plays a very important role throughout the entire lifecycle.

In developed countries such as the United Kingdom, the number of informal financial investors is relatively small, but the investments involve all the industries and enterprises at all stages of growth. Because targets of informal finance are generally located near where investors live or work. This mode of investment reflects the investors' desire to play an active role in their investment. Therefore, through the angel investors, small enterprises receive a lot of useful business skills and business management experience. Thus, informal investors make up for both lack of financing and lack of experience and personnel issues that constrain the development of SMEs.

Moral hazard of informal finance is channeled into financial risk. Due to a lack of external restraints and supervision, informal finance can easily cause moral hazard and adverse selection problems, which may become financial risk.[1] Informal financial organizations lack the mechanisms that guard against financial risks and also lack a reserve and deposit insurance system, which are both compulsory parts of the formal financial system. The informal financial system, then, fully depends on credit to maintain its operations, often relying on violence to enforce payment; therefore, many informal financial organizations are associated with organized crime.

As the scope of informal credit is relatively small, financial risks cannot be effectively dispersed, so once the risk becomes a payment crisis, this can cause a series of crises that affect normal production and social order. Fraudulent fund-raising activities with a criminal nature directly harm the public and impact the macroeconomy and financial management as a whole. Some activities of informal finance, such as foreign exchange fraud, that allow underground cross-border capital flows seriously interfere with the normal operations of national foreign exchange income and expenditure, resulting in a substantial imbalance of international payments and the reduction of international reserves. If financial risk becomes serious, economic development will decelerate or even stagnate, output will deviate from a balanced level, and economic efficiency will be very low. Finally, national income and welfare will decline.

Positive Effects of Chinese Informal Finance

In the period of economic transition and private economic development, China's informal finance has become a key component outside of the formal financial system. At the same time, it is the private capitals' chosen result. Under the financial system of China, private capital cannot flow into formal banks' ventures freely; investors are unable to obtain the potential financial profits. Because informal finance is not well controlled, there are many nonstandard operating characteristics associated with it. Its organization and management are relatively weak as well, so it is riskier. The nature of informal finance has complex effects on China's social and economic activities.

Informal finance promotes the development of market mechanisms. In order to meet reform requirements and to extend the functions of the planned economic system under the financial support of the state-owned economy, the formal financial system allocates a great deal of financial surplus to state-owned enterprises. Since formal finance prefers the traditional economic system to the market economy system, funds monopolized by the traditional economic system would not flow to the emerging market economy without the support of informal finance (Dai 2002). This would leave some reform objectives behind. Informal finance provides strong financial support to the individual private sector and SMEs and creates conditions for the development of China's market economy.

To some extent, informal finance compensates for the lack of formal finance. Since China started the reform and the opening-up policy, its private economy has developed rapidly, but the formal financial sector has failed to provide the corresponding financial services. As modern economic development and financial support are inseparable, these private sectors can rely only upon informal financial support. A typical example is the type of private financial organization that appeared in the provinces of Fujian, Jiangsu and

Zhejiang at the beginning of the 1980s. Fujian is one of the coastal provinces that were opened earliest, and the private economy was growing rapidly, particularly in the southeastern Fujian coastal areas, such as Fuzhou, Quanzhou, Xiamen and other cities. Private economic development has become an important driving force in the region, while the formal financial sector does not provide corresponding financial support. In the absence of formal financial services, the private economy in Fujian has depended on self-financing and private financing. Wenzhou city in Zhejiang province faces the same situation: according to an investigation by the Policy Research Office of the Wenzhou city government, in 1988, 21% of the start-up funds of 50 private enterprises in nine coastal counties (cities) was from private lending, and 23 was from bank loans; in the Liushi Town of Yueqing County, which is called the "Electric Kingdom," more than 50% of the overall funding of township enterprises comes from private lending; the scale of private funds in Qiaotou Town, "the East's largest button market," was about 30 million yuan, and almost every individual businessman has somehow been involved in private lending. One can say that China's private economic development is inseparable from informal financial support.

Informal finance has some positive effects on formal finance. Informal financial institutions are more efficient than formal ones. The ratio of non-performing loans in informal financial institutions is very low, because informal financing often occurs in a community in which both lenders and borrowers know each other, and community members have close social and economic contact with each other, reducing information asymmetry. For example, informal finance is very flexible and can operate 24 hours a day, and the traditional customs and shared morals of the same community make informal financial institutions mutual ones, reducing transactions costs and increasing profit levels. The existence of informal finance can place the pressure of competition on formal finance and compel formal financial institutions to change their management attitude and improve service quality and service efficiency.

Negative Effects of Chinese Informal Finance

Informal finance may weaken the effects of financial macroeconomic policy. Informal financial institutions may inevitably take part of the funds from public financial institutions out of the formal system, forming another system of financial markets. If this change is not strictly controlled, it will have a serious impact on formal financial institutions. In theory, a country's total financial scale should be equal to the sum of informal finance and formal finance. If excessive funds flow into the informal financial market, the government's economic macro-control capacity will be weakened and the effect of policy will decline. For example, when the government wants to implement a tight monetary policy to control an overheated economy, the informal financial sector may instead provide funds that weaken the tight monetary policy, preventing the whole economy from achieving a "soft landing" (see Appendix A in this book).

The harmful effects of informal finance's risks are serious. High risks associated with the operation of informal financial institutions may cause confusion in financial order and lead to social instability. Some forms of informal finance, such as *hehui* and underground banks, belong to financial organization models in the initial phase of the commodity economy, whose internal control mechanisms are not strong enough. Due to lack of effective external supervision and restraint, those informal financial institutions may be used by illegal elements who are trying to obtain more funds by collecting public money and promising a high interest rate. However, the managers of the fund use the money not for real business, but for pleasure or speculation, accumulating a great deal of money to repay. High interest rates, however, are just bait to collect funds from irrational investors, so the activities of financing with an ever-expanding scale of capital progress more easily and attract more and more people's participation. Use of the credit is non-productive and must be repaid, so the final payment is bound to lead to a collapse of the chain, resulting in damage to the participants, causing social instability and disrupting the normal social and economic order. By the end of 1985, the incident of *taihui* in Pingyang and Yueqing of Wenzhou city involved more than RMB 200 million and spread around the 10 counties. The incident had caused a series of kidnappings and even killings, which had a serious impact on social stability in Wenzhou. In 2002–2003, the public security departments wiped out more than 60 underground banks engaged in money laundering and confiscated a great deal of money and goods, which had a total value of RMB 300 million. The examples above vividly demonstrate the negative impacts of informal finance on society and the economy.

The negative impact of informal finance on formal finance should not be overlooked. Informal financial organizations attract public depositors from the formal financial institutions by using high interest rates. Their procedure for financing is very simple. Familiar acquaintances or clients, who may be annoyed by fussy procedures in formal financial institutions, can accomplish the whole procedure with just a call. Informal financial institutions provide small scale and short-term funding, matching the characteristics of commercial capital flow, so informal financing is welcomed by individual industrial and commercial households and SMEs. Formal financial institutions are reluctant to lend to those businesses, so the business scale of formal institutions is shrinking. The existence of informal finance, under specific conditions, also indirectly increases the risk of credit assets of formal financial institutions, because enterprises that have both formal and informal loans will repay the latter first,[2] bringing uncertainty to the normal operations of formal financial institutions.

Legitimate forms of informal finance play a more positive role in economic development; however, the authorities do not know clearly what the scale and operating practices are, and informal finance is not under the national financial supervisory system, so it may have some passive effects on monetary policy and macroeconomic regulation. Standardization and transparency are the two key elements needed for informal finance to transform its passive effects into positive ones. And other informal financial institutions, which have criminal behavior and are harmful for the economy, should be seriously punished and prohibited.

We must not simply reach an arbitrary conclusion and claim that informal finance is reasonable, or very harmful, and should be banned. Different types of informal finance should be treated differently depending on their distinct situations. China's informal finance was formed in the special period after the planned economy gradually transitioned to a market economy, and the basic economic type changed from a centralized entity to an individual entity. Because informal finance lacks legal recognition and is usually attacked as a potential danger, it has to be in the form of "underground institutions," which lack efficient supervision and external constraints, causing bad effects and even financial fraud in some situations. Therefore, it is important to impose strict rules and standard regulations on informal finance.

Economic and Political Factors in the Development of Informal Finance

With recent roots in China's transition to a market economy, the formation of informal finance in China not only has characteristics similar to other developing countries, but also has some unique factors.

Analysis of the Demand for Informal Finance

From a demand perspective, there has been an asymmetry between the policies of formal finance and changes in capital demand during the reform process. In the process of China's gradual reform, the formal financial sector has been a source of inertia, preferring an economy of public ownership to a private economy (Qiao 2001; Du 2003). Along with the establishment and promotion of a market economy, the private sector developed rapidly with a corresponding demand for funds, but the formal financial sector has not been willing to provide financial services to the private sector. In order to obtain the necessary funds to maintain and expand its development, the private economy had to seek assistance from informal financial channels; therefore, informal finance became an important channel for raising funds and meeting the inherent requirements of economic development (Zuo 2005).

Compared with the publicly owned sector, the private sector has distinct characteristics: it is comprised of many small scale units, and it requires a wide range of funds. If the formal financial sector wants to expand its existing services, it would have to pay a great deal of money for the construction of networks, development of a credit assessment program, and monitoring of loans. From a cost–benefit perspective, the formal sector is not willing to develop such services because they are not that profitable. Therefore, the private economy is often isolated from the formal credit system.

Analysis of Informal Finance Supply

From a supply perspective, the increasingly abundant supply of informal capital is a catalyst for the development of informal finance. Since China began its reform and opening-up policy, the income of urban and rural residents has increased substantially, providing informal financial institutions with potential funds. Since China's deposit interest rates are still kept artificially low and the domestic investment channels are very limited, the main types of financial assets of residents are deposits and cash. Thus, it is very easy for informal financial institutions to absorb idle funds by advertising higher interest rates. Take Wenzhou city for example: the individual average monthly interest rate of informal finance is 25%, with the highest being above 30%; the average interest rate of enterprises is 20%, with the highest being below 26%, while the latest (till May 2008) official interest rate is 4.14% per year and 3.45% per month. According to a survey by Ran Zhang, a journalist for Xinhua Net, at the beginning of 2008, Zhejiang's underground financial interest rates continued to climb, and the short-term interest rate in areas was up to 15%, which is 20 times higher than the official standard rate. Informal interest rates are far higher than the official level of interest rates. Such high interest rates are very attractive, so it is not surprising that many people participate in informal financial activities and regard it as a good way to invest.

The supply of informal finance results from people's desire to chase potential income which cannot be obtained from the formal financial system. The context of present-day informal finance is new, having been rejuvenated in response to the rise of a market economy, since the interest rate of informal finance increases as the official interest rate increases.

Geographical Features of Informal Finance in China

Since 1979, China has embarked on a development path of combining the planned economy and the commodity economy. Based on more than 10 years of practice and experience, the authorities established the goal of building the socialist market economy. The framework of the market economy has now been formed, but financial control is still relatively strict, so that informal finance remains underground.

In the gradual process of reform, on the one hand, the components of the traditional system still exist and need to be protected to ensure stability of the reform, but on the other hand, the government must cultivate market forces to promote the development of the market economy. Therefore, reform has adopted the "first test, second promote" model, with the pilot areas usually concentrated in the southeastern coastal provinces. Underground finance has been brought out in regions in which the old system has been transformed to the new one; then over time, other regions emulate, so that regional differ ences, that is, between the north and the south, are formed with specific geographical characteristics.

"Zhemin model."[3] China's private economy was begun mainly in the experimental areas of economic reform (such as Jiangsu, Zhejiang, Fujian, and Guangdong). Because these areas have been at the forefront of reform and have strong market mechanisms, the private economy comprises a greater proportion of the economy with a huge demand for capital, while the stock of idle funds is also large. At the same time, the financial industry has not begun large-scale market-oriented reform, and financial institutions are still mainly state-owned banks, so the normal financing channel of the private economy is very narrow. Therefore, in the early 1980s, informal finance rose first in Zhejiang, Fujian, Guangdong, and then in other prov inces in this area. Informal finance provides short-term credit and little long-term borrowing. This type of credit is the main form of informal finance on the southeast coast of China called the "Zhemin model."

"Northern model." In most provinces of northern China, firms' infor mal financial activities involve fundraising societies, with fund-raising methods including equity channels, debt channels, trust channels, and de posit channels. Private stock-collecting in the start-up period is one kind of informal equity financing, and it is rational; however, if the enterprise collects funds from many indirect investors, some severe hidden credit risks may emerge. In the absence of external regulatory constraints, the mode of issuing debt certificates could easily give rise to moral hazard, and cases of bank ruptcy to escape debts are not uncommon. Some enterprises, which operate certain programs, issue benefit certificates to collect funds through trust channels. Some enterprises collect funds from the public by advertising a high interest rate and manage banking operations rather than providing nominal business services. In some cities of northeastern China, with the help of cooperative financial organizations in association with enterprises, large enterprises lend their loans from banks to other small enterprises, and gain a spread of about 2%–5%. The primitive modes of fund brokers called *qianzhong* and *yinbei* (Zhang Jun 1997) still exist in the vast rural areas in northern China, with a small-scale and little influence. Following is one example.

On December 17, 2000, in Baoji County of Shanxi Province, the local court sentenced Feng Xiang Yang to 1 year of imprisonment and a 500,000 yuan fine for the crime of misappropriating public funds. Yang was the leader of the board of the agricultural association, which was founded in 1996. The original purpose of the association was to help peasants develop the planting trade and popularize agricultural technology. But afterward, it changed totally. On October 8, 1996, Yang used the name of the association to accept people's deposits illegally. Then he lent to private enterprises and small-scale enterprises. When people discovered that some of these enterprises had asked to withdraw their deposits, Yang promised to repay on time, and some people trusted this lie.

Yang knew that the association would go bankrupt. He recalled that from October 20, 1999 to January 9, 2000, deposits were reduced by twenty million yuan in less than 3 months. On February 29, 2000, Yang declared bankrupty, and many victims appealed for help. Local social stability was deeply wounded.

From October 1996 to February 2000, deposits numbered 180 million yuan. Until February 29, 2000, 150 million yuan could still be found on the account records. Loans were 120 million yuan in total, more than 60 million yuan of which were bad loans. The percentage of bad loans was higher than 50%. This is attributed to his greed and bad management of the association. On March 5, 2000, Yang was arrested.

To summarize, the main faults of rural foundations are as follows. Firstly, ownership is not clear. Foundations are collective economic organizations with cooperative systems, so they are easily controlled by inside persons like Feng Xiang Yang. Secondly, they are influenced by the intervention of local government. Most of the administrators of foundations are assigned by the local government. So the management of foundations does not follow the regular requirements of financial organizations (e.g., maintaining deposit reserves and risk prevention mechanisms), and the administrative authority does not implement effective guidance and supervision. Thirdly, staff members in the foundations are not well-trained. They lack financial knowledge and management experience, which would mitigate risk.

The main problems associated with other irregular financial organizations such as economic service departments, financial service departments, professional associations, and private banks are as follows. Compared with regular financial organizations, their organizational systems, internal management mechanisms, and control systems are not standardized. They have no loan loss provisions or reserves against deposits. A fairly large percentage of businesses do not follow the rules strictly. Some nongovernmental financial organizations attract deposits with abnormally high interest rates and are willing to loan regardless of high levels of risk. They are still trying to escape financial supervision. Rural irregular financial organizations promote rural economic development, while they have met with serious problems and their weaknesses are very obvious.

In recent years, rural irregular financial organizations have acquired some new characteristics: before, they were underground organizations but now they are semi-overt or even overt; most of their businesses are still local ones but they have begun to have businesses in other villages, counties, and provinces; the proportion of large loans have increased unceasingly, the proportion of free-interest loans have been reduced gradually; in the past, most loan contracts were oral ones, which was consistent with the low education level of villagers; and finally, the purposes of loans have changed, for before most of them were used for consumption purposes such as weddings, funerals, and traditional agricultural investments, but now most of them are used for production purposes, which can have a short investment-profit period, such as machining, transportation, and aquaculture. Now the procedure has been normalized gradually, and dissensions have gradually decreased. Along with a higher risk consciousness, people need to obtain loans using mortgages such as deposit receipts, bonds, and real estate. Those rural nongovernmental financial organizations play an increasingly important role in rural economic development and have an increasing level of standardization.

Countermeasures for Regulating Informal Finance

Different forms of underground finance have different functions and influence on the social economy, which also affect the process of implementing governmental macroeconomic control. The unpredictable scale and influence of informal finance reduces methods of regulation. Some choices of regulation under these circumstances are as follows: Firstly, to eliminate the base of informal finance, legalizing is the best measure, that is, bringing informal organizations and activities to light. Secondly, to reform the financial service system, improving the legal and financial monitoring effects is necessary. Restraining the development of the underground economy and taking a strong stance against underground financial activities are critical in regulating illegal financial activities.

Underground finance that has negative effects on social economic development should be controlled. Underground financial organizations and activities which disturb the financial order, undermine social stability, or retard the growth of the economy must be eliminated. This type of financial activity has obvious criminal features. These may include illegally absorbing deposits from the public, financial fraud, money laundering, transferring illegal gains, obtaining foreign currencies, and financing through gambling. In the southeast and southwest trade zones, underground banks colluding with mafia forces are illegal. Regulation becomes more difficult when cross-boundary economic crimes are added to the list. Thus, cooperation among the Public Security department, financial organizations, and financial regulatory authorities becomes vitally important in regulating underground financial crime.

Having pursued underground financial crimes, on January 17, 2005, the Shanghai Public Security Bureau discovered Zou's illegal private bank. In mid-April 2005, Shanghai public security arrested 17 suspects, froze more than 70 related bank accounts, and captured U.S. dollars, yen, and RMB worth more than 10 million yuan.

That there are cases of big underground private banks in Shanghai is really beyond our imagination. We think that Shanghai is the most important financial center of our country and the most important international financial center of the Asia-Pacific area. It has many stock exchange, foreign exchange, and gold exchange centers; it is also home to the headquarters of some Chinese banks like the Bank of Communications, Pu Eastern Development Bank, and Shanghai Bank. There are also some international banks such as National City Bank of New York and Hong Kong Shanghai Banking Corporation. The financial system in Shanghai is well developed, and the financial market in Shanghai is active. Most important is the fact that risk management consciousness and financial investment consciousness of people and enterprises in Shanghai are strong. Shanghai also has underground financial organizations.

Three government departments in Shanghai cooperated in this case regarding the big underground private bank. The Shanghai branch of the National Administration of Exchange Control discovered the suspicious accounts through information from the anti-money laundering information center. The Shanghai branch of the People's Bank of China along with other commercial banks tracked suspicious capital flows and helped the office of public security freeze the suspicious accounts and suspicious capital in time.

Preliminary investigation results show that Zou offered illegal services such as international exchange for people and enterprises starting in 2004 in Shanghai, Jiangsu, and Zhejiang. His business dealt with a huge amount of money; in September 2004 alone, the turnover of his underground private bank being as high as 200 million yuan.

Looking at the characteristics of underground finance in northern China, the authorities should impose strict supervision on the fund-raising activities of private enterprise. The administrative departments of enterprises, associations of enterprises, branches of the central bank, and commercial banks are obligated to supervise fund-raising behavior. By monitoring deposits and money flows, financial institutions should estimate whether transactions are normal or suspicious. If authorities find problems, the institutions should submit the report to the branches of the central bank and the financial supervisory department in time, and after careful investigation, the administrative department of the financial sector should report the case to the security authority, or the security authority should investigate the case directly. Commercial banks should control their credit risk in lending to enterprises, and guide and monitor the behavior of enterprises.

Help the informal financial organizations which have positive effects become formal institutions gradually. Many informal financial organizations play a positive role in the rural economy and the development of SMEs, but the *hehui*, which are decentralized, small-scale, lack supervision, and have no protection, cannot withstand moral hazard and credit risks. It is not wise to ban these organizations or to let them develop uncontrolled. To achieve desired macroeconomic objectives, the authority should integrate informal financial institutions into the financial supervisory system and strictly supervise their capital flows and risk management. Let us turn to a case of an antipoverty informal financial organization.

Tuanshuitou village is the central village of Tuanshuitou town in Lin County, Shanxi Province. It is a large village. There are 1800 people in the village. It is obvious that Tuanshuitou village is the economic and cultural center of the Tuanshuitou town. But the village is still very poor: most young workers hunt for work outside, and the agricultural population live on crops such as corn, Chinese yams, and sunflower and castor-oil plants. Due to poor natural conditions, agriculture is highly dependent on the climate. An obvious example is that in 2003, because of the drought, the farmers got nothing for the whole year.

Tuanshuitou village lacks capital, and people there need loans in small amounts very urgently. People need loans to pay for tuition, medicine, wedding and funeral costs, and agricultural materials. But the local credit associations have strict restrictions on mortgages and guarantors which most villagers cannot meet. Therefore, people must turn to usury. It is said that before the formation of the poverty alleviation foundation, the usury interest rate was about 10% a month, which most people could not afford.

The poverty alleviation foundation in Tuanshuitou village was founded on September 15, 2001, and most of its capital is from the people in urban areas, while some is from the rich villagers. In the beginning, there were no shareholders, but by March 31, 2004, there were 83 shareholders. The initial funds of the poverty alleviation foundation amounted to only 13,000 yuan collected by Mao Yushi, and by 2004 they became 291,461 yuan.

The poverty alleviation foundation is entirely a grassroots organization. The funds of the poverty alleviation foundation can be divided into poverty alleviation funds and cost funds. The lenders of poverty alleviation funds do not receive interest, but the lenders of cost funds can obtain 6% interest a year, although 20% of all their interest income will be handed over to the tax bureau. If some cost funds cannot be repaid, the loss will be compensated for by the poverty alleviation fund.

The poverty alleviation foundation can offer two kinds of loans, those with interest and those without. The loans used for paying tuition and medicine are interest-free loans, but loans used in production require interest. Most loans should be repaid in 3 or 6 months, with the longest period being 1 year, although the debtor can apply for an extension. The interest rate is higher than that of the credit association but lower than that of usury, which is 1% in a month (i.e., 12% in a year). Until March 31, 2004, the poverty alleviation foundation had 402 loans, with a total amount of 568,700 yuan. The poverty alleviation foundation's small loans meet the urgent needs of villagers most of the time, so it is very popular.

In our most recent national survey, we were interested in finding out whether the foundation followed modern management principals. We discovered that although the foundation is still not perfect, the operation system has the most basic characteristics of modern management patterns: clearly established ownership, well defined power and responsibility, separation of enterprise from administration, and scientific management.

The ownership of the poverty alleviation foundation is clearly established. None of its capital comes from the government. Shareholders are various: some are collective organizations, some are individuals, some are from rural areas, and some are from urban areas. Shareholders include professors, college students, governmental officials, journalists, some very famous persons like Yushi Mao, Min Tang, and Yifu Lin, and some kind-hearted overseas Chinese individuals like Lianlian Shan and Yunhai Hua. We must mention that some villagers who benefit from this foundation also contribute to it. The diversification of the shareholders makes the foundation manageable. Clearly established ownership is the key point. The foundation has an unwritten principle that it will never accept any funding from the government. Here is an example. In 2003, the technology department wanted to invest 10 million yuan to promote the poverty alleviation fund but they refused. In the past, the rural foundations and credit associations suffered from a lack of separation from the administration so the government often intervened. Their failures show this shortcoming clearly. So the foundation therefore has a closer relationship with the local residents and protects their independence.

The president is Yushi Mao; the associate presidents are Min Tang and Aiwei Lin. The people who take the responsibility for most daily work are the accountant, Aiwei Lin, the cashier, Linshun Li, and the supervisor, Yongqin Li. They should strictly follow the rules according to fair principles. Every month Aiwei Lin, who is the principal of daily work, presents a report to Yushi Mao, who is the representative of the shareholders. The report includes business of the foundation, financial condition, feedback from villagers, and main goals. Secondly, in daily work, the accountant takes the responsibility for checking the loan applications from peasant households, determining the credit level of applicants, deciding whether or not to give loans to the applicants, and urging them to repay; the cashier takes the responsibility for recording and providing money and performing statistical analysis; the supervisor can check on the account at any time (generally once every week). Thirdly, when the credit level of applicants is hard to define or the amount is large (3000 yuan and above), the accountant, cashier, and supervisor must have a meeting to discuss the application; loans can be granted only if a unanimous decision is made. Fourthly, the election mechanism of the accountant, cashier, and supervisor has been perfected. Only the people who have combined ability with character are eligible. All their work should be under the surveillance of villagers.

According to the specific conditions in rural areas, the management of the foundation is different from that of financial organizations in the city. The foundation must do business only in its own village. As we know, the most prominent advantage of the small loans offered by the foundation is low risk. The foundation and villagers are very familiar with each other and the villagers know the financial situation of one another very well. So if the foundation were to give loans in other villages, the risk would increase. The foundation workers insist on being just, fair, and open. Records are published in the village theater, which is the center of the village, showing the persons who borrow and who repay money, to distinguish between excellent and poor customers. Meanwhile, any villager can look over the account books at any time.

The foundation is also very serious about the purposes of the loans and check on borrowers. Once the staff found that the actual use of a loan was not consistent with the reported one, they would publish the person's name and require him or her to repay the loans as soon as possible. What is worth noticing is that the foundation will never lend money to usurers or individuals who will use the funds for illicit activities, such as gambling.

Considering that the household is the main economic unit of the rural area, the loan applicant is the household. The loan is the joint liability of the spouses, (for unmarried borrowers, the loan is the joint liability of the son and father, or a similar relationship). And villagers do not need to mortgage anything to the foundation to obtain a loan. The foundation also has a system of household records in its credit history. Once households are defined as excellent credit risks, they can obtain a loan by completing only two forms. Villagers find that it is very convenient, and some people say that "if there is cash in the foundation, it usually takes 2 or 3 hours to get the money; if not, it usually takes 2 or 3 days. That is very efficient." However, at present the poverty alleviation foundation has a unique function, but the vitality of this kind of new financial organization and its applicability are still yet to be determined. So its development still needs to be monitored.

Determining risks and benefits is the inevitable challenge for all financial organizations. But there is an unjustified common opinion that the irregular financial organizations often value benefits more than risks, and they may engage in dangerous behavior that would result in bad outcomes, such as an "association collapse." The government supervision departments appear to emphasize the risks, so they have restrained various irregular financial campaigns since 1997. But in reality, the appearance and development of irregular financial organizations show that these organizations are trying to balance risks and benefits. Government supervision departments pay too much attention to the risks and neglect the benefits that irregular financial organizations bring to rural economic and social development. So we must take an unbiased look at irregular financial organizations and find a good way for their development.

Can we balance the benefits and the risks? The financial situation of the poverty alleviation foundation gives us a relatively clear answer. From September 15, 2001 to March 31, 2004, the total capital of the foundation was 290 million yuan, putting out 402 loans with the total amount of 568.7 million yuan, only two loans of which could not be repaid. The foundation also stipulates that the proportion of interest-free loans should be lower than one third. In this period, the total interest income was 26,867 yuan, and payments were 23,567 yuan.

In 2 years, the poverty alleviation foundation took in a profit of 3299 yuan, while the total management expenses were 14,310 yuan, with the average cost of each loan at 35.60 (14,310 over 402) yuan. Compared with another financial organization such as a credit association, costs are very low and it is effective. All the records show that the foundation possesses very strong vitality. But it still needs to reregulate and prevent risk.

We cannot ignore the risks of the poverty alleviation foundation. As we have learned, now there is no risk precaution mechanism in the poverty alleviation foundation, so the establishment of a risk precaution mechanism has become quite urgent.

The risk problem of the poverty alleviation foundation embodies two main aspects. One denotes systemic risk. As per our inquiry, there is no corresponding supervision system in the foundation; it depends upon direct confidence in the staff. This kind of subjective confidence is not robust. The existence of supervisors in the foundation is only an internal, rather than an external, supervision mechanism. The second problem is the risk of capital in the foundation. There is no capital risk precaution mechanism in the foundation, especially for bad loans. So if any serious problems in the capital chain occurred, the foundation could not do anything about them.

The bookkeeping method of the foundation is single-entry bookkeeping, which is clear and easy to understand, so it is welcomed by villagers. But its shortcomings are also very obvious. It cannot reflect the whole situation of the foundation, and it is hard for the supervisory department to check. When the business of the foundation increases and becomes more complicated, single-entry bookkeeping cannot meet the foundation's development in the future.

Staff quality in the foundation should be improved. The achievement of the former foundation shows that its staff members are very conscious of good service; they take responsibility seriously. Along with the standardization of the foundation, the expectations of foundation staff quality in financial theory, law, and accounting are raised continuously.

The personnel system of the poverty alleviation foundation is not well organized. One example is that Yushi Mao set up another foundation in another village before he founded the Tuanshuitou poverty alleviation foundation, but it failed. The initial capital was 50,000 yuan, but the principal ran away with all the money.

Besides rural cooperative foundations, irregular rural financial organizations also include economic service departments, financial service departments, professional associations, and private banks. They meet the needs of rural economic development to a certain extent, but some of them work with high financial risk and make the local financial system unstable.

The authorities should help informal financial institutions that have positive effects be legalized. Finance must be held to very high standards to be competitive. The characteristics of informal financial organizations, which are small scale and have weak risk prevention mechanisms, determine that informal financial organizations should satisfy the financing needs of rural areas and SMEs, and financial cooperation is a common form. However, there is no true cooperative bank in China's rural areas, and the traditional credit cooperatives do not support the rural economy.

The general direction of rural credit cooperatives' reform is not transitioning into commercial banks, but into true rural cooperative financial organizations. If rural credit cooperatives transition into urban commercial banks, the problems of low efficiency and risk could not be resolved, and rural credit cooperatives could not provide sound services to SMEs. The fund base of cooperative financial institutions is all from its staff and associates, and the institutions follow the principle of "continuing to operate depends on the results of operation." On May 31, 2005, the "small scale informal credit" discussion was held by the People's Bank of China and the China Banking Regulatory Commission, which decided to choose Shanxi, Shaanxi, Sichuan, and Guizhou as the four experimental provinces for "microcredit institutions of NGOs," which symbolizes the beginning of informal finance's opening to the public. And the Inner Mongolia Autonomous Region became another experimental province soon after the meeting. Informal finance still has some problems, but it has made the first step toward moving from the underground to open air. After legalization, informal finance should be integrated into the whole financial administration system and should include risk-protection mechanisms, such as the legal reserve system and the deposit insurance system.

Deepen the reform of the financial system and increase the effective supply of financial investment instruments. Chinese nongovernmental financial organizations have generally become more open. In July 2005, the People's Bank of China carried out a trial in Shanxi, Shaanxi, Sichuan, and Guizhou Provinces called "nongovernment credit experimental units," and the trial became a sign of the acknowledgement of nongovernmental financial organizations by authorities. The government began to pay attention to the important role of the nongovernmental financial organizations, tried to control its power, and attempted to standardize it step by step. However, the development of informal finance has its own natural laws and intrinsic regulations, so whether or not the arrangement from the government can work is dubious. The key to making nongovernmental financial organizations legal is to build up a supervision system based on their natural laws.

Small-scale credit organizations have arisen as a way of perfecting the rural financial system. In recent years, the central government has paid much attention to issues concerning agriculture, the countryside, and farmers, and has decided to increase farmers' income. So the reform of rural finance has received more support.

In January 2004, some State Council policies regarding the promotion of peasants' income stated: "to promote the small-scale credit loans to peasants" it also required the enlargement of small-scale credit loans and the encouragement of local financial organizations to attract capital from different channels no matter whether it is private capital, collective capital, or foreign capital.

In January 2005, the State Council pointed out that rural areas should have a "clearly established ownership, well defined function and division of work, and an effectively carried out supervision system." It also emphasized the importance of rural financial reform and innovation.

Pingyao County in Shanxi Province and Jiankou County in Guizhou Province were selected to be the place for the trial. A preparatory group for the small-scale credit organization was set up in Pingyao. The associate lead of the county was appointed to be the group leader. The leader of the local branch of People's Bank of China was appointed to be the deputy leader of the group. Then they decided that the preliminary capital scale of the small-scale credit organization should be twenty million yuan, raised from 5 sponsors. Afterward, the organization would accept entrusted capital.

The People's Bank of China declared that they would raise funds by themselves; they could not accept deposits and should take the responsibility for their own profits and losses.

It is a reasonable choice in that the fiscal revenue would not offer assurance for this kind of financial organization. However, government's participation in operations would be harmful to the independence of this organization. For example, the poverty alleviation fund offered by the government would be a source of the capital for small-scale credit organizations; the agricultural department, finance department, and financial supervision department in the government would become the members of the leading reform group. The organization has the risk of being "a governmental organization in which the government does not invest directly." So when the organization meets operative difficulties or has too many bad loans, the government would have to compensate all losses.

The large-scale reforms sponsored by the government may cause the small-scale credit organization to stop serving the peasants. The profit-seeking motivation of the sponsor may send the loan interest rate to a relatively high level against the wishes of the grassroots sponsors.

This small-scale credit organization initiated mainly by the government has not evoked the enthusiasm of nongovernmental investors. Most nongovernmental capital prefers commercial small-scale credit organizations with no governmental background. Though the trial has met with many problems, its formation is a good attempt at the legalization of informal finance organizations. But the sponsors must respect the natural laws of informal finance (Li 2006). These laws are as follows:

Natural law one: the objectivity of its existence. Informal finance is the inevitable outcome of social development; its existence belongs to the nature, economy, culture, and ethics of a society. The variety of informal finance indicates the "otherness" of different places.

Natural law two: balance between risk and profit. Informal finance does not depend on legal or national forces to control risk, but leans on internal operation mechanisms and trust. Credit associations and inter-enterprise benefit associations are all financial activities within small groups. As long as economic benefit s of lending and borrowing are closely connected, credit risk can be dramatically reduced. Unless someone can secure a big enough profit and disappear, he will never break the promise. In fact, the capital scale of nongovernmental financial makes this impossible.

Natural law three: externalism. Externalism associated with informal finance means removing financial capital from formal finance. Informal financial institutions attract deposits by using high interest rates, and this causes deposits to flow out of banks on a large scale. In some places, the scale of informal financial business exceeds the scale of formal financial business, which means that the formal financial institutions cannot conduct normal business. But if the financial support offered by informal financial organizations leads to improvements in the whole society, the externalism of informal finance is positive. Therefore, we should judge informal financial organizations based on their overall effect, not based on their impact on formal financial organizations.

Natural law four: survival of the fittest. The diversity of informal finance is determined by the law of survival of the fittest. When informal finance cannot meet the needs of the market, it will be superseded naturally. In this competitive market, the government financial management authority does not need to "supply" funds; the only thing it needs to do is to institute laws regulating market access. The more functions the government undertakes, the more moral risk the market incurs.

Natural law five: act according to actual circumstances. In different economic environments, different scales and structures of informal finance are needed. Informal finance is an endogenous financial system. Legalization of nongovernmental financial organizations is not a process of making them uniform. So we should not force them to become NGO small-scale credit organizations or be regulated to hold the same amount of capital. This is inconsistent with the natural law of financial development.

What the financial management authority must do is to monitor and prevent risks through advance macroscopic analysis, to build a relief mechanism for the systematic trouble of informal finance such as loan loss provision systems and a deposit insurance system, as well as a central bank lending system. And the nonsystematic risks in informal finance must be handled according to market regulation; the financial management authority has no duty to offer corresponding help, and the local government cannot act as the final guarantor.

Another task that financial management authorities need to set about is to guarantee a strong competitive environment and abidance of regulations.

We have not established relevant laws and regulation on informal finance until now. That is one of the most important tasks of the financial reform and development in the future.

We do not want to overemphasize the importance of deepening reform in the financial system, but we hold the view that deepening reform will further eliminate financial suppression, promote the development of financial market, increase financial investment instruments, and increase innovation in financial institutions. Now the liberalization of interest rates and building a more elastic exchange rate system are the main goals of financial reform, but there will be a long way to go for the central government because there are many difficulties. However, the direction of reform is correct, despite the fact that the method of implementing reform is not explicit. The reduction of financial suppression weakens the advantages of underground finance and enhances its operating cost; if formal financial institutions and financial markets have more room to innovate, investors will not purchase underground financial instruments with an associated high risk. Given this, underground finance will gradually lose its foundation and will finally face its demise.

There are different factors that have supported the development of informal finance in China, and informal finance has generally had positive effects on private enterprises and individual entrepreneurs, especially in rural areas. But underground financing harms formal financial institutions by reducing deposits and destroying the normal social order when the risks are exposed. The financial authority should, then, control and forbid the development of underground financial institutions and permit the legalization of informal financial institutions that are beneficial.

Notes

1. In many *hehui* (ROSCAs), the heads used members' money to build or buy houses and cars for their luxurious lives, and some of them use the collected money to gamble and lost all the money. As they could not repay to the members, the heads would leave their living places and changed their names or go abroad. Some members borrow money from banks and put the money into *hehui*, as the *hehui* go bankrupt, they could not pay back the banks. The informal financial moral hazard transferred financial risk.

2. Informal financial institutions have a more strict credit protect mechanism, if the borrowers would not repay the money, they may be threatened or damaged by the lenders. Most borrowers have to put their houses, stocks, goods or other assets up as collaterals. And the informal loan interest rate is usually higher than formal loans rate, so borrowers have a decline to repay the informal loan first.

3. Zhemin means Zhejiang and Fujian.

References

Dai, Dezhu. 2002. Financial system reform and the development of private economy. *Theory Magazine* 10: 56–57.

Du, Chaoyun. 2003. Causes and management ideas of the informal finance. *Statistics and Decision Making* 3: 19–20.

Qiao, Haishu. 2001. Financial constraints and relief in the development of the rural economy. *The Agricultural Economy* 3: 19–23.

Li, Jianjun. 2006. *China Informal Finance Survey.* Shanghai: Shanghai People's Press.

Tan, Liwen and Qinghua Xia. 2001. Comparative analysis of the life cycle of enterprises. *Finance and Trade Economy* 7: 41–44.

Tian, Xiaoxia. 2004. Small business finance theory and empirical studies reviewed. *Economic Research* 5: 107–116.

Xu, XiaoMing and Zhonglai Lu. 2002. Private enterprise life cycle. *Economic Theory and Economic Management* 5: 54–58.

Zhang, Jun. 1997. High interest rates "filter" risk. *Zone Herald* 11: 34–37.

Zuo, Chenmin. 2005. The review of informal financial. *The Shandong Institute of Business Journal* 6: 29–34.

Appendix A: Informal Finance, Monetary Conditions, and Economic Movements

Qiang Fu and Jianjun Li

The clandestine nature of informal finance makes it difficult to accurately measure its scale and modus operandi in economic movements through open statistical methods. Relying on the abnormal differences between the economic and financial statistical indicators to estimate the scale of informal finance is an important way. It is helpful to determine how informal financial activities work on monetary finance and economic movements from a macroeconomic perspective, based on the scale of informal financial indicators, to compile an informal monetary condition index. Further, it is important to study the relationship among the informal monetary condition index, the monetary condition index, and the economic movement index. On the basis of measuring the scale of informal finance, we construct statistical models; analyze the relationship among the informal finance index, the monetary condition index, and the early warning index of economic movements; and comment on how the informal finance works on the monetary and economic movements.

Calculation of the Scale of Informal Finance

The indicators of the scale of informal finance include stock indicators and traffic indicators. In the traffic indicators, the index which reflects the financial status of the informal financial sector is the informal net financial investment (IFNFI); and that which reflects the relations of allocation of funds between the informal financial sector and the foreign sector is the informal cross-border net financial investment (IFCBCF). Within the stock indicators, the informal loan (IFL) is most important. In this section, we will calculate the three major indicators reflecting the scale of the informal finance.

The Calculation of IFNFI

IFNFI is the result of the allocation of funds between the national economic departments and informal financial sectors, which reflects the relations of capital flows between the formal financial sectors and other informal sectors. The amount of capital flow is the net funds that the informal financial sectors absorb and release, which has changed the capital flows of the formal economy and impacted the balance of economic movements.

The Theory and Method of Measuring the Scale of IFNFI

The System of National Accounts (SNA) includes the transactions accounts of physical capital flows and financial accounts. Using matrix accounting, it reflects the flows of all kinds of economic transactions and financial transactions among the national economic sectors, other domestic sectors, and foreign sectors. All national economic departments are divided into five sectors by the accounting matrix, which include the household, nonfinancial enterprise, government, financial institution, and foreign department sectors. They are listed in the guest column of the accounting matrix. All financial transactions, classified by using different financial instruments, are included in the main column. One uses double accounting to record the value of all financial flows. Income and outlays are included in each sector to reflect the changes of financial assets and liabilities. The difference between income and outlays is the net financial investment (NFI), which reflects the deficit and surplus of each national economy department, and shows the allocation of funds in various departments.

According to the principles of the flow of funds table, the sum of the four domestic sectors' NFI (NFI_d) should be equal to the foreign sectors' NFI (NFI_f) in absolute values, but with the opposite sign. But for various reasons, such as statistical shortcomings, incomplete information, and unobserved economic factors, the domestic sectors' net capital flows and the foreign sector's net capital flows are different. An additional statistical error is set in the flow of funds table to deal with this problem. If statistical errors can be included in the informal economic and financial aspects of the basic premise, we assume there should be an informal economic and financial sector in the national economy. It is the counterpart of the domestic and foreign departments. The capital flow of the informal economic and financial sector is called IFNFI.

The formal economic sectors include households, nonfinancial enterprises, the government, financial institutions, and foreign departments. The household sector has two parts: urban households and rural households, which includes self-employed households. This department primarily engages in final consumption and self-production activities and also a few for-profit production activities. The nonfinancial enterprise sector is made up of all independent accounting units engaging in for-profit nonfinancial activities. Government departments are made up of the central government, the local authorities, and the social insurance fund. This sector provides nonprofit outputs to public units and individuals and assumes the responsibility for redistributing national income and wealth. The financial sector includes the central bank, policy banks, commercial banks, and other financial institutions, which provide insurance services. The foreign sector includes all nonresident establishments engaged in transactions with domestic institutions.

The informal economic and financial sector is an economic unit which cannot be measured by the SNA. It is made up of households, nonfinancial enterprises, the government, financial institutions, nonresidents and nonresident agencies, which engage in informal economic and financial activities, accessing private income.

The clandestine nature of informal economic and financial activities makes it impossible to measure the income and outcome funds of each type of economic unit. However, the results of informal economic and financial activities must be shown in the results of the final allocation of funds in the whole society, which distorts the links between various accounts, and causes some puzzling results. Through the differences between reasonable net capital flows and actual net capital flows, we can find the NFI scale of economic and financial activities, which will be helpful to measure the allocation of funds. The sum of NFI of the formal sector ($NFI_d + NFI_f$) and that of the informal financial sector (IFNFI) should be zero. Thus, we have a way to measure the investment scale of the informal net financial sector:

$$IFNFI = -(NFI_d + NFI_f) \qquad [A.1]$$

The Scale of IFNFI in China: 1982–2005

IFNFI of Physical Transaction Accounts

The domestic NFI of the physical transaction accounts (NFI_d) is the difference between the national disposable income and consumption and investment, which is the currency reserves of national residents. The net foreign financial investment (NFI_f) is the sum of the balance of international payments and the balance of capital transfers. In 2006, the National Bureau of Statistics adjusted the GDP data after 1978 based on the first national economic census data but did not adjust the data from 1997 to 2003 in the flow of funds table. So the data we obtained is different from that which the National Bureau of Statistics issued. Foreign capital transfers data after 1997 can be obtained from the international balance of payments. The absolute value of the data is very small, only tens of millions of dollars. But in 2005, the number suddenly changed to $4.1 billion, which relates to the expected appreciation of the RMB exchange rate.

IFNFI of Financial Transaction Accounts

The financial assets included in the financial transaction account[1] are as follows. Currency[2] is the cash in the market, including coins and banknotes. The currency is usually issued by the monetary authorities (People's Bank of China) for circulation. Foreign currency is the cash issued by the nonresident monetary authorities, held by resident units, and used in domestic circulation. Deposits have many forms, such as demand deposits, time deposits, savings deposits of households, financial deposits, foreign exchange deposits, and other deposits. Loans include various forms of loans that financial institutions provide to the nonfinancial sector, such as specific short-term loans, long-term loans, financial loans, foreign exchange loans, and other loans. Securities[3] include bonds and stocks.[4] Bonds include treasury bonds, financial bonds, central bank bonds, and corporate bonds. Insurance reserves refer to life insurance reserves and the pension fund's net interest, insurance advances, and outstanding claims reserves. Settlement funds are the banks' exchange in transit funds. Exchanges among financial institutions include trade, storage, and lending. Reserves include all financial institutions' deposits in the central bank and their statutory reserves. Cash in stock is the cash held by the banking institutions for domestic currency and foreign currency businesses. Central Bank loans are the central bank's loans to financial institutions. The others (net) are the net domestic financial transactions besides the financial transactions mentioned above. Foreign direct investment is foreign direct investment to China and direct investment of China's resident units to other countries. Other external claims and liabilities are all the domestic and foreign debt obligations except reserve assets and foreign exchange deposits. International reserve assets include gold, foreign exchange, Special Drawing Rights, International Monetary Fund reserve positions, and the use of credit funds. The errors and omissions of the international balance of payments are due to incomplete information, differences in statistics, statistical standards, statistics classification, and valuation standards.

The domestic financial sector's NFI actually equals the credit insurance income of financial institutions, adding insurance reserves and deducting the difference between its own funds and the use of funds. Households, nonfinancial enterprises, and the government are the same in the use of funds, which is precisely the source of the funding of financial sectors. Fund uses consist mainly of currency, deposits, equity, bonds held by residents, business insurance reserves, and settlement funds. Fund sources include loans, stocks, bonds, government bonds, enterprises' foreign direct investment,[5] and other external debts. Therefore, the domestic financial account for NFI (NFI_d) is equal to the sum of two terms, one being the sum of the net capital flows of households, nonfinancial enterprises, and government departments (NFI_{heg}) and the other being the balance of payments of credit and financial institutions:

$$NFI_d = NFI_{heg} + NFI_b \qquad [A.2]$$

Net Foreign financial investment (NFI_f) is equal to the international balance of payments' financial accounts balance. With Formulas A.1 and A.2, we can calculate the informal financial sector's NFI (NFI_{no}).

In the course of the calculations, some of the items cancel out with each other, such as the stocks and bonds issued by enterprises, whose investors can only be households or corporate entities, after the merging of households, enterprises, and government departments so that the net value is zero. Because the treasury bond is a fund source for the government and is a fund use for the household, the offsetting balance is the financial institutions' purchase of government bonds. Settlement funds can only be taken directly from the flow data table compiled by the People's Bank for financial institutions. Foreign direct investment and other forms of external debt are taken from the data released by the National Bureau of Statistics data. Foreign investment can only be taken from the international balance of payment statistics. Net errors and omissions are not included in the measure. Because the errors and omissions are included in the unobserved economic and financial scope, they should not be deducted.

Results have shown that there are big differences between the IFNFIs estimated from the financial transaction accounts and those estimated from the physical transaction accounts, although they should be equal in theory. In fact, there also exist disagreements regarding NFIs for physical transactions and financial transactions even in the capital flows table issued by the authority of the State sector. The People's Bank of China uses the additional item "other (net)" in nonfinancial business and the net errors and omission category in the international balance of payments to deal with the problem. The National Bureau of Statistics includes the item "statistical error" to deal with the net investment balance problems between the flow of funds of physical transactions and financial transactions compiled by the People's Bank of China. Statistical errors in fact reflect the difference between financial transactions and physical transactions of the informal economic and financial sector.

Furthermore, which better reflects the capital flow condition of the informal economic sector, the IFNFIs estimated from the financial transaction accounts or those estimated from the physical transaction accounts? We believe that it is the latter. The reason is that physical transactions are measured based on the macroeconomic data of the national accounts measure, which is the result of formal economic activity. GDP, consumption, capital formation, and the statistics of the international balance of payments are based on the data of formal economic transactions The flow of funds of the informal financial sector only reflects the difference between the unobserved domestic balance and the observable international balance, or the unobserved international balance and the observable domestic economy, which is not comprehensive. And in the results measured in financial exchanges, including the errors and omissions of the international balance of payments, is the result of the difference in the increase in domestic financial assets and financial liabilities, and the difference between the capital and financial accounts in international revenue and expenditure. Domestic informal economic income reflected in the increase of financial assets is more accurate than the IFNFIs estimated from the physical transaction accounts. Therefore, when analyzing the impact of the IFNFI on the balance of currency, we use the IFNFIs estimated from the financial transaction accounts.

Measurement of Informal Cross-Border Capital Flows

Cross-border capital flows of the informal financial sector (IFCBCF) are part of capital flight or capital inflow and are also part of the statistical error in the balance of payments. It has potential effects on both balance of payment and money equilibrium. The increase of IFCBCF may lead to a reduction in the domestic money supply, which in turn results in disequilibrium between demand and supply of money in domestic markets. Besides, it makes the determination of key factors of the monetary base implemented by the monetary authority more difficult and offers evidence of uncertainties created by the assault of hot money. The measurement of IFCBCF can provide more comprehensive data support on the analysis of the balance of payments and money equilibrium.

The Theory and Method for Measuring IFCBCF

IFCBCF refers to capital flows formed by economic and financial transactions both at home and abroad and items which are not calculated by the balance of payments statistical system. It has both inflows and outflows, and what we are measuring here are net flows, that is, the final result of flows of IFCBCF, which is the parameter value of the error term in the equilibrium table of the balance of payments. IFCBCF is also the result of capital flows within informal financial sectors—part of IFNFI. Its economic interpretation is to reflect the distribution of capital within different sectors.

The measurement of IFCBCF is built on the basic theoretical proposition that the result of flows of cross-border funds is reflected by changes in foreign financial assets held by inhabitants. The form of overseas foreign assets comprises official international reserves, foreign exchange deposits in the bank system, and foreign currencies in cash. Foreign currencies in cash cannot be disbursed infinitely, so that foreign currencies in circulation have certain quantities and the data cannot now be obtained. Therefore, we suppose that the quantity of foreign currencies in cash is zero in circulation. According to the basic principle used to work out the equilibrium balance of payments table, IFCBCF actually equals the value of the net error term. However, research and studies on the changes in foreign currency deposits both at home and abroad are not comprehensive, which may lead to abnormalities in error terms. With respect to domestic foreign assets, an estimated amount of capital has been included in the errors and omissions term of the balance of payments.

The change in domestic foreign assets (Δ FA) is equal to the change in official international reserves (Δ IR) plus the change in foreign exchange deposits in financial institutions and foreign currencies in cash (Δ FC). We can obtain the change in official international reserves from the balance of payments and international reserves statistics and we can also obtain the change of foreign currency deposits from financial statistical data. The foreign economic transaction record corresponds to changes in overseas foreign assets, is contained in the balance of payment statistics, and is the margin of the autonomous transactions item in the balance of payments (Δ AT). The autonomous transaction item is a monetary value transferred transaction made by economic activity entities on their behalf and its counterpart is an accommodating transaction, that is, the changes in reserves and bank assets corresponding to autonomous transactions. Autonomous transactions comprise the current account, capital account, and the direct investment component, security investment component, and all the items of other investments minus monetary and deposit items of the financial account. So, we get the following formula for the IFCBCF:

$$IFCBCF = \Delta FA - \Delta AT \qquad [A.3]$$

It can be transformed into

$$IFCBCF = \Delta IR + \Delta FC - \Delta AT \qquad [A.4]$$

The Scale of IFCBCF in China, 1982–2005

The financial statistical system in China for foreign asset measurement still needs to be improved. The Chinese government published the data on foreign exchange loans of financial institutions from 2002 and the data of foreign currency deposits can only be obtained from the internal statistical material of the People's Bank of China. However, China has implemented foreign exchange control. Before 1994, foreign exchange income was settled by designated banks, and was then resold to the central bank by those designated banks. Statistical data on official foreign exchange reserves is relatively comprehensive, but other reserve assets such as the reserve position of the International Monetary Fund, SDRS, monetary gold, etc. lack comprehensive direct data, which can be obtained from previous records since 1982. Let's put the basic data into Formula A.20, and we can get the result of IFCBCF.

The results obtained showed that the scale of China's IFCBCF appeared to fluctuate, which is consistent with the characteristics of the index of the net flow of funds. The years with positive values indicate the inflow of capital in those years, while the years with negative values indicate the outflow of funds in those years. After the reform of the exchange rate system and foreign exchange management system in 1994, the main stream of the IFCBCF is outflow. This outflow then turned into an inflow in 2000 and reached a maximum in 2004, which is correlated with the expected appreciation of the RMB; speculative arbitrage funds increased, turning once again into an outflow with the withdrawal of part of the funds again in 2005.

The Measurement of the Scale of IFL

IFL is formed by informal financial activities. It is the informal and underground asset of illegal financial intermediary organizations. It can also exist within some regular financial organizations.

The Theory and Method of Measurement of IFL

IFL serves the regular economy for most of the time. For example, loans obtained from irregular, underground, and illegal financial organizations by small and medium-sized enterprises, individual business households, and peasant households are used for maintenance and production, and a small part of them is used for informal economic production activities. However, some parts of the loans provided by regular financial organizations are used for irregular, underground, and illegal production activities. Which is greater, the scale of loans obtained from informal financial activities and used for regular economic productions or loans obtained from regular financial organizations and used for informal economic productions?

We need ratios on loans to measure the scale of IFL, that is, the ratio of loan balances to the total GDP. To measure the scale of informal loans by informal economic scales,[6] we need the following hypothesis as the premise: the ratio of loans to IFE and GDP is the same, that is, IFL/IFE = L/GDP. According to the hypothesis, we can extrapolate the following measurement formula:

$$IFL = L \bullet IFE/GDP \qquad [A.5]$$

The Scale of IFL in China, 1982–2005

The result of measurement of the scale of IFL shows that the relative scale of IFL and the change in the informal economic factor to GDP are the same. Financial activities are determined by economic activities and the relationship between the unpaid loan balance and the economic scale can reflect the change in IFL. The absolute scale of IFL was relatively smaller from 1982 to 1988 and measured at less than 200 billion Yuan, which indicated that the scale of informal financial organizations and activities were small at that time, but the informal financial activities had certain effects in some areas. Shuxia Jiang (2003) stated that from the fall of 1985 to early 1996, there was an upsurge in *taihui* in Chu Leqing County. Within 1 year, 12 *taihui* were established and the money input amounted to 2.2 billion Yuan. This was just within one county in Zhejiang, so it was not strange that we found that the scale of IFL increased rapidly from 1985 to 1986. The IFL exceeded 200 billion Yuan in 1989, 500 billion Yuan in 1992, 1 trillion yuan in 1995, 2 trillion Yuan in 2002, and 3 trillion Yuan in 2003. The number decreased sharply in 2004, but increased again in 2005 and amounted to 2.85 trillion yuan.

The change of the scale of IFL bears a close relationship to the development of the economy and to the country's macro-regulation and control. As an example, we look at the economic and regulation policies since 1990. The People's Bank of China decided to lower the interest rate in April 1990 in order to overcome the poor economic situation and to mitigate the pressure of employment. It reduced the interest rate twice within the following 2 years and the 1 year deposit interest rate was reduced from 11.34% to 7.56%. This action left room for underground financial organizations to offer deposit services with high interest rates and this also created the opportunity for them to expand their credit. IFL expanded rapidly from 1991 to 1993. In May 1993, the People's Bank of China decided to increase the interest rate in order to control the overheated investment and restrain inflation. It increased the interest rate again in July during the same year and the 1 year deposit interest rate increased from 7.56% to 10.98%. It also controlled credit during the same time. However, fixed asset investment continued to overheat and some individual economic entities continuously expanded, using loans from irregular, underground, and illegal financial organizations. The scale of IFL exceeded 900 billion yuan in 1994. In 1995, the macroeconomic "soft landing" policy became effective so that inflation was controlled within a certain range. In order to prevent recession, the People's Bank of China implemented interest rate reduction policies again in May 1996. By February 2002, it reduced the rate eight times and the 1 year interest rate was reduced from 10.98% to 1.98%. In order to confront the deflation caused by the financial crisis in Asia, interest rate reductions were relatively frequent and large.

IFL expanded rapidly from 1997 to 1998, influenced by the financial crisis in Asia, and most of the credit capital poured into the illegal exchange markets. The topic of RMB depreciation was rather hot. The exchange rate was stationary between 1999 and 2000 and the economy functioned well. There were no obvious fluctuations and the scale of IFL decreased. However, it then expanded again between 2001 and 2003, influenced by China's access to the WTO and the expectation of RMB appreciation.

After the second half of 2002, talk of RMB appreciation appeared and became rather intense in 2003. At the same time, macroeconomic regulation policies were tightened. Regular financial organizations constricted their credit, but goods markets were still active and had high profits. Some economic entities borrowed from informal financial organizations and underground loans on speculative exchange rates were also increased. The sharp decrease of IFL in 2004 was influenced by the constrictive policy implemented by the central bank. In 2005, the scale of IFL increased again, because the formation of the exchange system made the expectation of appreciation even harder. At the same time, the prices of energy, real estate, etc. increased rapidly and also became essential factors in motivating the development of IFL.

The IFCI and MCI

The observable index in the macroeconomic—MCI—has the value of monitoring the informal finance. In practice, the MCI is generally defined as the weighted sum of real interest rates and the exchange rate, which reflects the strictness or looseness of monetary conditions, being an important basis for the monetary administration to coordinate monetary and exchange policies. This section will discuss the workout methods and the value of informal monetary index, and analyze its relationship to the MCI.

Theory of the MCI

The MCI is a macroeconomic concept, and it is the index numerical value which is calculated by a few economic and financial variables possessing a linear combination connection to monetary policies. The MCI generally reflects the monetary changes in value or amount, and the indicators which are involved in MCI always include the short-term interest and exchange index. In small open economic entities, the MCI primarily serves the short-term goals of monetary policy operation (Stevens 1998).

The MCI originates from the total demand determination model under the condition of a small open economy, which includes the real exchange rate and the real interest index. The assumption of the model is that monetary policy has a prominent influence on these invariables, especially in the short run. Therefore, the influential effect of monetary policy on total demand can be calculated using the linear combination connection. Since the MCI is a function of the real exchange rate, all of these factors will affect the MCI, slowing and changing trade conditions in foreign economic activities, but will not influence the interest rate.

The linear combination relationship between total demand and the interest rate and exchange rate should be

$$y = \beta_0 + \beta_1 r + \beta_2 q + \epsilon \qquad [A.6]$$

where y is the logarithm of total demand, r is the real interest in the form of a percentage, q stands for the nature logarithm of the real effective exchange rate, and the exchange rate takes the indirect quotation, in which one unit of domestic currency equals a certain amount of foreign currency. Increases in q show an appreciation of the domestic currency, with 1997 as a base year for the exchange rate equaling 1, ϵ is the residual, which is the effect of all the other variables on total demand. β_1 and β_2 are the flexible index of total demand on the real interest rate and the real exchange rate, respectively; the expected values of β_1, β_2 are negative, $0 \leq \beta_2/\beta_1 \leq 1$. The calculation function of MCI is

$$MCI = r + (\beta_2/\beta_1)q \qquad [A.7]$$

The change in the MCI is meaningful, but the number itself is meaningless, since the change in the MCI reflects the degree of tightness of the currency. It reflects the degree of tightness at the two different points in time. The increase in MCI means that monetary conditions are beginning to tighten, while the decrease in MCI means that monetary conditions are beginning to loosen.

Because the MCI is the linear combination of two variables, there may be some MCIs that equal each other, but these are generated by different interest and exchange rates; therefore, interest and exchange rates may have big changes themselves but have little to no impact on the MCI, whereas in a fixed MCI, especially on the condition that the transformation of monetary policy has a time lag, the differences between interest rates and exchange rates themselves have different outstanding revelations regarding real output and inflation. Now that the expectancy of β_1 and β_2 may have the same expression, the interest rate r and the exchange rate q may move in the opposite directions, while the MCI may not or may barely change.

Since the real interest rate and exchange rate demands are usually calculated in frequencies not less than one month, if one calculates the MCI more frequently than one month, the MCI is meaningless. In practice, the calculation of MCI usually uses nominal interest rates and nominal exchange rates, as this data is immediately obtainable.

The Measurement of China's MCI

Description of Date Sources

The date of the real loan interest rate comes from the 1 year benchmark interest rate which is declared by the People's Bank of China. The years 1991–2005 use a benchmark interest rate, while the years 1978–1990 have no standard benchmark loan interest rate. Therefore, we take the rate that banks use in providing loans to industry and business as the standard, and in fact these two loan interest rates are the same. Industry and commercial loans are short-term, but fixed asset investment loans are long-term. When the influence of inflation is removed from the nominal interest rate, we obtain the real interest rate, r. The inflation is measured by CPI.

The nominal valid exchange rate must be calculated by weighted sum of the nominal rates adjusted by using the trade exchange rate and trade amount between China and all of its trading partners. Because of the difficulty of getting the data, it is impossible to search out all the data of the 1980s. Another method is to incorporate the total amount of exports and imports from customs, using the total trade amount in RMB divided by the trade amount in dollars, getting an average valid exchange rate. Using the CPI index for America and China, we transformed the nominal valid exchange rate into the real exchange rate. To calculate the MCI, we use the common logarithm of the exchange rate under the indirect exchange rate quote, so we need to change the RMB real valid exchange rate into the indirect quote exchange rate. Taking 1977 as the base year, we convert the nominal exchange rate into the real valid exchange rate and design the real valid exchange rate index; then, taking the log of real exchange rate index, we finally get q from Function A.1.

Refer to Formula A.6 to calculate the elasticity coefficients, β_1 and β_2, of total demand of the real interest and exchange rates. We take the real GDP growth rate instead of the logarithm of real GDP to show the change in the total demand, so we get

$$\beta_1 = -0.110956, \quad \beta_2 = -0.085373, \quad \beta_2/\beta_1 = 0.7694$$

The Results of MCI

When the financial administration bureau of Hong Kong calculates the MCI, it uses the real exchange rate index which adapts the logarithm of the real valid exchange rate, Δreer. To compare the different conclusions, using Formula A.7 to calculate MCI_1, we still take the real valid exchange rate to substitute the logarithm of real valid exchange rate to calculate MCI_2. We also assume that, for the real interest rate and real exchange rate β_1 and β_2, using different simulation calculation methods and using the data from different periods, we will get different results. In fact, the sum of β_1 and β_2 should be 1, and the flexible index of total demand on the exchange rate is connected to the degree of the openness, especially the degree of trade openness (the total amount of exports and imports/GDP). Therefore, we take the yearly post-reform data as the flexible index of total demand on the exchange rate, while one minus the degree of openness will be taken as the flexible index of total demand on the interest rate, adapting the logarithm of the real valid exchange

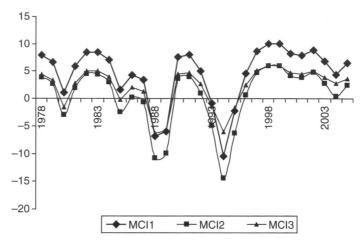

Figure A.1 China's MCI.

rate, to calculate MCI₃. The moving trend of the three MCIs can be seen in Figure A.1.

From Figure A.1 we can see that the three MCIs are quite close to each other. According to MCI theory, the bigger the index number is, the tighter the monetary condition will be, while the converse is also true. When the monetary condition is tight, the Central Bank usually implements a loose monetary policy, and when the monetary condition is loose, the Central Bank usually implements a tight monetary policy. In the overheated economic years of 1985, 1988, and 1994, the money supply was loose, and in the years of the recessionary economy, 1990–1991 and 1998–1999, the money supply was tightened.

Broad Statistic Caliber MCI

Broad statistic caliber MCI is based on the real interest rate and the real exchange rate and is calculated by adding other monetary movement variables. Some experts suggest, in addition to using the interest rate and exchange rate, the money—supply rate of increase be taken (Bo and Zhou 2004), with the assumption that the amount of money supply can reflect the change in monetary policy; others suggest the rate of loan increase be taken, with the assumption that monetary policy is mainly completed by credit loans (Peng and Liang 2005). Choosing the rate of increase in loan balances of financial institutions is more suitable, since the data is of better quality. Monetary policy regulators take seriously the industrial and commercial loans, under the assumption that regulating loans can directly and indirectly influence broad money supply M2. The loan index (L) follows monetary policy, whereas the money supply has a time lag in following monetary policy. The formula of broad statistic caliber MCI is

$$MCI_w = r + (\beta_2/\beta_1)\Delta reer + (\beta_3/\beta_1)L \qquad [A.8]$$

Total demand changes in the direction opposite to the appreciation and depreciation of the real interest rate and real exchange rate, but changes in the same direction as credit loan increases. Applying the linear connection between the total demand increase and the interest rate and exchange rate and calculating to get the flexible index of total demand on each variable, we have

$$\beta_1 = -0.118592, \ \beta_2 = -0.084261, \ \beta_3 = 0.034589, \ \beta_2/\beta_1$$
$$= 0.7105, \ \beta_3/\beta_1 = -0.2917$$

Applying Formula A.8 and using the same basic data as the MCI, we are able to see the two broad MCIs (MCIW) with different statistical calibers (see Figure A.2).

We can see that, due to the increase and instability in the credit amount, the center of broad MCI is lower than that of the MCI, but the monetary policies reflected are the same. The broad statistic caliber MCI better explains the degree of monetary policy tightness.

The Design of the Informal Financial Conditions Index (IFCI)

If we can compile the IFCI by using FCI to reflect the informal financial conditions, we will be able to build a relationship between IFCI and MCI as well as between IFCI and Economic Movement Alert Index (EMAI), which is used to determine the extent of the interference of informal finance in monetary and economic movements quantitatively.

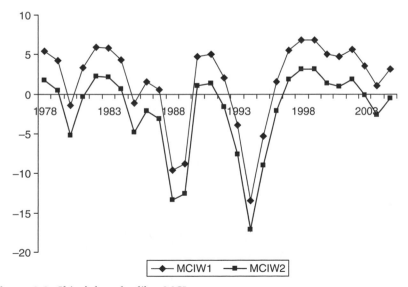

Figure A.2 China's broad caliber MCI.

IFCI and Variable Selection

IFCI should be a weighted index that includes the civil lending rate, the shadow exchange rate, and the size of informal credit to reflect the scale of informal finance.

Based on the method of compiling the FCI, the variable IFCI should combine the two basic monetary price elements of the interest rate and the exchange rate, which here must reflect the informal lending and borrowing rate, as well as the black market rate. The national interest rate data since reform in 1978 is not available. Although some regional data could be obtained, it is not continuous.

Looked at from the aspect of black market data, the RMB exchange rate has been the unique official exchange rate since reform began. The regulating exchange rate began in 1986, and the exchange rate in the black market of foreign currency was often higher by 20% to 50% than the regulating exchange rate. After 1994, as a result of the overall reform in the Foreign Exchange Control System and in the exchange rate mechanism, a market supply and demand-based, single, and managed floating exchange rate mechanism was formed and foreign exchange rate control turned to be loose, which made the black market for foreign exchange gradually lose its foundation and disappear in most cities.

We cannot find an informal interest rate and a black market exchange rate for calculating the IFCI, so we have to look for incorporate substitute variables.

The substitute variable for the interest rate is the Proportion of IFNFI to Equilibrium GDP (IFNFI/EGDP). IFNFI is the net allocation of funds between the informal economic and financial sector and the formal economic sector. The net outflow is expressed by a positive number, while the net inflow is expressed by a negative number. The net money position between the two sectors actually reflects the difference in interest rates between the two sectors. The amount of money to be allocated depends on the GDP size. IFNFI/EGDP shows the attraction of the interest rate difference to the funds. A positive and increasing value means the real rate in the formal sector is rising while the informal rate is falling; a negative and decreasing value means the rate in the informal sector is higher than the real rate in the formal sector, and money in informal sector is in short supply. Since a positive MCI indicates a tightening while a negative one indicates loosening, IFNFI/EGDP multiplied by -1 can be used as a substitute variable to reflect the extent of monetary conditions in the informal economic and financial sector.

A substitute variable for the exchange rate is the Proportion of Informal Cross-Border Flow to Equilibrium GDP (IFCBCF/TB). Since IFCBCF depends on the overvaluation of the exchange rate, under the imbalance in the exchange rate the speculative funds will flow over the border in both directions through shady channels. Generally speaking, the funds flow out when the exchange rate is overvalued and under devaluation pressure; capital flows in when there is an undervalued exchange rate and the domestic currency faces the pressure of appreciation. A positive IFCBCF indicates a depreciation of the shadow exchange rate and an unobserved loosening of the exchange rate; when the IFCBCF is negative, it shows a shadow exchange rate appreciation and a tightening of the informal exchange rate. Thus, IFCBCF/TB multiplied by -1 can reflect the extent of monetary conditions for the informal economic and financial sector from the angle of the exchange rate. A negative value represents a loosening monetary status and a positive value represents a tightening monetary status.

The Measurement of the IFCI

IFCI reflects the monetary tightness of the informal sector. A positive and a bigger index indicates a tightening monetary situation in the informal sector and the need to absorb monetary funds or financial resources from the formal sector; a negative value of bigger absolute value indicates a loose monetary and financial situation in the informal sectors, so that there is a need to release monetary or financial resources to the formal sector.

The informal sector's monetary and financial situation has a direct impact on the scale of the informal economic factor. The variables in IFCI are IFN-FIEGDP (the proportion of IFNFI to equilibrium GDP) and IFCBCFTB (the proportion of Informal Cross-Border Flow to equilibrium GDP). They have a linear relationship with the real informal economic factor (RIFE). That is

$$\ln \text{RIFE} = \beta_0 + \beta_1 \cdot \text{IFNFIEGDP} + \beta_2 \cdot \text{IFCBCFTB} + \epsilon \qquad [\text{A.9}]$$

Using the data from 1982 to 2005, we obtain the following:

$$\beta_1 = -0.013291, \ \beta_2 = -0.025616, \ \beta_2/\beta_1 = 1.9272$$

The results of β_1 and β_1 show that the informal economic factor is more sensitive to IFCBCFTB. The formula of IFCI is

$$\text{IFCI} = \text{IFNFIEGDP} + (\beta_2/\beta_1)\text{IFCBCFTB or:} \qquad [\text{A.10}]$$

$$\text{IFCI} = (\beta_1/\beta_2)\text{IFNFIEGDP} + \text{IFCBCFTB} \qquad [\text{A.11}]$$

The absolute value of results from Formulas A.10 and A.11 may differ slightly. However, the trends reflected are the same. Now we use Formulas A.10 and A.11 to obtain the respective IFCI and put them on Figure A.3.

From the changes in the index, we see that the informal monetary and financial situation was more lenient in the years 1985–1986, 1989, 1991–1994, 2000–2004 and relatively tight in the years 1982–1984, 1987, 1990, 1995–1999, and 2005.

Informal Monetary Conditions Index in the Wider Sense (IFCIW)

IFCIW will bring the informal credit or informal monetary index into IFCI. Calculating the informal credit or informal monetary index as one element is difficult, since the informal credit or informal monetary index is based on the

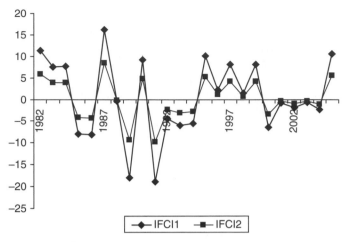

Figure A.3 IFCI in China.

informal economic scale. There exists a high degree of correlation between the two variables and the informal economic factor, and the elasticity is quite high. If both lnRIFL and lnRIFM$_2$ are included in the demand determination model of the informal sector, one can draw the following conclusion: that elasticity of IFNFIEGDP and IFCBCFTB is too small, while the elasticity of lnRIFL and lnRIFM$_2$ is too high, which makes IFCIW too high to observe and analyze. So we use the elasticity of the real informal economic factor to informal credit or informal money, converting the two to logarithmic form and putting them in IFCI. Since informal credit, informal money, and

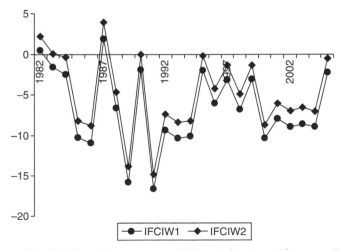

Figure A.4 China's informal monetary conditions index in a wider sense (IFCI$_W$).

informal economic factor change in the same direction while IFNFIEGDP and IFCBCFTB move in the direction opposite to the informal economic factor, we obtain the IFCIW as the following:

$$IFCIW = IFCI - \beta_C \cdot \ln RIFL \text{ or:} \qquad [A.12]$$

$$IFCIW = IFCI - \beta_M \cdot \ln RIFM_2 \qquad [A.13]$$

Using the data from 1982 to 2005, we obtain the following results: $\beta_C = 0.9045$ and $\beta_M = 0.6608$. Bringing the factors of informal credit and informal money factor into IFCI$_2$, the two groups of IFCIW can be obtained and the trend is seen in Figure A.4.

Compared to the IFCI, the center of gravity has moved downward, but the change tendency basically remains the same.

The Relation between the IFCI and the MCI

The MCI reflects the degree of money tightness or looseness at different points in time, which is influenced by monetary policy. The degree of money tightness or looseness is decided by many factors, including the condition money circulation during the period, economic expectations, and so on. Informal financial activity changes the track of money to a certain extent, so it should be considered as a factor that affects the money currency, although it is usually neglected. What relationship is there between the IFCI and the MCI, and can we calculate the degree of influence that the IFCI has on the MCI using a linear relationship?

The IFCI and the MCI

The IFCI's calculation method is as same as that of the MCI, and the two indices' economic attributes are also the same. The former reflects the degree of tightness or looseness of the overall money supply, and the latter reflects the degree of tightness or looseness of the informal financial money supply. When the index is bigger, the informal financial money supply is tighter, while if the index is smaller, the money supply is looser.

We look to find out whether changes in the Informal Financial Conditions cause movements in the MCI. To analyze from a theoretical angle, Informal Financial activity divides or configures society's money and financial resources, which influences the movement of currency, so it should be one cause of movements in the MCI. We next analyze using data. Using the Granger Causality Test method on the IFCI and the MCI from 1982 to 2005 in different calibrations, we find that the probability that the three groups of the Monetary Conditions Indices are not the reason for the IFCI's movement is above 99% and 82%, but the probability that the two groups of the IFCI are not the reason for the MCI's movement is only 44% and 27%. The IFCI has influenced the MCI although the influence is not very remarkable.

Now that we have found that the IFCI is one reason for the MCI's movement, we can create a linear relationship between the MCI and the IFCI:

$$MCI = \beta_0 + \beta_1 \cdot MCI \ (-1) + \beta_2 \cdot IFCI \qquad [A.14]$$

MCI (-1) is the MCI of the last period, β_0 is the constant term, β_1 is the coefficient of the MCI of the last period, and β_2 is the coefficient of the IFCI.

The currents reflected from the six results are basically consistent. The coefficient of determination (adjusted R^2) of the model is not high, about 0.37, but the collective significance of the model (F test value) is comparably high. Among the variable coefficients of the model there is one constant term in two combinations (IFCI$_1$, MCI$_2$ and IFCI$_2$, MCI$_2$) that seems comparably low, while the significance of β_1 is the highest. The test value of the coefficient of the IFCI, β_2, is 1.86, which is close to 2, so it has certain significance. The flexibility coefficient of the MCI to the IFCI is 0.13, 0.20, 0.25, and 0.38. Estimated according to the integer significance of the model, the long-term flexibility relations 0.20 and 0.38 are more believable, which indicate that the Informal Financial Department Conditions Index has a certain influence on the MCI.

The IFCI and the MCI of Wide Aperture

The calculation method of the wide aperture IFCI is the same as that of the wide aperture MCI, and their economic attribute is consistent. The influence of the informal financial sector on monetary conditions can be reflected according to the flexibility relations of the two indices. To see whether there is a linear relationship between the two, we first carry out a causal relation test on the time series data of the two indexes.

The causal relation tests show that the possibility that the wide aperture MCI is not a reason for the state of the wide aperture IFCI is about 88%, while the possibility that wide aperture IFCI is not a reason for the state of the wide aperture MCI is only 43%–45%. The causal relation between the data sets is not so marked, but it can also explain some degree of influence that the informal financial conditions has on monetary conditions. So we use a linear relationship model of the wide aperture IFCI and the wide aperture MCI as follows:

$$MCIW = \beta_0 + \beta_1 \cdot MCIW \ (-1) + \beta_2 \cdot IFCIW \qquad [A.15]$$

MCIW (-1) is the wide aperture MCI of the last period, β_0 is a constant term, β_1 is the coefficient of the wide aperture MCI of last period, and β_2 is the coefficient of the wide aperture Informal Financial Department Conditions Index. Substituting the wide aperture Informal Financial Department Conditions Index and the wide aperture MCI with a different calculation method into Formula A.15, we obtain a model of different explanatory variables.

The collective significance of the four explanatory variables with the explained variable combination model is comparably high. The coefficient of determination (adjusted R^2) of the model is about 0.35, not so great. The value of the constant term is not so high. The flexibility coefficient of the wide aperture MCI to the wide aperture IFCI is about 0.36; t value is 1.7, which is substantial. The results of the four models show that when the Informal Financial Conditions influence the MCI the two indices change in the same direction. When the IFCI increases, the real interest rate will rise, and it will divide the more financial resources from the public economy, and promote an increase in the public economy's real interest rate. When the IFCI decreases, the real interest rate will drop, and the financial resources will be released to the public economy, and then it will become one of the forces that push the real interest rate down.

The Policy Significance of the IFCI

The IFCI has reflected the degree of looseness and tightness of the informal finance currency condition comparatively well. If we can calculate the IFCI continuously, we can monitor the informal financial movement conditions intuitively as well as grasp their influence on the overall currency movements in the public economy. This would have a significant impact on looking at monetary policy.

First, the fact that the IFCI and the MCI change in the same direction may provide the foundational reference to regulate the informal interest rate policy. The interest rate substitution variable in the IFCI is the proportion of the IFNFI to the Equilibrium GDP (IFNFI/EGDP). When the index is increasing, and the interest rate substitution variable's function is bigger than the exchange rate substitution variable, this means the net amount of money is oversized in the informal financial department, and also means the real interest rate in the informal financial department is higher than that in the public economy. Otherwise, when the index decreases, this means that the net money current is effused in the informal financial department and the real interest rate will decrease, while the currency tends to be loose. In periods of prosperity, inflationary pressure is enhanced, and the Central Bank will increase the interest rate, leading to increases in the real interest rate, reductions in cash currency, and reductions in the foundational money supply, which suppresses the influence of informal financial activities. Certainly, in periods of economic stagnancy, through reductions in the interest rate, the informal financial department's real interest rate will drop as well. It will be beneficial for informal finance to support the production and management activities associated with small informal economic activity in order to promote economic resurgence.

The IFCI is also significant for exchange rate policy implementation. Floating capital within the informal financial sector is related to the degree of deviation in the exchange rate. In the IFCI, the exchange rate substitution variable—the proportion of the IFCBCF to the total amount of trade—is comparatively higher than the proportion of the interest rate substitution variable. When the IFCI increases and the exchange rate substitution variable is greater than the interest rate substitution variable, the informal interstate floating capital outflow is high and prompts exchange rate policy to control capital flight and to reduce depreciation expectations, eliminating the overestimation of the exchange rate. When the informal currency condition index decreases, the informal interstate floating capital inflow is high, the exchange rate revaluation pressure is quite great, the ratio of domestic currency to foreign currency is obviously underestimated, the Central Bank should adopt a policy to eliminate the exchange rate depreciation, and the exchange rate will surely be close to the actual effective equilibrium exchange rate level.

In terms of credit policy, the wide aperture IFCI may be used as a reference for policy makers. When the wide aperture informal financial department condition index decreases, informal credit is active, and the loan supplies are abundant, so that the Central Bank faces a situation in which the informal credit substitutes, to some degree, formal financial institutions, so that the effect of macroeconomic control is counteracted. When the Central Bank tightens the money supply to control bank loans, most borrowers switch to borrowing loans from informal financial institutions. So the total loan scale of enterprises does not go down and the credit policy effect is not obvious. At that time, the Central Bank also needs to use the interest rate method and exchange rate method to adjust and increase the financial condition index. In times of economic stagnancy, in which the credit growth of formal financial institutions is weak, the Central Bank would use the interest rate method to stimulate informal credit.

The IFCI and the Economic Movement Index

As a reflection of the overall state of economic movements, the national EMAI can show the "hot and cold" state of the economic cycle. The MCI of the Informal financial sector is an indicator of financial tightness in the informal sector. Therefore, the relationship between the MCI of the informal financial sector and the national EMAI is the link that reflects the extent of disturbance in the informal financial sector due to national economic movements. This section will explain, using quantitative methods, the relationship between the MCI of the informal financial sector and the EMAI, estimating the extent of disturbance of informal finance to economic movements through compiling the annual national EMAI.

National EMAI

Description of the EMAI Compilation

The two respective compilation systems for the national economy alert index prepared by China's Economic Information Center and the National Bureau of Statistics include 10 most important economic operation indicators within a unified alert index using a weighted average method. Within the two index systems, 9 out of 10 indicators are exactly the same, and the names of the indices and their weights are as follows: industrial production index, 1.2; the completion of fixed asset investment, 1; retail sales of consumer goods, 1.2; total imports and exports of foreign trade, 0.8; financial income, 0.8; total profit of industrial enterprises, 1; disposable income per capita of urban residents, 1.2; loans of financial institutions, 0.8; and consumer price index, 1.2. For the 10th indicator, China's Economic Information Centre uses commercial housing sales, while the National Bureau of Statistics uses broad money M2, with the same weight for each of 0.8. Since the index of real estate has been compiled since 1998, but we can design the EMAI since 1978, we adopt the system of the National Bureau of Statistics, using broad money M2 rather than real estate sales. We now explain those indicators for which complete data is difficult to access.

The index of industrial production is one of the indicators reflecting the pace of development of industrial production. The National Bureau of Statistics decided to compile a trial industrial production index from 1997 onward. The index of industrial production shows the comprehensive pace of development based on a weighted composite of the output of a variety of products. According to state regulations, there are about 1000 kinds of annual representative products, and about 500 monthly products. The weights are the indicators defining the importance of the individual products in the process of the formation of the production index. The higher the proportion of product or industry to the industrial total, the heavier the weight, and the higher the impact to the production index. Whether the selected weight is right or not has a direct impact on the accuracy of the index.

The existing index of industrial production compiled by the departments of authority can be traced back to 1990. Although there is a base year difference across the indices of different departments, the index, formed by taking the year before as 100, can be easily converted into a unified standard index. The index of the period 1981–1989 uses the total value of industrial production as a replacement index. The data declared by China to the United

Nations, before the compilation of the industrial production index, is directly the total value of industrial production instead.

Total profits of industrial enterprises are also an index that needs to be explained. The National Bureau of Statistics started to announce economic indicators of state-owned enterprises and non-state-owned ones above the scale from 1999 onward, while the index released before is the financial indicator of independent accounting industrial enterprises, which has an item of total profits. Since state-owned enterprises account for the principal part of the economy before 1994, the use of total profits of state-owned industrial enterprises is fine. The indicators used should be converted into the growth rate. Hence, the index of the profit growth of industrial enterprises before 1995 is the indicator of profit growth of independent accounting state-owned industrial enterprises. Starting from 1996, based on a total profit of independent accounting industrial enterprises in 1995, the corresponding profit growth is worked out.

Other indicators of the data, which can be obtained through public channels, will no longer be mentioned here.

The EMAI for 1982–2005

The annual alert index from 1982 to 2005 is obtained through the use of weighted data on national EMAI. As for the demarcation standards of the index reflecting the borders of economic cycles, China's Economic Information Center is based on the following criteria: an index greater than 41 is defined as "overheating," more than 35 but less than or equal to 41 as "approaching overheating," more than 25 and less than or equal to 35 as "stable," more than 19 but less than or equal to 25 as "approaching a cool down," and less than or equal to 19 as "a supercool down." Elicited from experienced judgment, this standard is suitable to the judgment of the monthly index. Some problems may occur, however, if the standard is used for the judgment of China's economy during 1982–2005; China's economy does not show any year of "approaching a cool down," not even to mention the "supercool down." Moreover, the period of "overheating" appeared to occur over 9 years, which was not in line with economic reality and, therefore, the criteria need to be adjusted somewhat. If the index average value 39.55 during 1982–2005 (equivalent to about 40) is taken as a standard upper limit of stability, the original standards are all increased by five points, with the overheating standard as 46, approaching overheating standard 40, stability standard 30, approaching a cool down standard 24, and then the criteria based on such judgments will be in line with the actual Chinese economic performance.

Figure A.5 shows the alert index of the national economy. It better reflects economic cycles, except for the economic "overheating" in 1988 by the original standards but economic "approaching overheating" by the new

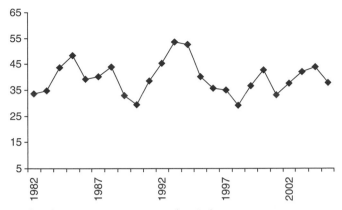

Figure A.5 China's economic movement alert index.

ones, which are slightly inconsistent with the reality of the economic movement. Other years are all able to illustrate the economic cycle characteristics. According to the new standards, the reflected economic cycle characteristics are more in line with the actual situation. Based on the new standards, the years of economic overheating are 1985, 1993–1994; the years of economic approaching overheating are 1984, 1987–1988, 1992, 1995, 2000, 2003–2004; the years of economic approaching a cool down are only 1990 and 1998; the remaining years are a time of economic stability.

The Relationship between MCI and EMAI

The MCI is compiled based on two major factors of currency prices: real interest rates and actual exchange rates, reflecting the degree of tightness of monetary conditions. From the perspective of economic theory, when real interest rates and actual exchange rates rise, both investment and exports will likely decline to different extents, and overall demand will then be restrained, while the economic growth rate may drop. When economic growth rate declines, alert index reflecting the "hot and cold" degree of economic movements may also drop. When real interest rates and actual exchange rates decrease, total demand will expand, economic growth will speed up, and the EMAI may rise. Therefore, the relationship between the MCI and EMAI should show changes in the opposite direction. The financial impact on economic movements can be observed through the inspection of changes in the elastic coefficients of EMAI to the index of monetary conditions. From test results of the correlation between the two types of indices, the correlation coefficients of the EMAI and the three groups of monetary conditions indices are −0.54, −0.54, and −0.50, respectively. Although the data itself does not show a high degree of correlation, the negative correlation indicates the existence of reverse relations between the two types of indices. Therefore, we establish in the following model characterizing the relationship between EMAI and MCI:

$$\text{EMAI} = \beta_0 + \beta_1 \cdot \text{MCI} \qquad [\text{A.16}]$$

Substituting the sequence data of different MCI into Formula A.16, fitting results can be obtained. Three fitting results show that the constant and the elasticity coefficient of MCI are relatively significant; the t-test values are all greater than 2; the F-test value of the overall model is also relatively significant; and only the coefficient of determination, the adjusted R2, is not high. But the model can explain the equilibrium relationship between MCI and EMAI. In comparison, the first two results are more accurate than the third one. It should be said that the regulation effect of monetary policy on the economy is relatively strong. When MCI changes by one unit, EMAI will change by about 0.6 in the opposite direction.

The Relationship between IFCI and EMAI

Since there exists a linear correlation between the MCI of the informal financial sector and the MCI, the problem of multicollinearity could appear if the both indices are included in the model for the economic movement index. The test results of correlation and causality prove that the MCI of the informal financial sector is not the main explanatory variable for the EMAI. It is therefore impractical to establish a univariate model of the economic movement index including only the MCI of the informal financial sector, and the data does not support the linear relationship between the two indices. As there are many determinant factors for the economic movement index, in order not to omit the other influential factors and to intuitively judge the impact of informal financial factors, we add a comprehensive variable to the model. The comprehensive variable is expressed as Other Factors Effects (OFE) The sequence data of the comprehensive variable is either 0 or 1, and rules of the choice of 0 and 1 are the following: the year is denoted as 1 if the EMAI is higher than the average value of 39.55 over the period of 1982–2005, and 0 if it is lower than the average value of 39.55. Thus, we have established the following model of the relationship between EMAI and informal monetary conditions index (IFCI):

$$\text{EMAI} = \beta_0 + \beta_1 \cdot \text{OFE} + \beta_2 \cdot \text{IFCI} \qquad [\text{A.17}]$$

Substituting the sequence data of IFCI and OFE variables obtained using the two different estimation methods into the above model, the fitting results can be achieved: compared with the results of Model A.14, the two results of Model A.17 have a higher degree of confidence; the model variables can easily pass through t-test; the elasticity coefficient is very significant; the model overall significant F-test is also very high; and the adjusted coefficient of determinant R2 is 0.688, however. The fitting results of Model A.17 show that changes in the IFCI promote the reverse changes of EMAI. A unit change in the IFCI may lead to about 0.17–0.34 points of changes of EMAI in the opposite direction.

―――

The Relationship between MCIW and EMAI

As with Model A.14, replacing MCI by MCIW, we can obtain a model of EMAI and IFCIW:

$$EMAI = \beta_0 + \beta_1 \cdot MCIW \qquad [A.18]$$

We can obtain the fitting results of Model A.18. The difference between the two results is relatively small; the constant and the coefficient of broad caliber MCI can all pass the t-test, and the variable is statistically significant. The F-test value regarding the model's overall significance is also high, but the model's adjusted coefficient of determinant $\bar{R}^2$ is relatively low. One unit change of MCIW may lead to about 0.62 points of reverse changes in the economic movement conditions index. By adding the variable credit, the impact of broad caliber MCI on EMAI has increased, comparable to MCI without the variable credit, but not significantly.

This means that EMAI has a certain policy impact on the elasticity changes of broad caliber MCI, that is, the changes of policy variables like interest rates, exchange rates, and so on have much stronger economic effects than those generated by credit scale changes. This is because the scope of the credit policy effects is smaller than that of interest rates or exchange rates policy effects. The changes of interest rates or exchange rates can affect not only the actual changes in economic variables directly, but also economic entities psychologically, being able to adjust the expectations and behavior of economic entities.

―――

The Relationship between IFCIW and EMAI

In order to avoid multicollinearity among the variables included in the regression model, broad caliber informal MCI and broad caliber MCI can not appear in the determinative model for EMAI at the same time. Other factors are taken into the model as a comprehensive unified variable called OFE. Therefore, we get the model of EMAI and IFCIW as follows:

$$EMAI = \beta_0 + \beta_1 \cdot OFE + \beta_2 \cdot IFCIW \qquad [A.19]$$

We can obtain the fitting results of Model A.19. Compared with Model A.18, the fitting results of Model A.19 are statistically more significant. Both constant and variable coefficients are able to pass the t-test; the overall F-test of the model is also relatively significant; the coefficient of determination-adjusted R2 reaches 0.688. The two fitting results showed that the elasticity coefficients of EMAI to broad caliber informal MCI are both −0.334, indicating that the impact of informal MCI on economic movements cannot be ignored. Every single unit change of IFCIW will lead to about 0.334 points of change in EMAI in the opposite direction.

The elastic relationship between the MCI of the informal financial sector and EMAI indicates that if 1 is taken as a standard of comparison (the most influenced), then the disturbance of informal financial activities to national economic movements will be around 0.33, having an obvious influence. If the central bank's monetary policies take the impact of informal financial activities into account, the policies will be significantly enhanced.

Notes

1. According to the tabulated flow of funds compiled by the People's Bank of China, some data of financial transactions cannot be assembled, such as equity, commercial credit, and certain projects receivable and payable.
2. The amount of RMB in circulation abroad and foreign currency in domestic circulation are still not countable for the moment.
3. The current statistics of the People's Bank of China do not include equity rights and the amount of shares issued but cannot be transacted in stock exchange transactions.
4. The current statistics of the People's Bank of China contain only the amount of shares issued and transacted in stock exchange transactions.
5. The difference between foreign direct investment (FDI) and direct investment abroad from home enterprises.
6. Cf. the measurement methods: Li Jianjun (2005), 62–66.

References

Bo, Yongxiang and Qing Zhou. 2004. China's monetary conditions index and its use in the monetary policy. *Journal of Financial Research* 1: 30–42.
Jiang, Shuxia. 2003. *China's Informal Credit.* Beijing: Chinese Financial and Economic Publisher.
Li Jianjun. 2005. *Study of the Scale of China's Underground Finance and Macroeconomic Impacts.* Beijing: China's Financial Publisher.
Peng, Wensheng and Weiyao Liang. 2005. The mainland of China's monetary conditions index. *Quarterly Bulletin of Hong Kong Monetary Authority* 6: 5–14.
Stevens, Glenn. 1998. Pitfalls in the use of monetary conditions indexes. *Reserve Bank of Australia Bulletin* August: 34–43.

Appendix B: The Story of an Entrepreneur's Financing Experience in Shanxi

Guangning Tian

This story reveals the difficulties of entrepreneurial financing in China and shows why entrepreneurs depend on informal financing. This is a real story that came out of this author's fieldwork on informal finance in Shanxi in 2005. In this story, there are two individuals named Zaixing Zhang and Junsheng Liu, who are individual entrepreneurs in different businesses. But both had the same experience when their businesses turned from prosperity to financial difficulty.

Deng Xiaoping, when he was in his southern tour in Shenzhen in the spring of 1992, used the following words to describe the role of finance: "Finance is very important; it is the core of modern economy. If finance goes well, the economy can go well."[1] It is also the core of the rural economy. The rural financial system plays an important role in the development of agriculture and rural areas and in improving peasants' income.

In the summer of 2004, Zaixing Zhang's eldest daughter from Zhucheng village was admitted into Hainan University as an eleventh grader. The whole family was very happy, but Zhang was not entirely happy. Tuition and other fees put together added up to 7000 yuan, which was more than his income for a whole year. The transportation to Haikou, the capital of Hainan province, was also very expensive. The girl also needed some new clothes and other necessities. Combining the cash and the deposits, the family only had a little more than 2300 yuan. The term was to begin in 40 days, and so Zhang wondered how he could possibly make so much money.

Just past four o'clock in the morning, Zaixing Zhang awakened, but he still did not want to get up. However, thinking about her daughter's tuition, he jolted awake. Hastily putting his bicycle and two big baskets in order, he ate a cucumber and hurried to get onto his bicycle. He would ride two hours to go to an orchard to buy peaches and then would take them to villages to sell. Selling peaches, he could earn 0.2 yuan every half kilometer. If the peaches tasted good, he could earn 0.3 yuan, and they would easily be sold out. Two big baskets of peaches would be sold out before 5 or 6 p.m. Zhang could earn 30 yuan in one day. But he had to go to the far orchard to obtain the best-tasting peaches, so that customers would buy his peaches again and again. For this, he had to leave at four o'clock in the morning and pedal his bicycle all day. Although it involved a lot of hard work, the income was good. During the midseason that lasted only for a short time in the summer and autumn the fruits came to market. He had to take advantage of it and earn a little more.

Zhang began his fruit business last year because he had no other choice. Before this, he had tried, among other things, repairing motorcycles, collecting scraps, and selling sesame cakes. But he did not succeed in any of these. He had also been a driver, driving a truck and a reaping machine; however, now the truck was sold and the reaping machine was useless. His future was unpredictable. A few years before, he was a famous person in the village since from the end of the 1980s to the beginning of 1990s transporting coal was a profitable business. But it is a dirty, tired, and dangerous job. Zaixing Zhang's family did not want him to buy a truck, for even a second-hand one was too expensive. Regardless of their objection, Zaixing Zhang borrowed a loan from the rural credit association. And this second-hand truck changed his life completely in a few years.

During the initial years of his transportation business, he was very young and vigorous, so he worked very hard. Within 5 years, he paid off the entire loan of 70,000 yuan. The living standard of his family improved. His daughter and son were born in succession. Villagers saw his success and some people followed in his footsteps. Several villagers also began to transport coal. They traveled with each other, and the work became easy but less profitable due to competition. With help from his army friend, he joined a new coal mine. After 4 or 5 years he had saved more than 100,000 yuan, but he did not want to continue this line of work. This business was no longer very profitable. Because of his hard work, he usually would not have meals on time, so he came down with a stomach illness. However, he wanted to seek a new line of business to make money.

At that time he was one among the richest people in his village and hoped to build a house. Building or buying a house is the major event in a rural person's life. It symbolizes the wealth of a household and can influence the marriage prospect of one's children. His wife was very sensitive about their reputation and had been hoping to build a new house for a long time. Zaixing Zhang had calculated that to build a very good house, he would need

40,000 yuan. This meant that he would still have 600,000–700,000 yuan left, so he decided to lend Sanbao Yang, his neighbor, 500,000–600,000 yuan to buy a joint reaping machine. Both he and Sanbao Yang felt that this machine could make money for them. But Zaixing Zhang and his wife had a big difference of opinion on how to build the house. His wife wanted to build a house like the one she had seen on a TV show, which would require at least 800,000 yuan.

Zhang's wife was sensitive about the family's reputation and the birth of their third child led Zhang to make a concession. He spent a large amount of money to build a top grade house. In 1 year, the new house was built, with wide corridors and wall lamps in every room and ceramic tile on all walls, and it also had all kinds of fashionable electrical equipment. It was exquisitely furnished. The house being the admiration of the neighborhood, the middle-aged couple felt very satisfied. However, in order to build this house Zaixing Zhang had to borrow 30,000 yuan from the credit association, for 60,000 yuan was all what he had previously estimated for house construction. The excessive expenditure of the new house and the fines for the third child, for violating the population control policy, cost Zhang all his savings.

When buying the joint reaping machine with Sanbao Yang, Zhang spent 130,000 yuan, including a 60,000 yuan loan. Then he borrowed another 70,000 yuan for the new house and for the fines for the third child. He left a good impression on the credit association because he looked very kind and honest, and also had repaid the truck loan of about 70,000 yuan on time; besides, he had a top grade house. So using the reaping machine as collateral, he did not have any trouble in getting the loan. However this new machine was not a good way to make money. He and Sanbao Yang could drive the reaping machine, but they had no customers. Because the land of every household is very limited and scattered, the reaping machine was useless and expensive in this situation. Zhang found he had to default on the loans in that year. Of course, their living standards were declining. Zaixing Zhang considered doing the transportation business again, but he soon decided against it. He was never willing to engage in the long-distance transportation business again because it was so tiring, and he could not spend time with his family.

He then sold the 10-year old truck at the price of 20,000 yuan to meet his emergency financial needs. At the beginning of the spring in the next year, he went to nearby counties in Henan and Hebei to find the areas where there was large-scale planting. Zhang did find some customers and earned 30,000 yuan, but after repaying the loans Zhang's family did not have enough money for their daily life. Gradually his wife grew dissatisfied with the situation. After the summer harvest Zaixing Zhang lost his customers again. The reaping machine he owned was not fit to reap the sorghum, bean, and the corn reaped in the fall. So in the second half of the year they only had payments but no income.

Zaixing Zhang was also very worried. He began to repair motorcycles but this business was very slow. Many households in his village had motors but people did not ride them very often, so fewer motors needed to be repaired. He earned only about 1000 yuan for 4 or 5 months and could not support the family this way. In the spring of the third year, he went out to participate once again in the reaping business, but yet again, after the busy summer, he did not have any work. He found gleaning and collecting scraps to be a good business, which did not need any capital but only labor. But the wind in autumn and winter blew the scraps everywhere in the courtyard, and his wife complained that it was too dirty. Also as a new entrant into this business, he was given a hard time by others. His income was still too low to support the family.

In the winter of the fourth year, he had repaid 60,000 yuan but there was still the 70,000 yuan principle and 30,000 yuan interest remaining. Then Zaixing Zhang, who had never cooked before, decided to learn how to cook and sell sesame cakes. That was really a failure. In the city, this business is quite good, since at mealtime people need to queue to buy sesame cakes. Because most people are on duty and do not have time to cook, the business is very prosperous. In Zhucheng village, however, most housewives cook at home and they can prepare many kinds of wheat foods. So only a few people buy cakes. Zaixing Zhang's family had to eat the sesame cake that was leftover everyday, and he did not earn much money. That summer after the reaping, he followed the fruit peddler to peddle fruit. Zhang was able to sell out all his fruit everyday. He had customers buy his peaches again and again, with some even waiting for his peaches. So the business was quite good.

At noon, it was very hot and there were few pedestrians in the street. Zaixing Zhang would rest in the shade, thinking about his daughter's expense. When he repaid the loan after the summer reaping, he wanted to reserve some money for his daughter, but the credit association urged him to repay, seeing his poor situation in recent years. Sitting under a tree, he looked at the pedestrians and waited for them to buy the peaches. He spent his noon like this every day. One day, he saw a man speaking into a mobile phone on the steps of the local branch of the Industrial and Commercial Bank of China. He recalled that the man was a student of his teacher Mr. Shi. The student, Junsheng Liu, was a factory owner. Zaixing Zhang thought he would ask his teacher to tell his situation to Liu and see if Liu could lend him money. He thoughthis teacher could certainly help him with this. That afternoon, he visited his teacher. Mr. Shi was very kind and gave Junsheng Liu's address and telephone number to him.

A few days later, Zhang visited Junsheng Liu with some gifts. He wanted to have a chat and borrow 5000 yuan. He believed that Junsheng Liu being a factory manager would possibly be able to lend 5000 yuan. Zaixing Zhang would promise to repay the loan the next summer.

When Zhang arrived, two other people were having a chat with Junsheng Liu. They were staff of a credit association, urging Junsheng Liu to repay his loans. Hearing that, Zhang felt it might be hard for him to borrow money since Liu's factory seemed to be in trouble. After the two people left, Junsheng Liu said he also had some financial trouble recently, but he was still willing to lend 3000 yuan to him and congratulated his daughter. Zhang very much appreciated that, and asked about his factory.

Junsheng Liu is a straightforward person and he told Zhang his experiences. After his retirement from the army, he worked in a local wine factory. Then he retired again and started a business by himself. Liu was a vigorous, flexible, and social person. He got a loan to start a little toy factory. The turnover of the toy factory was not large but his toys sold very well in towns and villages because of their low prices. After several years he saved 70,000–80,000 yuan. Afterward, the toy market was not as prosperous as it had been before, and he sold the little toy factory. He then came to know that someone made big money by breeding a certain kind of sheep with a short tail. He spent a large amount of money to buy a herd of sheep from Xinjiang. He expected that those sheep could grow up to be sold in 10 months, and he could make the profit of 2000–30,000. But he had never bred any livestock before and had no previous experience. He did learn something on his own but found that was not enough and met with many troubles. Some sheep caught diseases over time, which the local veterinarian had never dealt with before, because those sheep were so different from the local sheep. There was no information in any material he could get about this disease. In a short time 30 sheep died, so he had to sell all the leftover sheep at a relatively low price, losing most of his money. Junsheng Liu was not disappointed and he still believed that market economy would prefer people like him who were full of courage.

Liu thought to himself, people in Shanxi Province would like eating vinegar; every household would eat it everyday. This time he familiarized himself with every aspect of the business, including raw material purchasing, processing, packaging, and marketing. He borrowed 100,000 yuan from the credit association. He cooperated with his friend with whom he was very familiar to open a vinegar factory. In the first 2 years, the output was not large. Their vinegar sold well in nearby counties and their benefits were quite good. Workers could get 400 yuan in one month, much more than workers in collective ownership factories, so some of his friends asked him to employ their sons or daughters. Liu not to offend them employed their sons and daughters, and the workers in the factory increased from 8 to 34 successively. Output was twice what it was before but the sales increased very slowly. So the profit rate of the factory declined. It was still a new brand and not very famous, while there were some very famous brands. Junsheng Liu believed that he could succeed only if his vinegar had some characteristics which those famous ones did not have. But his idea that they could develop a new kind of healthy vinegar, which was based on the trend that most people are more and more sensitive to their health, was opposed by his partner. He worried that this might cost too much and be too risky. They could not persuade each other. His partner used as an excuse his son's wedding and pulled out all his money which was about 30% of the total capital of the factory, but left behind the workers he had introduced. All of this put Liu into a hopeless situation.

Junsheng Liu used the vinegar factory as a mortgage to borrow 80,000 yuan to seek a new technical cooperation. At that time he had a 120,000 yuan loan in total and had to pay for about 30 workers. Liu's sincerity made him earn the support of the Institute of Agricultural Science in his province. After this new vinegar was developed, he spent another 200,000 yuan on a new productive machine, and new packing, but his new production was still not accepted as a healthy food by the authority concerned, so this new kind of vinegar could not be sold in healthy food stores. In general, the price of traditional vinegar was 2 yuan for 500 mL, but the price for this healthy vinegar was 3.8 yuan for 280 mL, so this expensive and unknown vinegar could not sell well.

Junsheng Liu spent 300,000 yuan on the new product, but customers did not accept it. Liu believed that capital could help him recover. He could not get a loan from the local credit association again; he had already borrowed money from all his friends who were willing to lend to him, but he did not repay them. Those two people of the local credit association had visited him to ask him to repay part of his loan as soon as possible, for their supervision department would check on their accounts soon, and they promised to loan him money again after the inspection. Junsheng Liu, who was about 50 years old, seemed very tired to handle all these difficulties.

Junsheng Liu's situation made Zaixing Zhang feel very depressed, for they had similar experiences. At first, they had great ambition but all ended in trouble. Zhang knew his problems now; first the reaping machine was not applicable in this area, and second he spent too much on his house. He never had so much money before so he lacked experience in managing his finance. The heavy pressure of daily life expenditures and loan repayments made him lose self-confidence gradually. But he felt Liu did not commit a serious fault: he had to rely on his social relations to handle all things, so accepting some workers introduced by acquaintances was inevitable. Seeking a new type of production was also wise enough. Zaixing Zhang thought that to get more loans was the best solution, but Junsheng Liu also needed a very capable person to help him with his business. Such a person would usually demand at least 1200 yuan a month, which means three workers would be fired. That was really hard.

Junsheng Liu was still in financial difficulty a year after I had visited him and Zaixing Zhang had borrowed money for his daughter's tuition.

Note

1. See *Selected Works of Deng Xiaoping* Volume 2. Beijing, People's Press p. 366 1993.

Index

!